✔ KU-372-862

Organizational change and innovation

Organizational change and innovation have been at the centre of much recent management literature, which has in the main been informed by debates in organizational behaviour and strategic management. A theoretical contribution from work and organization psychologists is welcome. The psychology of how people in organizations adapt to and manage change is key to our understanding of the processes by which such changes can occur successfully.

Organizational Change and Innovation brings together the recent research findings of leading European work and organization psychologists, who take stock of existing theories about organizational change in the light of new case material. Their findings, from a range of cultural and national contexts, challenge some previously accepted models and set a new agenda for future research. In particular, the volume provides new perspectives on the person–organization relationship; the political qualities of organizational change; the input–output model of organizations as entities; and finally on research methodology.

Dian Marie Hosking lectures in Organizational Behaviour and in Organizational Planning, Development and Change at Aston Business School. She is co-editor of *The European Work and Organizational Psychologist* and on the committee of the newly created European Association of Work and Organizational Psychology. She has published in the areas of leadership, small groups, organization theory, decision making and gender. **Neil Anderson** is Lecturer in Organizational Psychology at the University of Nottingham. He has published in the areas of innovation at work and personnel recruitment and selection. He is consultant editor of *Selection and Development Review* (formerly *Guidance and Assessment Review*).

Organizational change and innovation

Psychological perspectives and practices in Europe

Edited by
Dian Marie Hosking
and
Neil Anderson

CHESTER COLLEGE

ACC. No.
00924076

DEPT.

CLASS No.
658.406019   HOS

LIBRARY

London and New York

First published 1992
by Routledge
11 New Fetter Lane, London EC4P 4EE

Simultaneously published in the USA and Canada
by Routledge
a division of Routledge, Chapman and Hall, Inc.
29 West 35th Street, New York, NY 10001

© 1992 Dian Marie Hosking and Neil R. Anderson

Typeset in Times by LaserScript, Mitcham, Surrey
Printed and bound in Great Britain by
Mackays of Chatham PLC, Chatham, Kent

All rights reserved. No part of this book may be reprinted or reproduced or
utilized in any form or by any electronic, mechanical or other means, now known
or hereafter invented, including photocopying and recording, or in any
information storage or retrieval system, without permission in writing from the
publishers.

British Library Cataloguing in Publication Data
A catalogue reference for this title is available from the British Library.

ISBN 0–415–06314–0

Library of Congress Cataloging in Publication Data
has been applied for

ISBN 0–415–06314–0

Contents

Figures

Tables

Preface

This volume has its origins in the Fourth West European Congress of Work and Organizational Psychology, held in Cambridge, England in March 1989. The theme we chose for the Congress was 'Working with Change'. The chapters in this text were selected from the many excellent presentations on the Congress theme; there were others which we would like to have included but sadly could not. Since our initial selection, we have worked closely with the authors to produce a coherent set of chapters, each of which has developed enormously since the first draft. We would like to thank the authors for being so willing to work with our requests and suggestions, particularly when working in a language which was not their own. It is to their credit that the chapter contributions presented here are now exactly that; it is to our debit as editors that the reader must attribute any omissions, inconsistencies, or *non sequiturs*.

From the very start is was our desire to provide a state of the art review of European psychological perspectives on change, innovation, and organization. Innovation and change have become increasingly important themes in work and organization (W/O) psychology in recent years. This is perhaps not surprising, given the extensive and often radical changes in European economic, social, political and environmental systems in the last decade. As a part of this change, W/O psychologists increasingly have been building their understandings and developing their competencies across Europe. In recent years, we have seen the growth of pan-European networks, conferences, research programmes, consulting practices, and organizational change efforts.

The story of the West European Congress is one which reflects these patterns. The Cambridge Congress was the fourth in a series which began as a result of a small number of persons, from W/O networks in different European countries, agreeing that it would be good to organize a European congress. Originally this was called the West European Congress, in order to avoid the 'imperialist' claim that all Europe was participating. The first congress came out of collaboration between representatives of the British Psychological Society (BPS) Occupational Section, and W/O associations from the Netherlands (NIP), West Germany (BDP) and Belgium (VOCAP). Each partner made a financial commitment and contributed through a European Congress Committee. Over the years, the organizing committee grew. It did so by embracing new networks and associations who also were able to contribute to the costs and financial risks. Further informal and organic growth also occurred by welcoming 'liaison' persons from countries where relevant networks, at that time, did not exist. By the time of the fourth congress in Cambridge, the congress committee combined contributions from the UK, Netherlands, Belgium, West Germany, Spain, Italy, France, Switzerland and Austria.

As the congress grew and flourished, so too did mutual understanding and a sense of communality. We came increasingly to recognize the need to create and support many different ways of connecting with one another, and to do so in ways which would enable anyone in W/O psychology to help and be helped.

In 1991, after many years of building the necessary knowledge and trust, we were able to create the European Association of Work and Organizational Psychology (EAWOP) – an association which any individual or network of W/O psychologists in Europe may join. The challenge now is to give our association a truly European outlook, to be fully European in its membership (not just West European), facilitate local networks and activities, and help interchange and collaboration amongst European W/O psychologists. Perhaps this collection may contain some lessons for us – helping us to build EAWOP as a relational setting which will enable W/O psychologists better to help others.

Whilst speaking of help, there are many whose contributions we would like most gratefully to acknowledge. We can begin with the Fourth European Congress – from which came the contributions in this volume. This congress followed meetings in Nijmegen, Aachen and Antwerp. For the fourth congress, Dian Marie Hosking (BPS Section representative to the congress committee) was asked to take on the job of president and to obtain the assistance of the BPS Occupational Section to form a British Organizing Committee. This committee was composed of Dian-Marie Hosking, Chris Brotherton, Neil Anderson, Sandra Simpson, Phil Leather and Colin Fraser. Our colleagues deserve all our thanks for making the Cambridge congress such a huge success. Thanks must go also to those at the head office of the BPS who, as always, were such a pleasure to work with. Last, W/O psychology in Europe owes an enormous debt to the unstinting generosity of those who, over the years, have given so much of their time to the European Congress Organizing Committee and, more recently, to the founding of EAWOP.

As we stated earlier, it was always our intention that this text should present a state-of-the-art review of European psychological perspectives on change and innovation at work. It is our sincere hope for the future that the challenges which this text poses for European W/O psychology are acknowledged, embraced, and acted upon by both academic researchers and practising organizational psychologists.

Dian Marie Hosking, Birmingham, UK
Neil Anderson, Nottingham, UK

1 Organizing change and innovation
Challenges for European work and organizational psychology

Dian Marie Hosking and Neil Anderson

THE CHANGING CONTEXT OF EUROPEAN WORK AND ORGANIZATION PSYCHOLOGY

The emergence of organizational change and innovation as issues for concern among academics and practitioners alike has been noted in several quarters of late (British Psychology Society 1988; Arnold, Robertson and Cooper 1991; Hollway 1991). Separate literatures have emerged on innovation and on change, although the nature of this distinction has been seldom theorized. Given the tumultuous political and socio-economic developments in Eastern Europe, and given the derestriction of the labour market within the European Community, it is not surprising that work and organization (W/O) psychologists are recognizing organizational change as an emergent theme of enormous importance.

It is therefore timely to take stock of our current understanding of organizational change and innovation within European W/O psychology. Regrettably, the literatures confuse innovation and change. For this reason, when we speak here of change we include innovation; although we would argue that talk of innovation must imply change for the better (Hosking and Morley 1991; Anderson and King 1991).

On examining the literature, some quite fundamental issues and shortcomings quickly became apparent. These key issues resurfaced time and time again throughout the editorial process of this volume. European W/O psychology lacks theoretical integration, validated models and modes of action, and even appropriately tested methods of research and intervention to tackle the multifaceted, multi level of analysis and multi-perspective nature of organizational change and innovation. In summary, we fall far short of Roe and Ten Horn's (1991) call for the development of generic theories and integrated models in organizational psychology capable of explaining observed similarities and differences across national and cultural contexts. More serious, in our view, is that there is a clear need for radical and fundamental changes in the ways we theorize, understand, and research organizational change.

It is our intention that this volume should be integrative in two ways: first, by providing a state-of-the-art review of knowledge in the areas of strategic change, innovation, technological change and work organization, and change methods and methodologies – accordingly the text is divided into four sections; second, by highlighting the crucial themes which emerge from the individual chapter contributions – to some extent in the section editorials, but more importantly in this overview editorial chapter – we intend to present a distinct but constructively controversial challenge to the established orthodoxy within W/O psychology. We argue that there is a demonstrable need for W/O psychology to develop new perspectives on person and organization, and thus on organizational change.

CHALLENGES TO EUROPEAN W/O PSYCHOLOGY

The topic of change has become increasingly popular in the literatures on management and organization. A major reason for this lies in the common assumption that organizations today must deal with environmental changes of a speed and complexity never before experienced. Given this assumption, it is argued that management and organizations must innovate, for example by creating new and better products, and must be able to change – preferably in a planned and strategic manner (see for example Peters and Waterman 1982; Kanter 1983, 1990; Nystrom 1990; and chapter 2 in this volume).

The fields of W/O psychology have long contributed to the understanding of change 'in' and 'of' organizations. These contributions, of necessity, are grounded in certain understandings about the relationship between person and organization; often these are left implicit. We will outline the implicit understandings which seem to characterize W/O psychology's treatments of change and organization. We will do so in order to expose the ways change has been understood in relation to organization and to highlight perspectives and issues which have been neglected.

The 'challenges' which we refer to in the title of this chapter emerge from these neglected issues and dimensions of change. In essence, we argue that there are four central challenges to be addressed:

1 To generate new perspectives of the person–organization relationship.
2 To retheorize relational processes in ways which do not rely on the traditional input–output model of organizations as entities.
3 To recognize the intrinsically political qualities of organizing and change.

4 To develop alternative methodologies and to foster reflexivity in our methodological assumptions toward organization change processes.

Overviewing challenges

First, we discuss the ways in which W/O psychology typically has understood the relationship between person and organization. Discussions of change in relation to organization have tended to reflect a very particular and restrictive view of this relationship. We outline this perspective, placing particular emphasis on epistemological arguments. W/O psychology, and treatments of change in these literatures, has been dominated by relational assumptions grounded in subject-object differentiation, in methodological individualism, and in an emphasis on 'objective reality'.

Challenge One is to develop a new perspective of the person–organization relationship – which is 'generative' (Gergen 1982) and which offers new ways to understand change and organization. We are especially keen to develop a perspective which focuses not on what is seen as objective fact but on the relational processes involved in creating reality when the underlying assumption is subject–subject, not subject–object (see Dachler and Hosking, 1991). Our discussion in this chapter reflects our first small steps in this direction.

Our 'small steps' are taken by examining selected features of the literatures on change, identifying themes which have resulted from the traditional perspective on person–organization relations. Our second theme – deriving from the first – concerns the common assumption that powerful individuals, or dominant coalitions, can design changes in organizations (from conception to implementation) in ways which, in principle, are predictable. Illustrations are given to show how popular this view has been in W/O psychology, but equally how inaccurate it is as a view of change – an anomaly we term 'the illusion of manageability'.

Challenge Two is to retheorize relational processes in ways which do not rely on the traditional input-output model of organizations as entities. In particular, it will be necessary to theorize the reflexive and emergent qualities of these processes. From this perspective – and in contrast to the traditional perspective – what emerges is, in principle, not predictable or designable.

Third – and again building on earlier arguments – we suggest that W/O psychology usually has ignored or has trivialized political processes. Treatments of person-organization relationships have been such that the political qualities of change could not be recognized except in very limited ways. Organizational politics have been individualized – viewed as self-serving 'behaviours' of individuals, rather then as being inherent in the processes of organizing and change. Here then is Challenge Three: to give due recognition to the political qualities of organizing and change – not as behaviours of individuals, but as qualities of the relational processes which characterize organizing. Clearly this will depend on achievements with respect to the first two challenges.

Developing these themes leads to our fourth challenge, which follows on from and reflects the previous three. Challenge Four is to encourage reflexivity in the practices of W/O psychology as a profession, particularly in relation to methodological assumptions over, and methods used to research into, organization change. So, for example, we would like to see more critical examination of 'how we do' W/O psychology, the issues we do and do not address, our valuational stances, normative arguments and the ethical aspects of these. Notice, however, that such a 'critical examination' looks very different when conducted from a subject–subject perspective, as compared with a subject–object perspective. We examine this issue as an integral part of Challenge Four, and conclude by highlighting some of the professional and ethical issues involved.

Challenge One: to generate new perspectives of the person–organization relationship

Perhaps the first text to name the area of organizational psychology was the one bearing that name, published by Edgar Schein in 1965. He rightly noted that, to understand organizational psychology, it is necessary to understand something about organizations. We would add that for organizational psychology to contribute to an understanding of innovation and change, the same also is true. How then does W/O psychology understand 'organizations'? More precisely, given that psychology deals with 'questions that involve human beings' (Schein 1980: 3), how does organizational psychology understand the relationship between person and organization?

The answer seems to be that person and organization usually are categorically distinguished and set apart from one another. That is, relations between person and organization are understood as subject–object relations. Depending on the particular interests of the researcher, persons may be treated as subjects or objects; the same is true of organizations. To illustrate, persons are treated as objects when they are understood to be manipulated by the objective realities of their contexts; this is the 'culturalist fallacy' in which agency is located in the context, not the person – indeed when this perspective is adopted, the contributions of persons often are ignored (Hosking and Morley 1991; see also Chapter 2 in this volume). Interestingly, it most usually is organizational members who are studied as objects, rather than top management. An example directly relevant to change and organization is found in the perspective which characterizes human resource management. More narrowly, W/O psychologists have studied, for example: change strategies as they might more or less success-fully influence the values, competencies, actions, and commitment of organizational members; training techniques; quality of working life (QWL); participation; organizational development; and the restructuring of work organization (see for example Guest 1984; Porras and Silvers 1991).

Subject–object differentiation can be the 'other way round', so to speak: persons may be treated as subjects. Here it is persons who are understood to manipulate, they who are viewed as agents, separate from and inde-pendent of their contexts; dominant over and able to manipulate those contexts. This perspective is reflected in treatment of change in which persons (often top managers or change agents) are viewed as the architects of organization and change: captains of their own managerial or leadership styles, the architects of organization structures, the designers of strategies and organization–environment relationships. Typical accounts in this vein are to be found in the literatures of strategic choice and organizational change (e.g. Child 1972, 1984; Pettigrew 1985, 1988). We will say more about these literatures and alternative treatments of change in the develop-ment of our second theme – the manageability of change.

We have defined subject–object differentiation as being the key element of the predominant perspective in W/O psychology. We also have noted that the focus on the person as subject usually is adopted in relation to senior management. When speaking of the person as the agent or creator (subject), Schein (1980) refers to 'the manager . . . acting on behalf of the organization'. He goes on to say that this is a 'kind of "organizational" perspective, but should not be construed to mean that the organization acts as an abstract entity; rather, it acts through the individual behaviour of certain key members in crucial managerial or leadership roles' (Schein 1980: 4).

Schein's language is revealing. The subject–object differentiation of which we speak goes together with a methodological individualism which treats organizational wholes as made up of aggregates of individual pro-perties – values, competencies, attitudes and the like. It is understood that decisions, development and change of individuals cause organizations to change: through training, organizational development, mobilizing power, innovating in their work roles, imposing their visions of the organization upon other less powerful actors, and the like (French and Bell 1984; Peters and Waterman 1982; Glendon in this volume).

The subject–object perspective we have outlined pays little attention to the processes by which realities are created. Instead, the focus is on the objects of creation (structures, cultures, resistance to change, learning

climate, etc.). Yet it is through these processes that the 'objects' are understood (Dachler and Hosking 1991). This subject–object perspective makes
it impossible to view the subject as an integral part of that which is created;
yet this is precisely the understanding we would like to see developed.

This brings us to our first challenge. We would like to see W/O psychology take up the challenge of exploring a new perspective on organization and change – one which focuses on the relational processes through
which realities are created when a subject–subject perspective is taken.
This is a very different way of understanding the relationship between a
person and their context – be the context considered as other persons,
procedures, rules, hierarchy, environmental complexity, pollution, or whatever. The process of reality creation in subject–subject relations is a process
of mutual creation: a process of co-construction where each to some extent
makes the other. Our subsequent discussion of related challenges will
develop this theme, and explore exactly what is meant by W/O psychology
moving toward a subject–subject perspective of organizational change.

*Challenge Two: to retheorize relational processes which do not rely on
the traditional input–output model of organizations as entities*

We have argued that W/O psychology traditionally has understood the
relationships between person and organization as a subject–object relationship. One expression of this lies in the treatment of persons as active
subjects: subjects able to design and manage objects – the 'objects' of
interest here being organizations. Many examples of this perspective can be
found in the discussions of change and organization (e.g. Kanter 1983; Van
de Ven, Angle and Poole 1989). The ubiquitous assumption across these
literatures is that change processes are actually under the direct control of
the dominant coalitions within organizations. Their ability to instigate, plan
and direct all forms of organizational change has been taken for granted,
creating a present-day misinterpretation appropriately termed 'the illusion
of manageability'. By this we mean that the extent to which managers are
able to direct or predict change processes is overestimated, and the way in
which they might contribute to change is fundamentally misconceived.

It is possible to trace the origins of this illusion to the seminal writings
on organization development in the 1950s and 1960s (e.g. Lewin 1951;
Leavitt 1965; Bennis, Benne and Chin 1969). In principle, organizational
change was depicted as an orderly journey from point A to point B, the
process being couched in terms of planned shifts in the 'quasi-stationary
equilibrium' (Lewin 1951), which were to be enacted through a series of
discrete, linear stages (e.g. unfreeze–move–refreeze). Crucially, the entire
process was at all times seen as being under the control and direction of

management. Resistance from interest groups affected by the change was to be expected, but a proliferation of strategies and techniques to 'overcome resistance to change' was preferred (e.g. Coch and French 1948; Lawrence 1954; Watson 1966; Zaltman, Duncan and Holbek 1973).

More recently there has been a resurgence of practitioner interest in 'how to manage change' – at least if one is to judge from the popularity of texts in this vein published in the USA in the 1980s (e.g. Kanter 1983, Peters and Waterman 1982). The underlying assumptions remain basically unaltered: that change is manageable, its outcomes predictable, and capable of being directly influenced by those possessing organizational authority. Nonetheless, there exists a considerable volume of evidence to suggest that change processes may be far from managerial control, and can at best be influenced only to a limited extent (Sauer and Anderson 1992; Pool and Van de Ven 1989; Angle and Van de Ven 1989; Nicholson, Rees and Brooks-Rooney 1990).

In this volume, two chapters in particular cast pertinent doubts over the management of change. In Chapter 2, Crouch, Sinclair and Hintz explode what they call the 'myths' of managing change, arguing that a common response to environmental change was for managers in their study to initiate endogenous changes within their own organizations, which often resulted in pleasant feelings of coping with anxiety-provoking events.

In Chapter 14 Ernecq presents results which typify the experiences of managers and change agents involved in OD interventions, showing that the actual intention of the intervention often is usurped by outcomes which were neither expected nor intended. We would argue that the 'illusion of manageability' has flourished precisely because W/O psychologists have understood relationships between person and organization from a subject–object perspective. European W/O psychology needs to incorporate a subject–subject perspective of change processes; a prerequisite will be to jettison the traditional view of organizing processes as causal links between inputs and outputs (see Challenge Four). A W/O psychology which reflects a subject–subject perspective is one which sees reality construction as a process of mutual creation in which person and organization each to some extent makes the other. Relational processes, when understood in this way, are assumed to reflect the connection, rather than the separation, of the subject–object perspective. The challenge can now be seen to lie in finding new ways to theorize relational processes of reality construction – ways which do not rely on the traditional input–output model of relationships.

In the traditional perspective the subject is understood to form the object. Therefore a further relational assumption is that the causal model, however else it is developed, is in principle fundamentally understood from subject to object. Arguments about feedback loops and non-linearity of

effect are simply variations on the same theme and do not alter the fundamental relational assumptions. Importantly the implication of this for the
understanding of change is that the processual qualities are lost in that
change is understood to be revealed in the new form of the object and
understood to be produced by the characteristics of the subject. That is,
interest is restricted to the content characteristics of inputs and outcomes.

The challenge for W/O psychology is to consider how change might be
understood when the processes of reality construction are located in
subject–subject relations which, in turn, are understood as relations of
mutual creation. These processes, in principle, have a reciprocal quality
(Hosking and Morley 1991); put crudely they are circular rather than
(primarily and in principle) one-way. The quality of mutual creation or
mutual influence means that relational processes have an intrinsically
emergent quality. Note that from a subject–subject perspective the meaning
and significance of 'emergent' process is very different from that implied
in a subject–object perspective in that, in contrast to the traditional perspective, what emerges in relational processes is neither predictable nor
designable.

We know of little work in W/O psychology which takes this perspective
and considers its implications for the ways change and organization may be
understood. We are particularly struck by the enormity of the implications
of a subject–subject perspective for research methods and methodologies of
intervention (these implications are examined further under Challenge
Four). Potentially important contributions come from, for example, developments in theories of organizing (Weick 1979; Hosking and Morley 1991),
in constructivism (e.g. Watzlawick, Weakland and Fisch 1974; Watzlawick
1984) and in the emerging area of relational theory (Dachler, 1991).

*Challenge Three: to recognize the intrinsically political qualities of
organizing and change*

In our introduction we noted that W/O psychology has tended to ignore
political issues – however politics is defined. More narrowly, politics as we
wish to define them – as processes, as texture intrinsic to organization and
change – are entirely ignored (see Hosking and Fineman 1990; Hosking and
Morley 1991). On the rare occasions when political issues are mentioned,
they are understood in the context of the subject–object perspective we
have outlined. For example, it has been common to focus on the 'outcomes'
of strategic decision-making. These, typically, are treated as if they were
politically neutral. Of course, describing outcomes in terms of performance
against objectives, quality criteria, and the like as 'organizational'
properties is a very good way to sanitize what otherwise would have to be

linked with the valuations of particular individuals or groups. Studies of strategic decision making often take for granted that it is actually possible to measure the quality of a strategic decision *as a property of the decision (object) itself*. In this way, the underlying model is understood to have normative value for management – helping them to manipulate decision processes so they may make 'better' strategic decisions (e.g. Child 1972; Hickson *et al.* 1986; Johnson 1987).

Recently, some authors have expressed disenchantment with the intrinsically apolitical treatment of change processes found within much of these literatures (Anderson 1990; Anderson and King 1991; Hollway 1991; also Thompson and McHugh 1990). Although there is certainly room for studies taking an explicitly radical Marxist or labour process perspective, or which discuss the different interest groups affecting and affected by organization change processes (Anderson and King 1991), such approaches remain within a subject–object perspective. It is necessary for European W/O psychology to make a quantum leap in its conceptualization of the politics of change to reframe the meaning of politics within a subject–subject perspective. But what would this mean in practice? Some have argued that W/O psychology has been essentially apolitical because the prevailing concept of person has treated the latter as fundamentally passive, in need of being activated, motivated, led, and so on. They have argued that a political model follows from the recognition of persons as fundamentally active, self-determining actors (see e.g. Lee and Lawrence 1985). However, this argument continues to rest on the subject–object differentiation with which we are familiar; people are argued to behave more or less rationally and change processes are understood in the context of input–outcome relationships between persons and context (Kipnis, Schmidt and Wilkinson 1980). In other words, an adequate political perspective requires not just the assumption of activity, but also the assumption of subject–subject relations.

In the pluralist perspective, individuals and groups are understood to mobilize power (with varying degrees of success) in order to further their own individualistic interests. Politics is understood in relation to the traditional concept of power within a subject–object perspective. Politics is power, persuasion, dominance and exchange – a view which makes sense only within a perspective which separates subject and object (see Dachler and Hosking 1991). Why then do we claim that W/O psychology is intrinsically apolitical? Our arguments lie in our earlier account of the predominant perspective on relations between person and organization and the emphasis on persons as subjects who structure their (objectified) settings. A political perspective, however defined, has been lacking because of the focus on individuals and groups, and the reliance on methodological individualism. More generally, the reasons lie with the prevailing epistemology, which takes for granted that what is important is the treatment of organizations as objects which 'exist in their own right', independently of the subjective appreciations and actions of humans.

We are arguing for more attention to be given to political aspects of organization and change. However, by now it should be clear that we take the term 'political' to mean something quite special. We take the view that the 'assumption of activity', described above, makes most sense when set in the perspective which understands the relationship between person and context as a subject–subject relation. As we have said, this relationship must be seen to be one of mutual creation. An important part of what this means is that relational processes are processes in which realities are created through processes of co-construction. We shall develop our argument on processes of co-construction initially by describing how we see intersubjective understandings being created, and then by explaining the notion of political texture and its implications for our reconceptualization of power and politics in organization change.

Realities are co-constructed and reflected in a person's cognitions, that is 'appreciations' (Vickers 1968); realities may be more or less widely agreed upon as intersubjective understandings; realities are co-constructed through dialogues and multilogues, through social action and social processes of interaction, or, more generally, in the social practices of social cultures. The relational processes through which realities are constructed are understandable as a 'process of ongoing negotiation about who shall be whom and what order shall obtain' (Gerson 1976: 796).

This brings us to the point where we can explain what it means to us, in the context of a subject–subject perspective, to say that relational processes have a political texture. The relational processes of reality co-construction are performed by persons who differ in their relationships with their context; who work with different people – and therefore construct with different people; who perform different tasks, have different personal histories, and so on. This is of considerable significance. First, it means that actors also differ in their 'appreciations' (Vickers 1968), that is, in their constructions of objective reality. Individuals and groups will differ in how they 'see' things and in the realities they enact. Second, their different relationships with their contexts mean that actors differ in their views about what is important, what they wish to change, and why they may wish to stay the same and what they are able to do about it. But remember, these arguments must be understood, and their significance grounded in connection, not separation. This is our third challenge to W/O psychology: to find ways to reconceptualize power and politics in the context of a relational perspective.

To summarize, we have sketched the main themes of subject–object and subject–subject perspectives of the relations between person and organization. At the risk of oversimplification, we have suggested the former sharply separates person and organization, treating them as relatively stable and distinct entities. Each entity then is only related at the level of implicit assumptions through methodological individualism. In contrast, the relatively undeveloped subject–subject perspective adopts a very different set of relational assumptions in which person and organization are understood to 'co-construct' each other. This perspective places the process of co-construction at the centre of person–organization relationships. This means that change also is centred, rather than being treated as a deviation from the stable norm.

We develop this latter point in our fourth and final challenge. The last challenge we wish to pose ourselves, and all W/O psychologists, is to explore the implications of a subject–subject perspective in terms of how we conduct research or interventions into organization change processes.

Challenge Four: to develop alternative methodologies for research/intervention and to foster reflexivity in our methodological assumptions toward organizational change processes

Embracing a subject–subject perspective has major implications for research and practice: for the way we understand reflexivity, for the methods we employ, for the ways we understand and conduct our relationships with our clients (broadly defined) and for our understanding of ethical concerns. This is not the place for an extended discussion of these issues. Further, we have found very little in the literature which helps us in thinking about them. Our intention here is not to offer prescriptions, but rather to highlight the series of questions we believe to be critically important .

It was argued under Challenge Two that organizations commonly have been understood within a subject–object perspective. This view of organizations has shaped the methods utilized to study organizations and, therefore, organization change. Facets of organizations have been operationalized as variables interacting with one another; the aim of much research has been to evaluate and quantify the strength of hypothesized linear relations between variables or clusters of variables. Change *per se* has been treated largely as aberration from the 'normal' smooth running of the system – as an interruption to the ongoing productive process of transforming inputs into outputs (physical, social, or cultural), and as such a diversion from the real process of the organizational entity. In essence, change in W/O psychology has been depicted in subject–object relation terms, only the contents being of concern.

We are struck by the shortcomings of our traditional methodologies, and the ways they have been employed and interpreted almost exclusively in the context of a subject–object perspective. Process typically has been reduced to content: the content of change being revealed in the altered form of the object (e.g. organization, structure, climate, etc.) as a result of the actions of the subject. In contrast, in a subject–subject perspective it is in the process of forming that organization and change are located. These, as we have argued, are processes of co-construction.

But, assuming W/O psychology does develop a subject–subject perspective, what methodological assumptions and research methods are to replace traditional approaches? We have implied that research methods and intervention strategies will need to focus not upon the content of change, but upon the process as change. By conceiving of change as endemic to organizations it follows that our research methodologies and methods need to facilitate understanding of construction processes as they characterize organizing processes. But how are we to reflect processes of co-construction in our accounts? How can we appreciate the complexities of person–organization relationships, and how are we to do justice to their multi-faceted, multi-level nature in our research reports? We must find the means to reveal political textures as we have defined them here.

In discussing this fourth and final challenge to European W/O psychology we hope to stimulate discourse amongst colleagues, and – as our wording of Challenge Four states – 'to develop alternative methodologies of research into organization change processes'.

CONCLUDING COMMENTS

In conclusion, we wish to place these four critical challenges firmly on the agenda of European W/O psychology. As issues concerned with organization change become increasingly prevalent within W/O psychology, so it becomes important to retheorize the predominant notions of person–organization relations from merely subject–object, as presently seems to be the case, to subject–subject relations as described in this chapter. The extent to which we are successful in contributing towards an understanding of change processes will be fundamentally determined by our responses to these challenges. The deconstruction of meanings, critical examination of theories and concepts, disection of methodological assumptions and concomitant methods as practised/employed are in our view, necessary precursors to overcoming the narrow and one-sided subject–object perspective of organizational change which is predominant within the wider management and psychology literatures, and which threatens to engulf W/O psychology.

REFERENCES

Anderson, N.R. (1990) 'Innovation in work groups: current research concerns and future directions', paper presented at the Fourth West European Congress on Work and Organizational Psychology, Cambridge UK, March 1989.

Anderson, N.R. and King, N. (1991) 'Managing Innovation in organizations', *Leadership and Organization Development Journal* 4: 17–22.

Angle, H.L. and Van de Ven, A.H. (1989) 'Suggestions for managing the innovation journey', in A.H. Van de Ven, H.L. Angle and M.S. Poole (eds) *Research on the Management of Innovation: The Minnesota Studies*, New York: Harper & Row.

Arnold, J., Robertson, I.T. and Cooper, C.L. (1991) *Work Psychology: Understanding Human Behaviour in the Workplace*, London: Pitman.

Bennis, W.G., Benne, K.D. and Chin, R. (eds) (1969) *The Planning Of Change*, New York: Holt, Rinehart & Winston.

British Psychological Society (1988) *The Future of the Psychological Sciences: Horizons and Opportunities for British Psychology*, Leicester: BPS.

Child, J. (1972) 'Organization structure, environment and performance: the role of strategic choice', *Sociology* 6: 1–22.

Child, J. (1984) *Organizations: A Guide to Problems and Practice* (2nd edn), London: Harper and Row.

Coch, L. and French, R.J. Jr. (1948) 'Overcoming resistance to change', *Human Relations* 11: 512–82.

Dachler, H.P. (1991) 'Management and leadership as relational phenomena', in M. Von Cranach, W. Doise, and G. Mugny (eds) *Social Representations and the Social Bases of Knowledge*, Bern: Haupt.

Dachler, H.P. and Hosking, D.M. (1991) 'Organizational cultures and relational processes: masculine and feminine perspectives and practices', paper presented to the Tenth EGOS Colloquium, Vienna, July.

French, W.L. and Bell, C.H. (1984) *Organization Development*, Englewood Cliffs, NJ: Prentice-Hall.

Gergen, K. (1982) *Toward Transformation in Social Knowledge*, NY: Springer-Verlag.

Gergen, K. (1990) 'Toward a relational theory of power', paper presented to St Gallen Research conference – Social Organizational Theory: From Methodological Individualism to Relational Formulations, St Gallen, Switzerland, August.

Gerson, E.M. (1976) 'On the quality of life', *American Sociological Review* 41: 793–806.

Guest, D.E. (1984) Social psychology and organizational change', in M. Gruneber and T. Wall (eds) *Social Psychology and Organizational Behaviour*, Chichester: Wiley.

Hickson, D.J., Butler, R.J., Cray, D., Mallory, G.R. and Wilson, D.C. (1986) *Top Decisions: Strategic Decision-Making in Organizations*, Oxford: Blackwell.

Hollway, W. (1991) *Work Psychology and Organizational Behaviour: Managing the Individual at Work*, London: Sage.

Hosking, D.M. (1990) 'Critique of a relational theory of power', discussants commentary presented to St Gallen Research Conference – Social Organizational Theory: From Methodological Individualism to Relational Formulations, St Gallen, Switzerland, August.

Hosking, D.M. and Fineman, S. (1990) 'Organizing processes', *Journal of Management Studies* 27 (6): 583–604.

Hosking, D.M. and Morley, I.E. (1991) *A Social Psychology of Organising*, London: Harvester Wheatsheaf.

Johnson, G. (1987) *Strategic Change and Management Process*, Oxford: Blackwell.

Kanter, R.M. (1983) *The Change Masters: Corporate Entrepreneurs at Work*, London: Allen & Unwin.

Kanter, R.M. (1990) *When Giants Learn to Dance: Mastering the Challenges of Strategy, Management and Careers in the 1990s*, New York: Routledge.

Katz, D. and Kahn, R.L. (1966) *The Social Psychology of Organizations*, New York: Wiley.

Kipnis, D., Schmidt, S. and Wilkinson, I. (1980) 'Intraorganizational influence tactics: explorations in getting one's way', *Journal of Applied Psychology* 65 (4): 440–52.

Lawrence, P.R. (1954) 'How to deal with resistance to change', *Harvard Business Review*, May/June.

Leavitt, H.J. (1965) (ed.) *Applied Organizational Change in Industry: Structural, Technological and Humanistic Approaches*, Chicago: Rand McNally.

Lee, R. and Lawrence, P. (1985) *Organizational Behaviour: Politics at Work*, London: Hutchinson.

Lewin, K. (1951) *Field Theory in Social Science*, New York: Harper and Row.

Nicholson, N., Rees, A. and Brooks-Rooney, A. (1990) 'Strategy, innovation and performance', *Journal of Management Studies* 27: 511–34.

Nystrom, H. (1990) *Creativity and Innovation*, Chichester: Wiley.

Peters, T.J. and Waterman, R.H. (1982) *In Search of Excellence*, NY: Harper & Row.

Pettigrew, A. (1985) *The Awakening Giant: Continuity and Change in ICI*, Oxford: Blackwell.

Pettigrew, A. (1988) *The Management of Strategic Change*, Oxford: Blackwell.

Poole, M.S. and Van de Ven, A.H. (1989) 'Toward a General Theory of Innovation Processes', in A.H. Van de Ven, H.L. Angle and M.S. Poole (eds) *Research on the Management of Innovation: The Minnesota Studies*, New York: Harper & Row.

Porras, T.J. and Silvers, R.C. (1991) 'Organization development and transformation', *Annual Review of Psychology* 42: 51–78.

Roe, R. and Ten Horn, D. (1991) 'Development and use of generic and specific models in organizational diagnosis', paper presented to the Fifth European Congress on the Psychology of Work and Organization, Rouen, France, March 1991.

Sauer, J. and Anderson, N. (1992) 'Have we misread the psychology of innovation? A case study from two NHS hospitals', *Leadership and Organization Development Journal* 13, (2).

Schein, E. (1965) *Organizational Psychology*, London: Prentice Hall.

Schein, E. (1980) *Organizational Psychology* (3rd edn.), London: Prentice Hall.

Thompson, P. and McHugh, D. (1990) *Work Organizations: A Critical Introduction*, London: Macmillan.

Van de Ven, A.H., Angle, H.L. and Poole, M.S. (1989) (eds) *Research on the Management of Innovation: The Minnesota Studies*, New York: Harper & Row.

Vickers, G. (1968) *Value Systems and Social Processes*, London: Tavistock.

Watson, G. (1966) *Resistance to Change*, Washington DC: National Training Laboratories.

Watzlawick, P. (1984) *The Invented Reality*, NY: WW Norton & Co.

Watzlawick, P., Weakland, J. and Fisch, R. (1974) *Change: Principles of Problem Formation and Problem Resolution*, London: WW Norton & Co.

Weick, K. (1979) *The Social Psychology of Organizing*, London: Addison Wesley.

West, M.A. and Farr, J.L. (1990) (eds) *Innovation and Creativity at Work*, Chichester: Wiley.

Zaltman, G., Duncan, R. and Holbek, J. (1973) *Innovations and Organizations*, New York: Wiley.

Part I
Strategic change

Introduction

Dian Marie Hosking

Organizing, of whatever kind, can be achieved in relation to a variety of logics, each of which makes sense in its own terms. The chapters in Part I share the theme of strategic change. This raises the question of what *strategic* might mean as a qualifier of the term 'change'. As will be seen, references to *strategic* cannot be taken to imply only one focus, perspective, theory, or unit of analysis.

Choice, be it implicit or explicit, perhaps comes closest to being a theme which is always implicated in discussions of strategic change. The issues which may then be explored are many and varied; they certainly are not all represented in this volume. At the risk of over-simplification we may say that at their most 'micro' the literatures consider the role of cognitive and personality characteristics of individuals and their effects on strategic choice processes and on 'outcomes' in the form of policy (e.g. Jervis 1976). Clearly many parts of psychology, not just organizational psychology, potentially could contribute to our understanding in this area. Others pursue their interest in strategic choice by treating organizations as entities – having particular properties or characteristics in the same way that individuals can be said to 'have' them. So, for example, more 'macro' interests include the consideration of organizations as strategic types – varying systematically in the ways they relate with their environments (e.g. Miles and Snow 1978; Miller and Friesen 1984). Of course, underlying these micro-macro emphases are assumptions about the relationship between person and organization. As we noted in Chapter 1, it is our view that organizational psychology has yet to fully embrace a debate on this issue. As a result, the concept of organization typically emerges from methodological individualism (see Hosking and Morley 1991).

It is perhaps because of methodological individualism that contributions to strategic change and organization which come from W/O psychology often focus on individuals and small groups. It is they who are understood to have agency – to exercise choice. Particularly popular has been the focus on senior management as the agents of change. This emphasis goes together with an interest in senior management, because they are the 'strategic apex' (Mintzberg 1979) and are understood to have the responsibility for strategic decision making.

An alternative focus has been to take strategic decisions themselves as the unit of analysis. This opens up the possibility of considering the contributions of different individuals and groups (see Pool and Koopman, Chapter 4). Organizational psychologists have been particularly interested in considering the desirability of organization-wide participation and industrial democracy. Even so, and perhaps surprisingly, they have been slow to question the predominant 'taken for granteds' about what is 'desirable' (see Chapter 1).

Interests in strategic change are often pursued through attention to the content characteristics of choices. So, for example, attention may be directed to questions concerning the kind of organization we want to be (structural characteristics, culture etc.), the kind of environment(s) we want to be in or the kinds of relationships we want with our environments. Attention also may be devoted to the processes of change over time. W/O psychology has contributed, for example, to whether decisions do, may, and/or should go through a series of stages; who or what may appear to influence the transitions; and what might be the 'levers' which might be manipulated to influence the decision process. Work of this kind is reported here. Glendon (Chapter 3) argues that the actions of the chief executive were the major source of effective influence. Pool and Koopman (Chapter 4) make choice opportunities the centre of their analysis of how the 'decision course' can be managed.

The first of the four chapters in part one falls within the tradition of interest in organization–environment relations. The authors' approach may be said to be psychological, because they focus explicitly on how individual managers respond to environmental changes. In this way Crouch and his colleagues set themselves apart from those who treat organizations as unitary actors and in so doing miss the different understandings, actions and influence of participants. By taking this approach, the authors also avoid the more usual treatment of environments as if they have the status of objective reality, existing independently of the social constructions of actors (see Chapter 1).

Crouch and his colleagues consider three questions: how managers perceive their environments; how they act; and how they feel about the changes. They use their research to investigate selected orthodoxies. First, that the objective features of environments 'force' themselves on the perceptions of individuals. Second, that individuals act to reduce the uncertainties they perceive. Third, that feelings primarily are those of resistance, stress, and anxiety.

The authors suggest that these orthodoxies might fairly be described as myths. So, for example, they argue that some people increase uncertainty (the authors' interpretation) by initiating changes, providing them with an opportunity for the exercise of mastery. They leave unexplored the possibility of a link between strategy and gender. Certainly 'exercising mastery' has been identified as a masculine identity script (see e.g. Gilligan, 1982).

In Chapter 3, two major perspectives are examined: the 'pluralist' and the 'radical'. They are described as perspectives because they reflect particular basic assumptions or ways of understanding in this area of organizational change. The pluralist perspective is characterized by the following assumptions. First, that all participants are able to achieve some degree of influence over organizational policies and practices. Second, that participants will differ in what they count as important, and therefore, in how they feel about changing or staying the same. Third, that conflicts over these differences are potentially capable of integrative solutions, that is, solutions which benefit all. The radical perspective rejects this third assumption, taking the view that influence relations may be so asymmetric that some participants may effectively achieve very little influence. As a result, organizational changes may not respect their (different) points of view and interests.

The author examines selected themes in pluralist models of change. He does so by considering the extent to which they 'fit' the events and processes which characterized an eight-year period of change in one organization – a British university. He uses his case study to critique the pluralist perspective. He concludes that in this case, a radical perspective offers the best fit. More generally, he suggests that different models are likely to be more or less appropriate, depending on the particulars of the actors, their processes and context.

In Chapter 4, Pool and Koopman take not the organization, but a decision as the unit of analysis. They present a model of strategic decision making synthesized from existing research and theory. They offer their model as a relatively comprehensive account of the ways strategic decision making may vary, and as one way to investigate organizational innovation and change.

The central purpose of the authors is to explicate the levers or mechanisms by which strategic decision making can be controlled. This raises an issue we addressed in Chapter 1 – the assumption that individuals and groups can plan and practically implement designed changes. In both the cases they report, top management achieved a considerable degree of influence. When read in conjunction with Glendon's paper this raises the question of whether a radical perspective might be required, and how their model might accommodate this. Does Pool and Koopman's model seem able to handle Glendon's findings? Could their model also suggest how such influence (dominance) could be contested? As we suggest in Chapter 1, there is room for organizational psychology to consider more seriously the political qualities of organization and change.

In the final chapter of Part 1, Waddington also adopts a decision-making approach. The author develops a social psychological perspective through which he seeks to account for a lack of strategic innovation. The author gives great emphasis to what he calls 'socio-historical' and 'cultural' variables. These he argues are of central importance to actors: interpretations of their context (what is happening); beliefs about possible courses of action (what can be done); and attempts to translate their understandings into actions (strategic choice and associated tactics).

Waddington devotes detailed attention to the 1984–5 strike by British coal miners. Selected social psychological literatures are drawn on, as are interviews with mineworkers, to consider why the union uncritically applied a previously successful strategy – strike action. They did so without seriously evaluating why this strategy had worked the last time, and why it might not work again. The author puts a question often posed in psychological approaches to decision making. The question is, 'Why was there no serious consideration of possible contextual changes which might be relevant to the success of their strategic choice?' Again, there may be a gender dimension which could be explored. It may be that the decision to strike was, in part, the expression of a masculine identity script (see earlier). Further, the seeming lack of contextualism on the part of the decision-makers fits with the description of masculine cultures identified in the literatures on gender.

REFERENCES

Jervis, R. (1976) *Perception and Misperception in International Politics*, Princeton, NJ: Princeton University Press.

Miles, R.E. and Snow, C.C. (1978) *Organizational Strategy, Structure and Process*, New York: McGraw Hill.

Miller, D. and Friesen, P.H. (1984) *Organizations: A Quantum View*, Englewood Cliffs, NJ: Prentice Hall.

Hosking, D.M. and Morley, I.E. (1991) *A Social Psychology of Organizing*, London: Harvester Wheatsheaf.

Mintzberg, H. (1979) *The Structuring of Organizations*, Englewood Cliffs, NJ: Prentice Hall.

IDE – International Research Group. *Industrial Democracy in Europe*, Oxford: Clarendon Press.

Gilligan, C. (1982) *In a Different Voice*, London: Harvard University Press.

2　Myths of managing change

Andrew Crouch, Amanda Sinclair and Philippa Hintz

Prescriptions defining how individual managers should manage change
are informed by myths or widely-shared, but not necessarily well-
substantiated, understandings. Three such myths are examined in this
chapter – that managers are perceiving unprecedented turbulence, that a
typical reaction to such turbulence is to minimize its impact with resistance, denial or inaction, and that the emotional experience of such
externally-imposed turbulence is overwhelmingly unpleasant. Managerial responses to exogenous change were analysed in three circumstances: a field study of financial managers involved in the 1987
Stockmarket Adjustment, and in two complex business simulations. Our
findings challenge the myths, suggesting that managers do not perceive,
and consequently are not paralysed by, conditions of unprecedented
turbulence. Rather, managers act, colluding to increase the complexity
and rate of change engulfing them. Their emotional response to turbulence often is positive, particularly in the early stages of change and if
they perceive a capacity to influence outcomes.

INTRODUCTION

Can change be managed, and if so, by whom? Many management writers
argue that it can, and that managers are the people for the job. They offer
advice on how to develop organizational structures and cultures which are
conducive to creativity and innovation (Peters and Waterman 1982; Kanter
1985, 1989; Peters 1987). Decentralized structures, devolution of power,
teams, and 'loose-tight' cultural properties are some of the ingredients, as
are leaders who model change-embracing values and provide power tools
to innovators.

But perhaps these prescriptions are overtly optimistic. Nothing we know
about the traditional characteristics of managers and the management pro-

cess encourages confidence in them as change agents (Zaleznik 1977; Bennis and Nanus 1985; Starbuck 1985).

This research explores the responses of managers to change. When we embarked, we were part of a burgeoning stream of organizational and management researchers concerned about the impact of what seemed to be radical and dramatic changes in the environments of managers. How would they survive events like the 1987 stockmarket crash? How would they steer their organizations successfully through such events? As we planned the research and later analysed our data, it emerged that much of the work done on the management of change was based on assumptions about the nature of recent change and the sorts of responses managers have to it. These assumptions or myths have underpinned much of the thinking about change management; we argue they deserve closer scrutiny. Our results contradict several of the myths which we identified. The challenge to these myths is based on three empirical studies which, in different ways, examine managerial experiences of change.

MYTHS OF CHANGE MANAGEMENT

1 Managers are perceiving conditions of unprecedented turbulence

Modern times are widely characterized as turbulent, governed by unprecedented levels of change (Emery and Trist 1965; Toffler 1970; Drucker 1980; Naisbitt and Aburdene 1985; Morgan 1988; Baburoglu 1988). The 'information explosion', the technological and communications 'revolutions' provide uncontestable evidence of the acceleration of change, leading inexorably to the conclusion that change is the only constant. The language in which this turbulence is discussed is grandiose, with commentators competing for metaphor with which to convey its monumental scale:

> ... the swift spread of microprocessors ... biotechnology ... the electronicization of money ... the creation of startling new materials ... artificial intelligence ... accompanied by equally important social, demographic and political changes ... taken together add up to nothing less than a mutation in our way of life ... They threaten all our basic institutions .... When so great a wave of change crashes into the society ... traditional managers ... are thrown overboard.
>
> (Toffler 1985:3)

In the zeal to highlight turbulence, its scale may have been overstated and its forms oversimplified (Cameron, Kim and Whetten, 1987), but this has not, apparently, undermined the imperative to 'manage' change. These 'megatrends' (Naisbitt 1982) or artefacts of modernity are maintained to have profound effects on organizations and individuals whose working lives are driven by the demands of change. Both organizations and individuals are offered advice on how to 'manage' or 'ride' the 'waves' of change (Morgan 1988), how to 'thrive on chaos' (Peters 1987).

Managers must not only accommodate rapid change themselves, they must shoulder the strategic responsibility of steering their organizations through turbulence (McCaskey 1982). They must construct an organizational capability to manage change: 'managers of the future will have to ride this turbulence with increasing skills and many important competencies will be required' (Morgan, 1988:1). Tushman and Nadler conclude: 'In today's business environment there is no executive task more vital than the sustained management of innovation and change (1986:74). However, there is an increasing body of research that suggests that managers almost certainly do not share such a unified perception of turbulence and the resulting management imperative. McCall notes that commentaries like those cited are 'missing the important processes by which events are interpreted and their significance appraised', thus 'events have little objective meaning' (1977:116). Weick (1985), Isabella (1990) and others researching the cognitive bases for responding to change, have found that a manager's interpretations will be influenced by different properties of the organization and its culture, and they might also progress through phases built in to any change experience (Isabella 1990; Waddington, this volume).

2 Managers typically attempt to cope with turbulence by blocking or minimizing disturbance, through defences such as denial and inaction

The most thoroughly developed models of change management focus on the organizational or strategic level. The original contingency theorists (Burns and Stalker 1961; Thompson 1967; Lawrence and Lorsch 1967; Woodward 1965) and their successors who have refined particular contingency approaches (e.g. Donaldson 1985; Dunphy and Stace 1988) have matched organizational structures and managerial styles to particular circumstances of change. Staw, Sandelands and Dutton (1981) have noted that the 'anthropomorphic quality' of many of the 'macro-level' strategies, encourages us to confuse organizational (macro) with individual managerial responses to change. As they note, there may be an overlap between organizational and managerial responses – for example, where strategies are 'the product' of a single decision-maker. Further, there is evidence that 'many effects appear to generalise across levels of analysis' (Staw, *et al.* 1981:501). Thus the organizational effects of change, which have been well-documented, can clearly inform our understanding of how individual managers respond to change, though the two should not be confused as the same thing.

The focus of our research

The focus of our research is how individual managers construe and respond to change. This aspect of change is less well understood than macrochange, with particular deficiencies in 'the identification of maladaptive or pathological cycles of behaviour' (Staw *et al.* 1981:501). The work of Kets de Vries (1984) and Kets de Vries and Miller (1984) has partially redressed this, examining cases in which endogenous change has been a catalyst provoking irrational and neurotic managerial responses.

A small but growing body of research which attends to individual responses, does so in particular circumstances of organizational change such as closure or death (Hardy 1985; Sutton 1987; Cameron, Sutton and Whetten 1988). Much of this research understandably, though not totally justifiably, assumes that resistance will be the universal response. Resistance to the change may be mitigated by the way in which it is managed – the type and amount of information provided, the opportunity to participate in decision-making, the autocratic versus democratic style of leadership (Hardy 1985). However, the effectiveness of participation in ameliorating resistance to change has been a controversial and ideologically-charged debate, which suffers from an absence of firm conclusions (Lawrence 1969; Locke and Schweiger 1979; Cotton Vollrath, Froggatt, Lengrick-Hall and Jennings 1988; Rothschild-Witt 1986).

There is more research evidence in psychology, though much derived from experimental settings, and rarely looking specifically at managers. It focuses on psychological effects thought to be associated with change, such as stress, anxiety and arousal. This research encourages us to envisage managers as reluctant actors in the turbulence scenario, their primary stance being one of resistance. The expression of this resistance will be determined by the manager's distinctive portfolio of defence mechanisms – unconflicted inertia, defensive avoidance, hypervigilance (Janis and Mann 1977), denial displacement or regression (Martin and Meyerson 1988; Sinclair 1990).

Perceiving something new and contradictory to experience, the expectation is that managers will adjust stimuli to achieve consistency or preserve pre-existing gestalts (Postman and Bruner 1948) or to reduce cognitive dissonance (Festinger 1957). They will imbue ritual into new situations to make them seem familiar, and will use a variety of 'standard operating procedures' (Allison 1971; Starbuck 1985) or stereotypic behaviours to, subjectively at least, convert difference into what is known (Adler 1986). Externally induced change thus tends to set in train a complex psychological reaction, which will be likely to include 'stress, anxiety and arousal [which] often result in poor task performance and a tendency to persevere in well-learned courses of action' (Staw *et al.* 1981:507). The behavioural response is most likely to be an inability to match new stimuli with new behaviours, with managers psychologically 'sealing off new information' (Staw *et al.* 1981:502) and denying or avoiding the need to act in new ways (Waddington, this volume).

Traditionally managers have been advised to try and choose strategies which will eliminate the resistance of others (Kotter and Schlesinger 1979). However, there has been more recent recognition that resistance is often expressed through a complex pattern of defences, and to attempt to eliminate or circumnavigate is a risky strategy. Goldstein (1988) argues the need to reframe resistance; on the basis of her study of forty managers, Isabella argues that 'resistances to change might alternatively be viewed not as obstacles to overcome, but as inherent elements of the cognitive transition occurring during change' (1990:34).

3 Managers experience change as difficult and emotionally unpleasant

Change, and particularly radical change, such as crises or disasters, tends to produce high levels of anxiety and stress which in turn 'elicits behavioural responses of withdrawal . . . reductions in critical information processing . . . and constriction in behavioural responses' (Staw *et al.* 1981:505). The relationship between exogenous events and stress has been supported in a managerial simulation context by Gladstein and Reilly (1985). Where change is threatening for the manager, in conditions such as resource scarcity, competition or reduction in the size of the market, these effects can be intensified, though as Staw *et al.* conclude from their exhaustive analysis of research, factors such as the manager's level in the organization may be important moderators. Generally, research leads to the expectation that managers will find change overwhelmingly unpalatable. It will produce negative emotions and a pessimistic mood, as well as maladaptive responses, particularly where the change threatens the status or security of the individual manager.

METHODOLOGY AND RESULTS

Empirical studies of managerial responses to change

Using three studies of organizational change, with distinct research methods and sample populations, this paper investigates these assumptions which underpin current perspectives on organizational change and its management. The studies were guided by the desire to understand organizational events and circumstances from the perspectives of senior managers who interpret their own and their organization's processes of change (Daft and Weick 1984). We sought to compare these experiences with the current ideology of change: widely perceived and inescapable turbulence, and the accompanying imperative to 'manage' change by reducing uncertainty, restoring order through resistance and denial: and of change being a generally unpleasant emotional experience.

The three studies build on each other in sequence. Study 1 investigates managers' reconstructions of the events of the 1987 Stockmarket Adjustment. At the time, this event was considered one of the most momentous changes to confront the finance industry worldwide in over fifty years. The following two studies examine the behaviour of a relatively small number of managers in quasi-experimental conditions which simulate abrupt and unexpected organizational changes. Study 2 is an investigation of managerial reactions to a sudden and radical change in organization structure. Study 3 involves managers in simulated organizations operating in a capricious environment which suddenly introduces a flood of new demands and variables, then, just as suddenly, becomes still.

The three myths which have been identified and described should not be treated as hypotheses which we set out to test. Rather our intention has been to scrutinize some aspects of the change-management orthodoxy using the results from three different studies. While we cannot claim to debunk it, we argue on the basis of the following studies that the responses of managers to change are complex and contingent on both psychological and environmental factors. This complexity has been obscured, rather than highlighted, by much of the contemporary work on managing change.

Study 1: Perceptions of change among senior executives in the finance industry during the 1987 Stockmarket Adjustment

The Stockmarket Adjustment of October 1987 was portrayed at the time as a sudden and dramatic change in world financial markets. This event presented itself as an opportunity to gain insight into the ways in which senior executives in organizations associated with the finance industry interpreted a turbulent environment.

In mid-1988 twenty-one managers from four organizations with direct exposure to the Adjustment were selected for interview. Their organizations included a stockbroking firm, an investment division of an insurance company, a merchant bank, and a friendly society. After a brief preliminary explanation of the research project each interviewee was asked for permission to record the interview and given assurances of confidentiality. A semi-structured interview was conducted using a small set of preliminary questions which focused attention on a respondent's experience of the Adjustment, after which respondents were encouraged with as little direct prompting as possible to talk about their experiences of change in their own professional lives. The average duration of interviews was 45 minutes.

Transcripts were verified for accuracy by interviewees and analysed using two techniques. The first was a content analysis (Goode and Hatt 1952), the second an interpretative analysis (Kets de Vries and Miller 1987; Daft and Weick 1984). Transcripts were read and reread by each of the authors until agreement was reached on the principal themes which could be best represented in content analysis. The result was a three-way categorization of references to change: a cross-classification of action, emotion and change. The unit of analysis for the transcript data was a phrase of speech by a manager. Using a list of category-relevant phrases constructed after developing familiarity with the transcripts, the authors searched the data to count the number of phrases which referred to change (or no change) in association with references to action and emotion. Change–action–emotion references were classified according to the criteria specified below and counted. This formed the 3 x 3 x 2 cross-classification shown in table 2.1. Classification of transcript data was conducted twice to check method reliability, no significant difference being found between codings.

Action responses were trichotomized. The first category included action by which a manager brought about some variation or change to his or her organization, creating some new role relationship, a new structure, adding a new external relationship, or changing technology. This category was termed 'increasing novelty'. The second category, termed 'decreasing novelty', contained those actions which deliberately prevented a new development in the organization, disallowing change in structure, technology or behaviour. The third was a neutral category which included those references to change (or its absence) in which a manager determined not to act at all, or to act in a way which neither increased nor decreased novelty. Emotional responses were trichotomized into pleasant, neutral and unpleasant associations, with change depending on the respondent's reference to his or her feelings. The change dimension was dichotomized into references to the recognized presence or absence of exogenous change to the organization. Since there were no significant differences in cross-classification between organizations or between respondents, the data were consolidated in one table (Table 2.1). Log-linear modelling procedures (Bishop, Fienberg and Holland 1987; Bonett and Bentler 1983) were used to analyse the underlying pattern of cell frequencies.

Table 2.1 Observed frequencies of reference to changing and unchanging organizational circumstances associated with the 1987 Stockmarket Adjustment

| | Reference to unchanging organizational circumstances | | | Reference to changing organizational circumstances | | |
| | Associated emotion | | | Associated emotion | | |
	Pos.	Neut.	Neg.	Pos.	Neut.	Neg.
Action to increase novelty	6 0.01	61 0.08	13 0.02	56 0.08	248 0.34	82 0.11
Action not increasing or decreasing novelty	12 0.02	38 0.05	17 0.02	10 0.02	62 0.08	25 0.03
Action to decrease novelty	0 0.00	22 0.03	6 0.01	3 0.00	61 0.08	4 0.01

Note: Upper figures are frequency counts, lower figures are proportions of the overall total frequency.

Results and interpretation

Given an open brief to talk about their experience of change, it is not surprising that 75 per cent of references counted in Table 2.1 refer to changing organizational circumstances of one form or another. What is perhaps surprising is the 25 per cent of references to no change. In other words, when asked to reflect specifically on personal and organizational change, using the Stockmarket Adjustment as a cue, many references were made to constancy and stability. The managers' mental schemas were apparently not focused entirely on matters of change, even when the framework for the conversation was a dramatic disturbance.

Managers' perceptions of change and their descriptions of its impact varied widely. Clearly, an objectively definable event such as the Adjustment was not experienced in similar ways, even for those working in the same department or organization, or in similar jobs. Also many managers eschewed describing the Stockmarket Adjustment, instead focusing on internal or local organizational events, for example, a change to a new job within the organization.

Responses to change were primarily actions which introduced novelty to the organization. As Table 2.1 shows, action to increase novelty accounts for 53 per cent of all references in the cross-tabulation, and it is associated with 70 per cent of references to change. This latter proportion far outweighs neutral action responses or those which decrease novelty. To illustrate, members of the top management team of one organization referred to processes of dramatic organizational growth, bringing forward visionary plans, introducing new technology, and attempting to achieve closer relationships with clients, all within the context of dramatic disturbances in the organization's environment. Despite their overwhelming propensity to novelty-increasing action under circumstances of change, the degree to which managers felt able to influence the course of events varied substantially: from one who expected to 'revolutionize . . . change the face of the industry', to another who lamented that 'they keep changing the rules on you'.

The interpretive analysis of the transcripts reinforces the pattern in Table 2.1, which shows emotional neutrality as the most frequent response to change. Some referred to change as fearful or exciting, but the majority registered little emotion: simply a part of the job, not a matter for strong feelings of any form.

Data interpretation was taken further in Table 2.2, by fitting a set of log-linear models to the data in Table 2.1. The objective here was to identify a descriptive model which provided a statistically acceptable and inter- pretable account of the pattern of observations. Only one model, other than the saturated model (aec), shows a non-significant discrepancy between observed frequencies and predictions. This is the second-order model (ae, ac) ($G^2 = 11.6$, df = 6, p = 0.07) which includes interactions between action and emotion and between action and change. The form of the interactions can be deduced from the significant standardized parameter estimates for the (ae, c) and (ac, e) models.

The underlying relationship between emotion and action described by the model refers to both high and low incidences of emotional neutrality. Action to reduce novelty is associated with emotional neutrality relatively frequently, as indicated by the parameter estimate describing the relationship between action and emotion ($a^-e^n = 3.9$, p<0.01). A low incidence of neutral emotion associated with both novelty-neutral and novelty-increasing action ($a^ne^n = -3.4$, p<0.01; $a^+e^n = -2.3$ p<0.01 respectively) is also indicated.

Relationships between action and change reveal a pattern of relatively high incidence of novelty-increasing action associated with the presence of change ($a^+c^p = 5.2$, p<0.01) and novelty-neutral action associated with the absence of change ($a^nc^a = 4.2$, p<0.01). The model predicts a low incidence of novelty-neutral action associated with the presence of ($a^n c^p = -4.2$, $p<0.01$) and a low incidence of novelty-increasing action associated with the absence of change ($a^+ c^a = -5.2$, $p<0.01$). That is, managers are more likely to take novelty-increasing action when change is experienced.

Table 2.2 Log-linear models of relationships among action and emotion in the presence and absence of change

Model fitted	df	Likelihood ratio chi-square G^2	p	Significant ($p<0.05$) standardized parameter estimates
a	15	640.4	<0.01	$a^+ = 16.5$ $a^n = -2.7$ $a^- = -9.4$
e	15	573.2	<0.01	$e^+ = -9.6$ $e^n = 18.0$ $e^- = -3.4$
c	16	740.2	<0.01	$c^p = 13.2$ $c^a = -13.2$
a, e, c	12	69.8	<0.01	
ae, c	8	48.9	<0.01	$a^- e^n = 3.9$ $a^n e^n = -3.4$ $a^+ e^n = -2.3$
ac, e	10	32.5	<0.01	$a^+ c^p = 5.2$ $a^n c^p = -4.2$ $a^+ c^a = -5.2$ $a^n c^a = 4.2$
ec, a	10	69.3	<0.01	
ae, ac	6	11.6	0.07	
ca, ce	8	32.1	<0.01	
ec, ea	6	48.5	<0.01	
ae, ac, ec	4	11.3	0.02	
aec	0	0.0	saturated	$a^- e^- c^p = -1.9$ $a^- e^- c^a = 1.9$

Notes: Change (c) c^p: Change present
                   c^a: Change absent
         Action (a) a^+: Action to increase novelty
                   a^a: Action neutral
                   a^-: Action to decrease novelty
         Emotion (e) e^+: Positive emotion
                   e^n: Neutral emotion
                   e^-: Negative emotion

Summarizing the findings of this study, considerable variation was found in the ways senior finance industry managers interpreted change and described their responses. Yet interestingly, when referring to change, there was a strong and consistent pattern in their associated actions. These managers spoke of initiating further change when faced with externally-induced change. Conversely, change-neutral action was associated with an unchanging environment, and in these circumstances the introduction of novelty was avoided. No evidence was found to indicate that a changing organizational environment was met with suppressive action. Managerial action to create novelty was not experienced as emotionally neutral. Such initiatives were apparently undertaken with mixed feelings.

The primary limitation of this study is its dependence on the retrospective interpretation of events by interviewees. Although the senior managers spoke confidently and without hesitation in recalling the 1987 Stockmarket Adjustment, suggesting no difficulty in remembering the circumstances, it is still possible that unknown systematic bias has influenced the pattern of results. In recognition of the dangers of inference from retrospective data, the research method employed in Study 2 simulated an abrupt organizational change which could be directly observed by the researchers.

Study 2: Simulated organizational acquisition

The primary objective of Study 2 was to cross-validate in a quasi-experimental setting the patterns of association among the variables identified in Study 1. To achieve this a business simulation was designed to investigate the behaviour of fourteen senior managers under conditions of abrupt organizational change. The simulation was conducted during a Master of Business Administration unit on the management of organizational change.

Students were introduced to the simulation with an outline of its objectives. These were to participate in an experiential exercise involving organizational change which would highlight managerial issues for later class discussion. To aid this discussion, students were asked to keep a personal journal recording their interpretations of important events during the simulation.

A computer-based competitive business environment was employed involving four simulated companies, each comprising three or four participants. One person was selected at random from each firm to occupy the role of General Manager. Firms were required to decide on complex strategic marketing, production and financial objectives over six simulated years. Six sessions of one and a half hours were set aside for the simulation, over a two-week period. At the end of each session, which simulated a year of business operation, firms submitted their decisions. These were processed by computer and the results returned in the form of financial statements and competitive analysis.

Unknown to the participants, the simulation was divided into three phases. The first, labelled *prechange* involved the first three decision cycles, during which members of the four firms became familiar with the computer-based decision-making processes and were fully involved in their operation within a competitive business environment.

The second phase introduced a dramatic change. Based on an analysis of the financial positions of the firms after the third session, an industry restructuring occurred as a part of the experimental design, resulting in two pairs of firms merging through acquisition. The General Managers in charge of the two firms in the strongest financial position were informed by a letter from their imaginary Boards that their firms had acquired one of the two in weaker positions. They were now responsible for their merged organizations. General managers of the acquired firms were informed by letter that their Boards had resigned and control of their firms had been passed to another firm. As leaders they were therefore displaced, being no longer responsible for their firm's performance. This was the *change* session. As the firms continued operations towards submission of subsequent decisions after the change in control, they moved into the third phase, which was *postchange*.

The sources of data collected were information from journals collected at the end of the simulation and from direct observation. Consistent with the three-category typology employed in Study 1, the journals were searched for references to behaviour and expressions of emotion by the General Managers during the *prechange* and *change* periods. A 3 x 3 x 2 cross-classification of managerial action, managerial emotion and change was prepared from the journal content search. As there was limited scope in the simulation to change task or technology, the threefold classification of action centred mainly on the managers' initiatives or otherwise in the formulation of role structures. The three categories were as follows: action which increased novelty by introducing new role structures through changing reporting relationships; neutral action which was consistent with or reinforced existing role structures; and action which actively decreased novelty by rejecting the development of new role structures. The rule of evidence established for these classes of managerial action required that a manager's report of his/her own behaviour was corroborated in journal entries by two or more members of a firm.

General Managers' journals were also scanned for references to their authors' emotional states during the *prechange* and *change* periods. These were trichotomized into three broad groups: positive emotions including satisfaction and pleasure, negative emotions such as frustration and anxiety, and statements of emotional neutrality. Table 2.3 tabulates these observations. Cross-classification was performed twice, with no significant differences between codings.

Table 2.3 Frequencies of reference to managerial actions and emotions in pre-change and change sessions of business simulation

	Prechange condition			Change condition		
	Associated emotion			Associated emotion		
	Pos.	Neut.	Neg.	Pos.	Neut.	Neg.
Action to increase novelty	0 0.00	1 0.03	1 0.03	4 0.11	4 0.11	5 0.14
Acquiring	0	1	1	2	3	5
Acquired	0	0	0	2	1	0
Action not increasing or decreasing novelty	4 0.11	1 0.03	2 0.06	1 0.03	0 0.00	6 0.17
Acquiring	0	1	1	1	0	1
Acquired	4	0	1	0	0	5
Action to decrease novelty	2 0.06	3 0.08	0 0.00	0 0.00	1 0.03	1 0.03
Acquiring	2	2	0	0	0	1
Acquired	0	1	0	0	1	0

Notes: Upper figures in bold type are frequency counts, lower figures are proportions of the overall total frequency.

Figures in rows labelled *Acquiring* are observations relating to General Managers in firms which acquired others during the industry restructuring.

Figures in rows labelled *Acquired* are observations relating to General Managers in firms acquired during the industry restructuring.

Results and interpretation

The log-linear models fitted to these data are displayed in Table 2.4. The model with the most satisfactory fit is the complete second order (ae, ac, ec) model ($G^2 = 2.79$, df = 4, p = 0.59). Compared with the model fitted to the Study 1 data, this model includes the additional ec interaction, describing an association between emotions and change.

Table 2.4 Log-linear models of relationships among action, and emotion in the presence and absence of change in business simulation

Model fitted	df	Likelihood ratio chi-square G^2	p	Significant (p<0.05) standardized parameter estimates
a	15	20.98	0.14	
e	15	22.78	0.09	
c	16	22.26	0.14	
a, e, c	12	18.64	0.10	
ae, c	8	12.9	0.11	$a^-e^n = 1.7$ $a^ne^n = -1.9$
ac, e	10	11.9	0.29	$a^+c^p = 2.4$ $a^-c^p = -1.7$ $a^+c^a = -2.4$ $a^-c^a = 1.7$
ec, a	10	15.3	0.12	$e^-c^p = 1.8$ $e^-c^a = -1.8$
ae, ac	6	6.3	0.39	
ca, ce	8	8.6	0.38	
ec, ec	6	9.6	0.14	
ae, ac, ec	4	2.79	0.59	

Notes: Change (c) c^p: Post-change
$\quad\quad\quad\quad\quad\quad\quad$ c^a: Pre-change
$\quad\quad\quad$ Action (a) a^+: Action to increase novelty
$\quad\quad\quad\quad\quad\quad\quad$ a^n: Action neutral to novelty
$\quad\quad\quad\quad\quad\quad\quad$ a^-: Action to decrease novelty
$\quad\quad\quad$ Emotion (e) e^+: Positive emotion
$\quad\quad\quad\quad\quad\quad\quad$ e^n: Neutral emotion
$\quad\quad\quad\quad\quad\quad\quad$ e^-: Negative emotion

Reviewing the significant standardized parameter estimates for the second-order interactions, substantial correspondence is found with the Study 1 model. With regard to relationships between action and change, novelty-increasing action is frequently associated with change ($a^+c^p = 2.4$, p<0.01) and infrequently associated with unchanging conditions ($a^+c^a = -2.4$, p<0.01). That is, managers act to introduce new, increasing change under conditions of exogenous change, and rarely do so under constant conditions. When conditions are unchanging the most frequent managerial response is to suppress novelty ($a^-c^a = 1.7$, p<0.05). Novelty-decreasing action, the suppression of change, is associated relatively frequently with emotional neutrality ($a^-e^n = 1.7$, $p<0.05$). In this study there is some indication that change is experienced as unpleasant ($e^-c^p = 1.8$, $p<0.05$).

It is clear from Table 2.3 that the total number of observations is relatively low, reflecting the detail recorded in the journals at the specified stages of the simulation. Despite small cell frequencies, which actually reduce the likelihood of cross-validation, the overall pattern of cell entries is largely consistent with the results of Study 1.

Interpretative analysis of the journals suggests that their interpretation of change has little relationship to the objective circumstances surrounding them. Further, as shown in the analysis of Table 2.3, changing events are most frequently associated with further change initiatives. Change becomes an opportunity for self-expression, for affirmation and the exercise of mastery over their working environment.

Interestingly, the highest incidence of emotional responses among the General Managers was negative after the change. This trend included both the acquired and acquirers. Those who now managed an organization of double the previous size took their responsibilities very seriously, expressing concern, frustration and worry about their decisions. Compared with the managers in Study 1 who experienced mixed emotions with the onset of change, these executives perhaps felt frustrated by the limited scope for change in their simulated organizations.

Although not reported in the content analysis, the feelings experienced by firm members are also revealing of the dynamics of change and emotional responses. Interpreting from the journals, individuals responded in positive and novelty-increasing ways with the onset of the change, depending on their perceived ability to influence outcomes through their actions. This varied between participants and over the course of the simulation. Where participants described a feeling of being able to influence changes, they took initiatives and made decisions, feeling excitement and optimism. They stressed the need to surmount events, 'take a big picture view', 'be structured and directive', 'show leadership' and 'focus on the future'. Other participants, who were encouraged to contribute to decision-making, though not to redirect the course of change, responded by being cooperative, sensitive and perceptive, 'observant'. In contrast, where participants felt unable to influence the course of events they resigned or withdrew to higher philosophical ground: they managed their sense of anxiety by dismissing the exercise.

Summarizing, the abrupt organizational change imposed from outside was interpreted by managers in a variety of ways which appear to be linked with the perception of their capacity to influence. In the case of the General Managers, whose roles provided such control, their actions were largely focused on creating new organizational structures. Once again in this study, as in the previous one, the concept of change has no unitary meaning within an organization. And the apparent managerial response to change is to create yet more change, further accentuating disturbances rather than limiting their impact.

Several limitations of this study need to be acknowledged. One is its inference from a small number of subjects in an experimental setting. However, the speculation about differences between response patterns in high and low-performing organizations does require further investigation. A unidirectional change in organizational circumstances is a second limitation arising from the experimental design. Both these shortcomings are addressed in Study 3.

Study 3: Organizational simulation with fluctuating environmental change

Study 3's objective was to investigate relationships between organizational performance and managerial responses to change. As in Study 2, a quasi-experimental design was employed, using the same computer-based competitive business simulation. Participants in a management development programme were formed at random into six firms of five or six people, comprising a General Manager and his or her staff.

The simulation involved ten decision periods run over a period of five weeks. In addition to the preset variations in market and financial conditions, the experimental design included a period of major environmental change. During the first three decision periods (t^1) firms responded only to the competitive behaviour of their organizational rivals and the changing market conditions. Then, without warning, the firms experienced a sudden increase in environmental turbulence. At this point (t^2) the environment became turbulent, ambiguous and unpredictable, exhibiting multiple sources of exogenous change. Each firm received demands from governments and trade unions, and threats to the cohesion of firm membership were experienced. Turbulent change lasted until time (t^3), then the environment became calm (t^4) with all extraordinary demands disappearing just as suddenly as they appeared.

Over the duration of the simulation two expert judges ranked the performance of the six firms on financial and strategic criteria. Averaging over the ten decision periods this resulted in three firms being ranked high in performance, and three low.

Information on processes of change was obtained from two sources during the simulation. One source was the journals which were completed during each decision cycle and submitted with completed decisions. The second was a short questionnaire which each person completed at the end of every decision cycle.

Following the lead of the previous studies, the questionnaire sought information about dimensions of emotion and action. Perceptions of three aspects of action within each firm were sought: implementation of new ideas, for example 'there is an emphasis on learning', decentralization of influence, for example 'team members influence each other through discussion', and direction and strategic review, for example 'the team has a clear sense of direction'. A measure of positive and negative emotional state used items from the Profile of Mood States (McNair, Lorr and Doppleman 1971). Seven-point Likert scales were used for items measuring each of the dimensions of action and emotion. Reports of action and emotion at each of the four critical stages of increasing and decreasing change formed a 2 x 4 (performance x time) repeated measures Anova design. Analysis of main effects and interactions was conducted using data for each of the five scale dimensions.

Results and interpretation

The key variable carried over from the previous studies is *action*: the introduction of novelty. In this study this was measured by the reported willingness to implement new ideas. Perhaps most interesting among the perceptions of action is the absence of significant shifts in behaviour with the onset and disappearance of environmental change. Apparently the alterations in behaviour which are most apparent are those which occur during change itself.

Two other variables not investigated in the previous studies were decentralization of influence and direction. Analysis indicated a trend towards a decline in decentralized influence over the period of environmental turbulence ($F = 2.86$, $p<0.10$) and a significant decline in direction for low performing firms during this period ($F = 4.58$, $p<0.05$). Table 2.5 indicates that regardless of performance of the firm, there was a decline in innovation over the period of environmental turbulence ($F = 5.64$, $p<0.05$). Together these results suggest that over a period of persistent change, decisions tend to become more centralized. Also the sense of direction during this time is lost, notably in organizations which are already limited in performance.

Variations in experienced emotions display a more complex pattern, according to the analysis shown in Table 2.5. First, high-performing firms displayed a significantly higher positive mood than low-performing firms over the duration of the simulation ($F=4.41$, $p<0.05$). Success and positive emotion apparently covary. Averaging across high and low-performing

Table 2.5 Mean scores for responses to abruptly increasing and decreasing environmental change in business simulation

	Firm performance	Change increasing $t^1 \to t^2$		Change decreasing $t^3 \to t^4$	
Action within firms					
Decentralization	High	17.5	18.0	17.4	17.2
of influence	Low	17.3	17.5	16.5	16.9
			-----------(1)-		
Implementation of	High	10.5	11.5	10.1	10.1
ideas and learning	Low	10.5	10.4	9.5	9.5
			----------(2)-		
Direction and	High	11.1	11.3	11.1	10.9
strategic review	Low	10.1	11.0	9.5	9.8
			----------(3)-		
Emotions reported					
Positive mood	High	36.8	38.1	34.7	36.4
	Low	34.2	33.2	29.8	31.5
			------------------------------(4)-		
			----------(5)-		
				-------------(6)-	
Negative mood	High	16.5	12.3	14.4	12.1
	Low	17.3	16.8	21.7	17.2
			----------(7)-	-------------(8)-	

Anova results
(1) F (1,25) = 2.86, p<0.10 (Time effect averaging performance)
(2) F (1,25) = 5.64, p<0.05 (Time effect averaging performance)
(3) F (1,25) = 4.58, p<0.05 (Interaction: performance x time)
(4) F (1,25) = 4.41, p<0.05 (Performance effect averaging time)
(5) F (1,25) = 4.82, p<0.05 (Time effect averaging performance)
(6) F (1,25) = 5.31, p<0.05 (Time effect averaging performance)
(7) F (1,25) = 4.22, p<0.05 (Interaction: performance x time)
(8) F (1,25) = 12.94, p<0.01 (Time effect averaging performance)

organizations, positive mood declines under conditions of continuing change (F=4.82, p<0.05), increasing once again when exogenous change ceases (F=5.31, p<0.05). This pattern suggests that managers feel unhappy as change persists, regaining their positive feelings once calm returns. The analysis of negative mood reveals a significant interaction with the onset of change. Managers in high-performing firms reported a significant decline in negative feelings during this time (F=4.22, p<0.05), whereas the negative mood of low performers was unchanged. Both groups experienced decreased negative feelings as the environment became calm ($F=12.94$, $p<0.01$). These results suggest a complex interdependency between the duration of change, the performance of the organization (and subsequently, perhaps, the perceived position of the manager) and emotions.

Journal accounts of events in Study 3 highlight the importance of a sense of efficacy in enabling individuals to act and therefore 'manage' change. So long as groups perceived a link between actions and outcomes, they continued to negotiate and generally felt positive about change. They elaborated roles and strategies, created new tasks and construed feedback from the environment to suit their ends. There was risk-taking, a readiness to operate with incomplete information, 'to give it a try'.

These perceptions, however, are a fragile group construction. Doubts about performance, discord, withdrawal of members, or one too many setbacks, extinguished efficacy. Groups then retrieved control by scapegoating, dismissing conditions as 'unrealistic', attacking the simulation organizer. 'As a result of government intervention . . . the syndicate was thrown into disarray . . . there was a consensus that [the game] was a waste of time and further, detracting from people's effectiveness in other sections of the course'. The 'shutdown' (of a firm's operations by a foreign government) was 'unrealistic' . . . the game was 'over' because the organizer 'has control of all the companies'. The mechanics of the game had made it unrealistic and therefore removed any opportunity for winning.

Group theorists (Slater 1966) observe that such a sense of helplessness produces mounting anger and eventually an attack on the perceived repository of power – in this case the simulation organizer. Journals of group members experiencing this loss of efficacy end with attacks on the organizer for various 'crimes' including 'controlling everything'. Others attacked with threats of not completing journals, and some were never submitted. The perception that efficacy has been extinguished by external events prompts resistance and withdrawal.

DISCUSSION

Our three studies clearly have limitations. The overall sample population of managers is skewed towards senior, rather than junior managers. Study 1 captures the recollections of survivors after the Stockmarket Adjustment, not those swept overboard. The two simulations reflect the inevitable constraints of experimental studies. Despite these and other acknowledged shortcomings, it is the consistency of our findings across three quite distinct and diverse sample populations and change experiences, together with the complementarity of methodological approaches, which encourages us to question the common wisdoms or myths. We propose an alternative set of propositions about managing change in organizations, which depart from the prescriptions of traditional change management ideology.

1 Managers perceive variable levels of change in their environment, and their interpretations derive from the interplay of organizational and personal characteristics

Change management research has tended to frame change as an objective phenomenon which can be imputed from indices of, for example, rates of diffusion of new ideas into new technologies. Change management strategies are prescribed which are based on these assumptions. Our findings support an alternative argument, placing emphasis on the variable ways managers interpret events, then mould or 'manage' meanings for others (Pfeffer 1981; Smircich and Morgan 1982; Daft and Weick 1984; Isabella 1990). Managerial interpretations may bear little resemblance to imputed commentaries of objective events. In fact, the journals from Studies 2 and 3 and interviews from Study 1 suggested that turbulence might be an example of the retrospective sense-making which Weick (1979) has argued we use to help us understand events after they have happened. Perhaps we decide we have experienced turbulence only with the benefit of hindsight.

Our research also suggests that how managers interpret change is likely to be determined by a complex interplay of organizational and personal characteristics, such as perceived performance and perceived scope to influence outcomes, which may be partially a function of organizational seniority. Our embryonic understanding of these factors should provide an important qualification to our willingness to prescribe change management strategies, since a manager's capacity to 'manage meaning' for others is clearly dependent on her or his own interpretations. Neither the perceptions, nor management, of change is free of a manager's interpretive framework, along with its biases and roots in past experience.

2 Managers do not respond to change with simple resistance or passivity, but rather favour action

Data from all three studies indicate that in response to a change, managers reported an increase in novelty-creation as their chosen action. The most frequent response to exogenous change was to generate endogenous change. The most favoured way to 'manage change' amongst our managers was to initiate change. Most commonly this took the form of elaborating or realigning the social structure in groups, perhaps to increase the likelihood of creating novel options from which to choose later.

In the interviews and journals, three clearly discernible responses to change were reported. The first was to initiate, issue directives and assume power by organizing followers. The second was to be co-operative, alert and look after immediate colleagues by being sensitive to their needs. The third was to remove self or withdraw, often by being 'philosophical' or 'an observer'. In some cases where managers perceived themselves as power-less to affect change, they regained their power to act by leaving the stage of action; by disengaging and reasserting control of themselves through the choice to withdraw. Other research (Murgatroyd, Rushton, Apter and Ray 1978; Ashford 1988) supports the hypothesis that individuals have different responses to change, and predispositions to act in certain ways.

The interaction of the event and the response it produces appears, from our studies, to be substantially governed by the individual's sense of control over previous and anticipated experiences. Bandura has termed this 'self-belief in one's capabilities to exercise control over events to accomplish desired goals' as efficacy (1988: 279). The importance of possessing a sense of control, rather than helplessness, has been substantially docu-mented by sociotechnical researchers and is the basis for arguments for worker participation and industrial democracy. Bandura's research shows that a sense of efficacy is an important determinant of performance, and that structural conditions can substantially enhance or detract from this sense of efficacy (Lock, Frederick, Lee and Bobko 1984).

Contextual as well as personality factors can influence response to change (Ashford 1988), and group effects are important. The responses we found can thus be seen as both characteristic responses used by particular individuals to change, and alternative responses used by groups at different stages of a change process. This finding is consistent with Bion's (1961) observations of groups as dominated by one of three 'basic assumptions'; fight–flight (action), dependency (co-operation and sensitivity), and pair-ing (withdrawal to a more elevated vision).

That managers have a predisposition for action is not a new insight. Indeed some might suggest that an obsession with action displaces reflec-tion and contemplation from management, and nurtures a management culture which thrives on action for its own sake (Anthony 1977; Starbuck 1983). But the impact of this propensity on change management strategies does not seem to have been widely considered. According to the change management mythology, managers will resist turbulence by denial, in-action, or action which is a retreat to the familiar. We propose an alternative interpretation, that managers respond to unfamiliarity by acting and therefore adding to it. They act in ways that convert exogenous into endogenous change. Ways of creating alternatives will perhaps be those that have produced previous success. Action in the face of unfamiliar change may be an attempt to recreate previous success or mastery; however, it is not a defensive denial of change, but rather a bid to better it. If action is the more common response to change among managers, then this implies a whole set of new problems and issues which are not anticipated in current change management models.

The notion that individuals and organizations construct the change that then impinges on them through their own actions has been explored by Abolafia and Kilduff (1988). In their version of enactment theory, they argue that crises are 'a social construction of self-interested actors' who respond to an exogenous shock by a process of action, attribution and regulation (189). Action consists of 'a deliberate effort to shape the environment . . . a political process [which] involves the mobilization of resources to shape or redefine the existing definition of reality' (1988: 180). Abolafia and Kilduff see change as the creation of groups of actors in response to other changes, which enables them to have greater control over events. Our research lends support to this view of change as a political process, in which managers obtain power by acting. By acting, seizing the initiative, the individual retrieves power over events. In the simulation studies, action enabled participants to control their activities. Failure to act, an inability or unwillingness to introduce the possibility of new alternatives and therefore a wider basis for choice and control, left a manager dejected. The hopelessness of dependence and lack of control became self-fulfillingly apparent, along with a feeling of being at the whim of the simulation organizer.

3 Change can be a pleasant emotional experience for managers, dependent on the duration of the change, perceived success and capacity to influence

In each of the studies which analysed emotional responses, it was clear that change was associated with mixed feelings. Although a higher proportion of references were made to experiences as unpleasant, under unchanging conditions the proportion of positive and negative feelings was not significantly different. We can conclude that unpleasantness and emotional distress are therefore not necessarily associated with change. Our research suggests that it may be more strongly associated with other factors a manager is perceiving. Journal entries registered feelings of exhilaration and excitement, particularly among those who had authority to command resources, enabling them to create more possible futures than those deprived of that authority.

CONCLUSION

Our findings challenge the view of managers in danger of being swept overboard by a tumultuous wave of change. According to our results, managers are more likely to embrace and create even more change: for some this offers the opportunity to learn how to swim! Whether or not they do this, and what sort of emotional response they have, is determined by a number of personal and contextual factors, including their perceptions of the degree of power they have to influence events. Our investigations cannot discount the claim that we live in turbulent times, although it should certainly suggest to us that 'change management' is not a new problem, just because it has a new label. What our evidence does do is question some conventional wisdoms about how managers respond to change. It joins with the growing body of research which argues that we need to refocus on managers' responses to, and interpretations of, change. It also reinforces the possibility that there may be some fatal flaws in the model which assumes that managers can manage the change of others, and attempts to prescribe activities to do just that.

REFERENCES

Abolafia, M.Y. and Kilduff, M. (1988) 'Enacting market crisis: the social construction of a speculative bubble', *Administrative Science Quarterly* 33(2): 177–93.

Adler, N. (1986) *International Dimensions of Organizational Behaviour*, Boston: Kent Publishing Company.

Allison, G.T. (1971) *Essence of Decision: Explaining the Cuban missile crisis*, Boston: Little, Brown & Co.

Anthony, P.D. (1977) *The Ideology of Work*, London: Tavistock.

Ashford, S.J. (1988) 'Individual strategies for coping with stress during organizational transitions', *The Journal of Applied Behavioral Science* 24(1): 19–36.

Baburoglu, O.N. (1988) 'The vortical environment: the fifth in the Emery-Trist levels of organizational environments', *Human Relations* 41(3): 181–210.

Bandura, A. (1988) 'Social cognitive theory', *Australian Journal of Management*, 13(2): 275–302.

Bennis, W. and Nanus, B. (1985) *Leaders: Strategies for Taking Charge*, New York: Harper & Row.

Billings, R.S., Milburn, T.W. and Schaalman, M.L. (1980) 'A model of crisis perception: a theoretical and empirical analysis', *Administrative Science Quarterly* 25: 300–16.

Bion, W.R. (1961) *Experiences in Groups*, London: Tavistock.

Bishop, Y.M.M., Feinberg, S.E. and Holland, P.W. (1975) *Discrete Multivariate Analysis: Theory and Practice*, Cambridge, Mass: MIT Press.

Bonnet, D.G. and Bentler, P.M. (1983) 'Goodness of fit procedures for the evaluation and selection of log-linear models', *Psychological Bulletin* 93: 149–66.

Bourgeois, L.J., McAllister, D.W. and Mitchell, T.R. (1978) 'The effects of different organizational environments upon decisions about organizational structure', *Academy of Management Journal* 21(3): 508–14.

Burns, T. and Stalker, G.M. (1961) *The Management of Innovation*, London: Tavistock.

Cameron, K., Kim, M. and Whetton, D.A. (1987) 'Organizational effects of decline and turbulence', *Administrative Science Quarterly* 32: 222–40.

Cameron, K., Sutton, R. and Whetton, D.A. (1988) *Readings in Organizational Decline: Frameworks, Research And Prescriptions*, Cambridge, Mass: Ballinger.

Cotton, J., Vollrath, D., Froggatt, K., Lengrick-Hall, M. and Jennings, K. (1988) 'Employee participation: diverse forms and different outcomes', *Academy of Management Review* 13(1): 8–22.

Daft, R.L. and Weick, K.E. (1984) 'Toward a model of organizations as interpretation systems', *Academy of Management Review* 9(2): 284–95.

Donaldson, L. (1985) *In Defence of Organizational Theory: a Reply to the Critics*, New York: Cambridge University Press.

Drucker, P.F. (1980) *Managing in Turbulent Times*, New York: Harper & Row.

Dunphy, D. and Stace, D. (1988) 'Transformational and coercive strategies for planned organizational change: beyond the OD model', *Organization Studies* 9(3): 317–34.

Emery, F.E. and Trist, E.L. (1965) 'The causal texture of organizational environments', *Human Relations* 18: 21–32.

Festinger, L. (1957) *A Theory of Cognitive Dissonance*, Stanford: Stanford University Press.

Gladstein, D.L. and Reilly, N.P. (1985) 'Group decision making under threat: the Tycoon Game', *Academy of Management Journal* 28(3): 613–27.

Glaser, B. and Strauss, A. (1967) *Discovery of Grounded Theory: Strategies for Qualitative Research*, Chicago: Aldine.

Goldstein, J. (1988) 'A far-from-equilibrium systems approach to resistance to change', *Organizational Dynamics* 17(2): 16–26.

Goode, W.J. and Hatt, P.K. (1952) *Methods in Social Research*, New York: McGraw-Hill.

Greiner, L. (1972) 'Evolution and revolution as organizations grow', *Harvard Business Review*, July–August: 37–46.

Hayes, R. and Watts, R. (1986) *Corporate Revolution: New Strategies for Executive Leadership*, London: Heinemann.

Isabella, L.A. (1990) 'Evolving interpretations as a change unfolds: how managers construe key organizational events', *Academy of Management Journal* 33(1): 7–41.

Janis, I.L. and Mann, L. (1977) *Decision Making: A Psychological Analysis of Conflict, Choice, and Commitment*, New York: The Free Press.

Kanter, R.M. (1985) *The Change Masters*, New York: Counterpoint.

Kanter, R.M. (1989) *When Giants Learn to Dance*, London: Unwin Hyman.

Kets de Vries, M.F.R. (1984) (ed.) *The Irrational Executive*, New York: International Universities Press.

Kets de Vries, M.F.R. and Miller, D. (1987) 'Interpreting organizational texts', *Journal of Management Studies*, 24(5): 233–47.

Kets de Vries, M.F.R. and Miller, D. (1984) *The Neurotic Organization*, California: Jossey Bass.

Kindleberger, C.P. (1978) *Manias, Panics and Crises: A History of Financial Crisis*, New York: Basic Books.

Kotter, J.P. and Schlesinger, L.A. (1979) 'Choosing strategies for change', *Harvard Business Review* 57(2): 106–14.

Lawrence, P. (1969) 'How to deal with resistance to change', *Harvard Business Review*, January/February (reprinted in HBR Classics: *Developing an Effective Organization* 145–53.

Lawrence, P.R. and Lorsch, J.W. (1967) 'Differentiation and integration in complex Organizations', *Administrative Science Quarterly* 12: 1–47.

Lazarus, R.S. (1966) *Psychological Stress and the Coping Process*, New York: McGraw-Hill.

Litwin, G.H. and Stringer, R.A. (1968) *Motivation and Organizational Climate*, Boston: Division of Research, Harvard Business School.

Locke, E., Frederick, E., Lee, C. and Bobko, P. (1984) 'Effect of self-efficacy, goals, task and task strategies on task performance', *Journal of Applied Psychology* 69: 241–25.

Locke, E. and Schweiger, D. (1979) 'Participation in decision-making: one more look', in B. Star (ed.) *Research in Organizational Decision-Making*, Connecticut: JAI Press: 265–339.

Lodahl, T.M. and Kejner, M. (1965) 'The definition and measurement of job involvement', *Journal of Applied Psychology* 49: 24–33.

McCall, M.W. (1977) 'Making sense with nonsense: helping frames of reference clash', in P.C. Nystrom and W.H. Starbuck (eds) *Prescriptive Models of Organisations/TMIS Studies in the Management Sciences* 5, North Holland Publishing Company: 111–23.

McCaskey, M. (1982) *The Executive Challenge: Managing Change and Ambiguity*, Boston: Pitman.

McNair, D.M., Lorr, M. and Droppleman, L.F. (1971) *The Profile of mood states*, San Diego, CA: Educational and Industrial Testing Service.

Martin, J. and Meyerson, D. (1988) 'Organizational cultures and the denial, channeling and acknowledgement of ambiguity', in L. Pondy, R. Boland and H. Thomas (eds) *Managing Ambiguity and Change*, Chichester: Wiley & Sons.

Miller, D. and Friesen, P. (1980) 'Momentum and revolution in organizational adaption', *Academy of Management Review* 23(4): 591–614.

Morgan, G. (1988) *Riding the Waves of Change*, San Francisco: Jossey Bass.

Murgatroyd, S., Rushton, C., Apter, M. and Ray, C. (1978) 'The development of the Telic Dominance Scale', *Journal of Personality Assessment* 42(5): 519–27.

Naisbitt, J. (1982) *Megatrends*, London: Macdonald.

Naisbitt, J. and Aburdene, P. (1985) *Reinventing the Corporation*, New York: Warner.

Peters, T. (1987) *Thriving on Chaos: Handbook for Management Revolution*, New York: Random House.

Peters, T. (1988) 'Facing up to the need for a management revolution', *California Management Review* 30(2): 7–38.

Peters, T. and Waterman, R. (1982) *In Search of Excellence*, New York: Harper & Row.

Pfeffer, J. (1981) 'Management as symbolic action: the creation and maintenance of organizational paradigms', in *Research in Organizational Behaviour*, B. Staw and L. Cummings (eds), Connecticut: JAI Press.

Postman, L. and Bruner, J.S. (1948) 'Perception under stress', *Psychological Review* 55: 314–23.

Quinn, J.B. (1980) *Strategies for Change: Logical Incrementalism*, Holmwood, Illinois: Irwin.

Quinn, J.B. (1985) 'Managing innovation: controlled chaos', *Harvard Business Review* 63(3): 73–84.

Rothschild-Witt, J. (1986) *The Co-operative Workplace: Potential and dilemmas of organizational democracy and participation*, Cambridge: Cambridge University Press.

Sinclair, A. (1990) 'Sponsoring self-management of change', working paper 16: Graduate School of Management, University of Melbourne.

Slater, P. (1966) *Microcosm*, New York: Wiley.

Smircich, L. and Morgan, G. (1982) 'Leadership: the management of meaning', *Journal of Applied Behavioural Science* 18(3): 257–73.

Starbuck, W.H. (1983) 'Organizations as action generators', *American Sociological Review* 48(1): 91–102.

Starbuck, W.H. (1985) 'Acting first and thinking later: theory versus reality in strategic change', in M. Pennings (ed.) *Organizational Strategy and Change*, San Francisco: Jossey Bass.

Staw, B.M., Sandelands, L.E. and Dutton, J.E. (1981) 'Threat-rigidity effects in organizational behaviour: a multilevel analysis, *Administrative Science Quarterly* 26: 501–24.

Sutton, R.I. (1987) 'The process of organizational death: disbanding and re-connecting', *Administrative Science Quarterly* 32: 542–69.

Thompson, J.D. (1967) *Organizations in Action*, New York: McGraw-Hill.

Toffler, A. (1970) *Future Shock*, London: Bodley Head.

Toffler, A. (1985) *The Adaptive Corporation*, London: Pan.

Tushman, M. and Nadler, D. (1986) 'Organizing for innovation', *California Management Review* 28(3): 74–92.

Weick, K. (1979) *The Social Psychology of Organizing* (2nd edn), New York: Random House.

Weick, K. (1985) 'Sources of order in underorganized systems: themes in recent organizational theory', in Y. Lincoln (ed.) *Organizational Theory and Inquiry: the Paradigm Revolution*, Beverly Hills: Sage: 106–36.

Woodward, J. (1965) *Industrial Organization: Theory and Practice*, London: Oxford University Press.

Zaleznik, A. (1977) 'Managers and leaders: Are they different', *Harvard Business Review* 55: 67–78.

3   Radical change within a British university

A. Ian Glendon

This case study documents a longitudinal perspective of a generally neglected organizational topic: size reduction. Research methods used were
participant observation and documentary analysis. Alternative theoretical
perspectives are reviewed as potential frameworks for explaining events
over an eight-year period of intense organizational change. The analysis
extends to a consideration of external demands which drive system
changes. The analysis reveals the inadequacy of a pluralist framework for
explaining events, a radical model being a more valid fit.

METHODOLOGY

Participant observation has an extensive pedigree in sociology and social
anthropology; it is much less used in psychology. In traditional participant
observer role classifications (Gold 1958; Junker 1960), the researcher plays
a 'participant-as-observer' role, combining a formal role within the organization with being an observer of it. With previous experience of a similar
role in an organization experiencing industrial conflict (Glendon 1977), it
was known that the advantages conferred by such a role include relatively
good access to documentary material, and direct experience of the emotional intensity associated with observed events. As a member of the local
AUT[1] committee throughout the period of intense change, the researcher
also was active in the change process, both inside and outside the organization. The main disadvantage of this role was the access limitations
imposed by role boundaries. The researcher's formal role changed four
times during the period, his departmental status changed five times, and his
faculty status changed three times.

The researcher's position within the organization inevitably means that
the analysis is partial, and to an extent interpretive. Although hindered by
lack of systematic data collection, there was no shortage of documentary
material. Further, retrospective analysis allows for meanings and

interpretations which were not always evident at the time. The historical perspective in retrospect confers the advantage of an interpretive approach (see, for example, Pettigrew 1985).

Finally, it should be noted that because anonymity for the organization is not possible in this case, this has, to an extent, influenced selection and presentation of material for illustrative purposes.

CASE INTRODUCTION

The case example is Aston University, where the author was a full-time member of staff from 1975. During this time the organization passed through a period of radical change. In 1979/80, Aston's full-time academic staff establishment was 537; by 1985/86 it had reduced to 279 – a 48 per cent reduction within seven years.[2] There were comparable reductions among support staff, and total student numbers fell from 5,700 in 1978/79 to 3,600 in 1984/85 – a 37 per cent reduction. In 1980, there were twenty-four departments in four faculties; these had become ten departments in three faculties by the end of 1985. Table 3.1 shows the chronology of key events.

Table 3.1 Chronology of key events

1966	– Aston granted university charter
1966–79	– Era of expansion
1979	– Aston's second Vice-Chancellor[3] retires
1979–80	– Caretaker Vice-Chancellor in post
July 1980	– New Vice-Chancellor appointed
July 1981	– University Grants Committee (UGC)[4] cuts Aston's grant by 31 per cent
1981–3	– Intense conflict and disruption
1983–5	– Major restructuring and staff reductions
Jan 1986	– Vice-Chancellor awarded knighthood
1986–90	– Consolidation of major changes; continuing minor changes

The task of presenting a detailed chronicle of events has been undertaken already (Aston University 1985, 1988a, 1988b; Walford 1987). The focus of this chapter is on selected aspects of the change process which illustrate issues of theoretical interest. In particular, the case illustrates the political nature of change and its challenge to the status quo, in which vested interests are revealed by power and authority relations. The case also highlights the quasi-planned nature of organizational change, showing how the intentions of key actors affect outcomes in a general way, even though the main unit of analysis is the organization. Finally, the particular contribution of a participant observation methodology as a basis for evaluating organizational change reveals a distinct offering from organizational psychology.

THE PROCESSES OF CHANGE

The issue of what constitutes change is problematic, given that change is an ever-present feature of all organizations. A typical formulation is that change follows a pattern of relative calm, interspersed with shorter periods of intense activity (see, for example, Pettigrew 1985). Elaborating upon Miller and Friesen's (1984) model of firms moving between periods of stability punctuated by transformations, Child and Smith (1987) maintain that clearly defined beginnings and ends are not necessarily characteristic of intense transformations, which can be separated neither from their genesis nor from their legacy. In their study of restructuring as a consequence of strategic redirection, Doz and Prahalad (1987) acknowledge that transformations follow a period of stability but that it comprises a series of relatively minor steps over time. Child and Smith (1987) reveal that 'transformations . . . typically combine the incremental extension of some existing policies and practices with other features that are more radically innovative' (p. 576), leading them to write of the 'interleaves of change and continuity' (p. 577).

This case represents an example of what Whetten (1980a) refers to as a 'neglected topic in organizational science', namely organizational decline – in respect of size. Noting the difficulty of overcoming labels which equate growth with success and accomplishment, and decline with failure (1980b), Whetten alludes to a bias in the organizational change literature towards the study of growth and its concomitants – diversity and increasing complexity, for example (1980a). Whetten also notes that the dominance of the growth paradigm poses problems for models in explaining behaviour under conditions of decline (1980b). For example, models of decision-making, leadership, conflict resolution and communication which are valid for organizations during growth phases are no longer likely to be so for organizations when growth is negative.

Where declining organizations were once seen as aberrant, now their ubiquity has generated a new term – 'downsizing' – as a euphemistic referent. In an extensive review (1980b), Whetten reveals that the research literature on organizational decline is broad, and mainly case study. Freeman and Hannan (1975) report on non-symmetric growth and decline processes in US schools, and the environmental demand changes which drive system changes. For example, demographic changes might lead to a period of rapid growth followed by slow decline. A more turbulent organizational experience might be expected from slow steady growth preceding a period of rapid decline. Political vulnerability is cited as one of four reasons for decline in Levine's (1978) typology, with young organizations – such as technological universities – being particularly vulnerable.

THE PLURALIST PERSPECTIVE

The pluralist perspective is used widely in the analysis of social and organizational change (e.g. Clegg 1979). Essentially, it maintains that all actors within a system have the potential to influence outcomes and that differences between them are inevitable because of their independent positions. Thus, while conflict is conceived of as an inevitable outcome of change, there are system balances which ensure that even if power is not shared equally among participants, there are opportunities for realistic participation in decision-making and implementation stages (e.g. Flanders 1965, Dunlop 1971).

From this description of the pluralist approach to organizational change, a number of themes which characterize this perspective may be identified. First, participants within the system are conceived of as being players in a potentially positive sum game, that is one from which all parties can benefit in terms of outcomes. Second, no long-term power imbalances are admitted – all participants are able to influence change and decision-making processes. Third, pluralist approaches frequently use a structured framework for describing events, for example a system of rules as found in industrial relations processes.

This section reviews relevant literature from pluralist change perspectives, using selected illustrations from the Aston case study to highlight key concepts used.

A prescriptive stage model

Surveying eighteen cases of organizational change, Greiner (1967) identifies eight features of successful change. Table 3.2 shows Greiner's eight features and illustrates these with examples from the Aston case study.

An interesting feature of Table 3.2 is that while acceptable parallels from the case may be found for the first six of Greiner's stages, the fit of the model breaks down thereafter. One reason for this is the problematic nature of the 'success' criterion, which although identified as a series of indicators by Greiner, would create methodological and measurement difficulties in their operationalization. In the absence of empirical data on these measures and because of the underlying unitary nature of the model – 'success' is equated with the objectives of the powerful group, and ignores any possibility of conflicting criteria arising from a plurality of interests – the

Table 3.2 A comparison of Greiner's (1967) success patterns and events in the change process at Aston University

Greiner success pattern	Aston examples to parallel Greiner stages
1 Considerable external and internal pressure for improvement long before explicit change is contemplated. Low performance/morale. Management groping for solutions.	Main pressure from UGC over period up to 1981 and specifically requiring radical changes 1981–4. Interregnum management weak during difficult period of finding a successor. Performance identified as poor by UGC.
2 'New man' known for his ability to introduce improvements becomes official head (or consultant).	New Vice-Chancellor appointed in July 1980 largely on the basis of these qualities.
3 Initial act of new man is to encourage re-examination of past practices and current problem.	Vice-Chancellor sets such a re-examination in process by collecting information (by questionnaire and lunchtime discussions with academic staff) and by communicating (by newsletter, circular and addressing mass meetings of staff) on the need for Aston to change.
4 Head of organization and immediate subordinates assume direct and highly involved role in the re-examination.	Vice-Chancellor and three immediate subordinates (dubbed the 'gang of four') attend fifty-seven meetings within the organization to discuss change with all university staff.
5 The new man engages several levels of the organization in fact-finding, problem-solving discussion to identify and diagnose current organization problems.	Administration set to work collating statistics about all aspects of the University and its staff. 'Task forces' are set up composed only of junior staff to address problems in their field and to suggest solutions. Individual interviews are held by the Vice-Chancellor with senior staff to review their positions.
6 The new man provides others with new ideas and methods for developing solutions to problems.	Vice-Chancellor mainly challenges assumptions made, particularly in respect of obtaining resources. Task forces and similar mechanisms are new to the organization.
7 Solutions and decisions are developed on a small scale and used to solve problems.	No real examples. Change occurs so rapidly that this stage seems to have been omitted!
8 Change effort spreads with each success experience and as management support grows, is gradually absorbed permanently.	Management support for Vice-Chancellor's approach does increase over time and changes are 'permanently' absorbed. However, 'success' criteria problematic.

Greiner model must be rejected as inadequate for a complete analysis of change processes.

One central feature of the Greiner model – that of the new chief executive as a change agent – is also identified in the organizational 'turnaround' literature, some of which indicates the significance for the 'turnaround' phenomenon of a new incoming chief executive (see for example, Slatter 1984). Doz and Prahalad (1987) contrast successful with unsuccessful organizational change, the former being associated with one individual obtaining a leadership position and bringing a new vision. However, Grinyer, Mayes and McKiernan (1987) note that new leaders characterize organizations which fail to manage change, as much as they are associated with organizations which manage change successfully.

A transitional stage model

The systems model proposed by Beckhard and Harris (1987) provides another potential framework for analysis of the Aston case. Downsizing is among the challenges for managing change identified by these authors, and the technical innovation and quality maintenance features of this particular challenge were salient components at Aston. The two principal examples of technical innovation during the period of contraction were the Centre for Extension Education (CEE), comprising three fully-equipped lecture rooms for videoing lectures, editing suites, viewing rooms, staff, etc., and the prestigious and successful Aston Science Park. Levine (1978) reports a divergence of views in respect of the relationship between decline and innovation, noting that innovations initiated under conditions of stress may contribute to system collapse. This was not evident in Aston's case.

Beckhard and Harris's model is centred upon present, future desired, and transition states for an organization, with particular emphasis upon managing the transition. The Vice-Chancellor at Aston expended considerable effort in mapping the demand system in the year following his appointment. For example, great initial emphasis was placed upon undergraduate student entry qualifications. The main initial quality-maintenance feature was A level[5] entry grades for admission to undergraduate courses, which rose from a mean of 7.4 in 1980 to a mean of 11.5 in 1988, with no student then being admitted with fewer than nine points. Aston's average A level entry points for all subjects surpassed the all-UK university average during this period, remaining at about one point above this figure thereafter. Quality criteria were also applied to such areas as postgraduate admissions, research, and sources of research funding.

In July 1981, the awaited letter from the UGC arrived, announcing a cut of approximately 30 per cent in Aston's revenue from this source. Once the contents of the letter had been digested, further effort was expended in communicating alternative projected deficits (the worst case being a deficit of £12m within three to four years) to all members of the organization. However, at no time did the Vice-Chancellor ever project a clear image of a desired future state, except in abstract terms or by inference. Thus, 'quality driven', 'excellence', 'attractive programmes' (courses) all found frequent expression, and it became widely known that certain subjects were favoured over others. But the dominant image projected was a negative one, reflecting what the fate of the university would be if certain actions were not followed.

Beckhard and Harris proceed to an essentially pluralist, yet prescriptive, perspective on organizational change. While many features of their model could be observed at Aston during the 1980-5 period, others seem to miss the target. For example, the notion of a 'critical mass' of support supposed to be required for change did not appear to develop at Aston. The concept of a 'critical mass' as a precursor to change may thus be challenged as being either unnecessary – change can occur without it – or as a *post hoc* attribution – if change occurred, then there must have been a critical mass to promote it. Another possibility is that the concept is relevant only within a pluralist framework – for example where change is negotiated – but that it is inapplicable to a period of intense radical change driven by unequal power relationships.

These selected elements from the Beckhard and Harris model suggest that it cannot provide a complete fit for the analysis of change in this case.

Other models

A model which is again prescriptive, but which concentrates upon key events and activities, is that of Plant (1987). Plant proposes a force-field analysis, and such an analysis for Aston in 1981 might look as shown in Figure 3.1. A force-field analysis gives some indication of the relative position and strength of the various forces operating, and immediately suggests an initial strategy for change. As Plant (p. 31) notes, 'The very process of *listening actively* to the resisting forces will have the effect of reducing them' (emphasis in original). This was a strategy pursued by the Vice-Chancellor who met regularly with all those who might wield power or have influence within the organization – for example, senior academics, other high-ranking staff and trade union representatives. It is impossible to quantify the effect that this exercise might have had, although it confirmed in the minds of those 'listened to' that the Vice-Chancellor was not only determined and resourceful, but more importantly was concerned with the appearance of listening, rather than being motivated by a genuine interest in the views expressed.

A feature of the force-field analysis is that the main driving forces – apart from the Vice-Chancellor himself – were environmental and techno-logical, whereas the main resisting forces were in the 'social' categories.

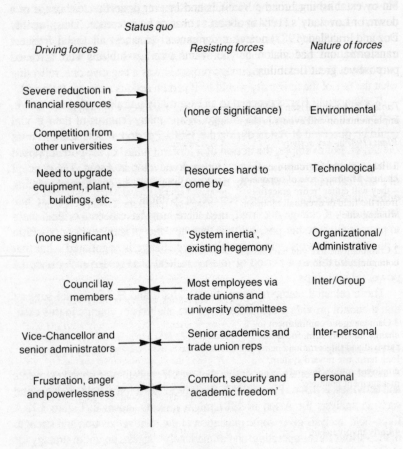

Status quo

Driving forces		Resisting forces	Nature of forces

Severe reduction in financial resources →

(none of significance) — Environmental

Competition from other universities →

Need to upgrade equipment, plant, buildings, etc. →← Resources hard to come by — Technological

(none significant) ← 'System inertia', existing hegemony — Organizational/Administrative

Council lay members →← Most employees via trade unions and university committees — Inter/Group

Vice-Chancellor and senior administrators →← Senior academics and trade union reps — Inter-personal

Frustration, anger and powerlessness →← Comfort, security and 'academic freedom' — Personal

Figure 3.1 Force-field analysis – Aston in 1981

Plant (1987) identifies six key activities for successful implementation of change. These are shown in Table 3.3, alongside examples from the Aston case. The last of these – avoidance of over-organizing – is particularly interesting, because the Vice-Chancellor was asked frequently during the years of frantic activity what his own plans were for the university. He was rarely believed when he consistently replied that he had no plan (in the specific sense). In retrospect, it seems most likely that he did not in fact have any plan, in the sense of having a particular organizational structure or set of functions in mind, but rather a generalized view of what the organization should be like in the future. His role was in line with that described by Mintzberg (1987) of crafting strategy not by planning detail, but by establishing broad guidelines and leaving specifics to those lower down, or Lovelady's (1984a) notion of change being created, not planned. Doz and Prahalad (1987) note that key executives who managed successful transformations had vision but no 'game plan', exhibiting constancy of purpose yet great flexibility.

Table 3.3 A comparison of Plant's key activities for successful change implementation and events in the change process at Aston University

Plant (1987) – key activity	*Aston examples*
1 Help individuals/groups face up to change. Minimize role of opponents – they will either 'retire gracefully from the field or eventually join the winning side'.	Much time and effort devoted to meeting groups to discuss change. Many opponents of proposed changes leave Aston, and others join winning side (professors initially vocal in their opposition to the Vice-Chancellor's approach later become pro-vice-chancellors).
2 Communicate like you have never communicated before.	A news sheet – *Aston Fortnight* – becomes a propaganda vehicle for internal and external consumption. Vice-Chancellor sends out vast amounts of material to all academic staff and to other parties, and holds many meetings.
3 Gain energetic commitment to change. In short term, focus on survival and the common enemy; in long term, use reward system, employment policies and management practices.	A week after the UGC letter of July 1981 is received, 23,000 letters are sent out to put Aston's case. Survival was the issue, and the UGC and the Government the enemy. Promotion system used to reward desired staff performance; only those with exceptional qualifications are appointed; [6]appraisal and evaluation systems introduced.
4 Early involvement.	Junior staff task forces.
5 Opportunity or threat – perceptions of change.	Conditional upon certain 'staff movements', the future is often presented as an opportunity for creating a better organization.
6 Avoid over-organizing – cannot completely control the change process. Have a generalized vision and allow structures to evolve.	A new faculty – Life and Health Sciences – is created in 1983, but survives for only 18 months.

A composite of the transition model of Beckhard and Harris (1987) and Plant's (1987) key-event model might result in the description of the Aston case shown in Figure 3.2.

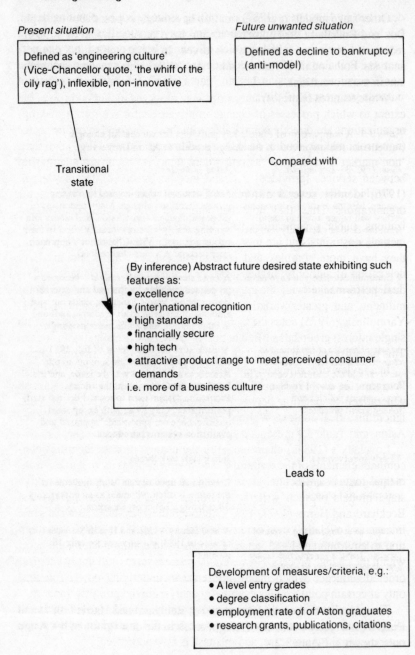

Present situation

Defined as 'engineering culture' (Vice-Chancellor quote, 'the whiff of the oily rag'), inflexible, non-innovative

Future unwanted situation

Defined as decline to bankruptcy (anti-model)

Transitional state

Compared with

(By inference) Abstract future desired state exhibiting such features as:
- excellence
- (inter)national recognition
- high standards
- financially secure
- high tech
- attractive product range to meet perceived consumer demands

i.e. more of a business culture

Leads to

Development of measures/criteria, e.g.:
- A level entry grades
- degree classification
- employment rate of of Aston graduates
- research grants, publications, citations

Figure 3.2 Transition model for Aston University *c.* 1981

Other stage models of transformation have been proposed. For example, Doz and Prahalad (1987) propose a four-stage process model of strategic redirection for cases which they observed. In Child and Smith's (1987) analysis, both cognitive framing and material structural change are important in transformations.

While features of these frameworks were observed in the Aston case, the extent to which processes of change in private sector (i.e. profit-making) organizations are directly comparable with those observed in public sector (non-profit making) bodies needs to be addressed. Downs (1967) defines a 'non-market organization' as one where there is 'no direct relationship between services [provided] . . . and income [received]'. Rainey *et al.* (1976) identify several differences between public and private sector organizations. Thus, they note that compared with private sector organizations, public organizations have less market exposure, more environmental constraints, and are more subject to political influence. As a result, they have more complex and contradictory goals, less autonomy, less delegation of authority, higher turnover, greater difficulty linking individual performance with incentives, lower worker satisfaction and commitment, and greater variation in member characteristics and abilities. Yarmolinsky (1975) notes the inability of universities to change because no single interest group has sufficient power to alter the organization's course. This pluralist position may obtain only during times of low external threat.

In a review of contingency approaches to human services organizations, Pettigrew *et al.* (1987) note that many writers, in seeking to establish generalized association between organizations and their environments, ignore historical context. Walford (1987) provides a historical context for Aston, and Table 3.4 presents a possible stage model for the case.

Lovelady's (1984a) chain model of the change process identifies concomitant elements of the reappraisal and review process as well as environmental features influential at each stage. Lovelady criticizes prescriptive stage models of such writers as Greiner (1967), Ottaway (1976) and Beckhard and Harris (1977, 1987), although these models share the same lineage as Lovelady's own iterative model. Lovelady's model draws attention to environmental and iterative processes in communicating elements within the change process. However, the process stages still imply a logical ordered sequence which makes reference to underlying power relations only at certain points, and is essentially analysis in the pluralist tradition.

The pluralist diagnostic frameworks examined, while providing useful insights into organizational change processes, fail to explain fully change outcomes in the Aston case, and this task is now addressed.

Table 3.4 Stages in the change process at Aston university

Year	Period descriptor	Main characteristics of period
1975–9	Complacency	*Laissez-faire*, growth, apathy, low involvement in decision-making
1979–80	Anxiety	Power vacuum at top, rumblings of impending change in university following election of Tory government
1980–1	Preparation	New Vice-Chancellor gathers information on the organization
1981–2	Mobilization	External threat mobilized to initiate major changes – leads to greater uncertainty, anxiety and defensive postures
1982–3	Confrontation	Positions increasingly polarized, AUT issue writ against compulsory redundancies, intense conflict
1983–4	Restructuring	Main period of staff departures, mergers and dismemberments affect all departments, strike of Aston technicians against redundancies
1984–5	Respite	New faculty structure emerges; threats against staff recede, uncertainty and anxiety persist
1985–6	Consolidation	Internal threat of imbalances and maldistributions used to mobilize further but less radical changes
1986–7	Development	Physical development of campus proceeds apace and visions of a better future are tentatively forecast
1987–8	Evaluation	Measures of all areas of activity – teaching, research and administration – established to compare individuals, groups, disciplines within Aston and the organization as a whole with competitors

BEYOND A PLURALIST ANALYSIS

The radical perspective may be likened to the pluralist approach in so far as it maintains that different parties within a system have different interests, and that conflict is therefore a likely, if not an inevitable feature of their relationship. However, it diverges crucially from a pluralist position in that it maintains that enduring power imbalances between parties critically determine their relationships (Fox 1974).

The essential differences which characterize either a radical perspective or a critique of the pluralist perspective (Lukes 1974) are that first, system players may well be engaged in a zero sum game, from which if one party emerges as a winner, then the other(s) will be losers. Second, power imbalances persist in both the long run and the short run. The significance of this is that some participants are unable to influence decision-making because of their lack of power.

This section offers a critique of the pluralist perspective in organizational change, again using selected illustrative material from the Aston case in order to critique one example of pluralist analysis (Plant 1987). The diagnostic framework adopted is based upon the unequal use of power in the pursuit of change within organizations, on which an extensive literature exists (see, for example, Pettigrew 1972, 1973; Pfeffer 1981; Handy 1985).

Critique of a pluralist model

From the analyses presented in the above section it should have become clear that the Vice-Chancellor was a prime mover not only in developing and influencing power structures within the organization (Lovelady 1984a), but also in 'mobilizing bias' in order to facilitate his role as a change agent and manager. For example, lay members of the University Council (its governing body) were targeted as part of the Vice-Chancellor's influencing strategy. An illustration of the failure of a pluralist analysis to proceed far enough may be demonstrated by a revised version of Figure 3.3 showing how power derived from the Vice-Chancellor's role (see following section) could be used to reinforce the key activities identified in the Plant (1987) model. This is shown in Table 3.5.

A comparison of the examples shown in Tables 3.3 and 3.5 against the same key activities (Plant 1987) shows that, while the initial pluralist analysis appeared on the surface to provide a satisfactory analysis of events, the power-based examples of Figure 3.6 demonstrate that this was a less than adequate analytical framework. Thus, a single powerful actor was able to dominate other actors, such that their influence was minimal. This observation calls into question the adequacy of a pluralist perspective in this case.

Power and the Vice-Chancellor

An issue which must now be addressed is the origins of the power of the Vice-Chancellor. Moodie and Eustace (1974) identify a number of ways in which power accrues to a vice-chancellor, and these are reviewed in the Aston context by Walford (1987). The most important ways are summarized in Table 3.6.

While the examples in Table 3.6 illustrate some of the mechanisms involved, they cannot do justice to another vital feature in this case – referred to by Lovelady (1984a) in the context of the importance of the role of social relationships in generating and implementing change. Among other characteristics, the Vice-Chancellor is an exceptionally skilled debater, and challenging him was never undertaken lightly. These relationship characteristics were relevant in that, combined with the sources of power theoretically available to any Vice-Chancellor, they allowed for

Table 3.5 A power-based perspective of Plant's key activities

Plant (1987) – key activity	*Aston examples*
1 Help individuals/groups face up to change. Minimize role of opponents – they will either 'retire gracefully from the field or eventually join the winning side'.	Individuals and groups are threatened if they fail to comply with Vice-Chancellor's current wishes, either directly by him or via department heads. Threats take form of cutting off research resources or telling individuals they are no longer required. Many opponents do not 'retire gracefully' from the field, but leave because they are forced out – professors have their departments dismembered and staff find that courses they taught on no longer exist. Many people leave in a state of anger, frustration and dismay.
2 Communicate like you have never communicated before.	Control of communication channels devolved to Vice-Chancellor. Academic Assembly publication *Viewpoints* – providing an alternative and opposing voice – ceases publication as funds are cut off.
3 Gain energetic commitment to change. In short term, focus on survival and the common enemy. In long term, use reward system, employment policies and management practices.	Individual bargains struck by Vice-Chancellor with all senior staff in the days following UGC letter to provide a platform for proposals for change to be pushed through at Senate a week later. The 'enemy' is within.
4 Early involvement.	Task forces' recommendations largely ignored – involvement essentially bogus.
5 Opportunity or threat – perceptions of change.	Varied use of opportunity and threat perspectives by Vice-Chancellor to destabilize structures.
6 Avoid over-organizing – cannot completely control the change process. Have a generalized vision and allow structures to evolve.	Generalized vision allowed for targets to be continually reset and for a state of uncertainty to be sustained. Fate of new faculty effectively sealed once detractors dub it the 'Faculty of Death and Disease'!

substantial hegemony. For example, by breaching traditional academic cultural codes of argument based upon expertise, academics and university managers could be coerced by a Vice-Chancellor willing and able to employ such resources.

Table 3.6 Ways in which power accrues to a Vice-Chancellor (after Moodie and Eustace 1974 and Walford 1987)

Moodie and Eustace criterion	*Aston case (Walford 1987)*
1 Nature of selection – appointment by Council and Senate	Hard for Council and Senate to oppose a Vice-Chancellor they appointed so recently!
2 Chairmanship of important committees	Vice-Chancellor chaired all committees of any importance, made occasional appearances at others, controlled agenda items and contents of minutes.
3 Focal point for communication	From the start the Vice-Chancellor made it his business to know about everything. He once remarked that 'not a sparrow falls without my knowing it'. (Dr Sparrow left soon after!)
4 Link between Senate and Council	Particularly important that most lay members of Council (mainly businessmen) saw Vice-Chancellor in a Managing Director role, with effective executive authority.
5 Chief administrator role	Use of age profiles, class sizes and A level grades as internal 'success' criteria for departmental survival. Quantitative data hard to challenge.
6 Control over new appointments	Vice-Chancellor a member of every appointments board for lectureships since his arrival, and uses his power of veto as he sees fit. No professors appointed between 1980 and 1988.
7 Influence over financial decisions	By channeling funds into physical development and other projects (e.g. CEE), fewer resources are available for staff, thus creating additional pressure to make staff redundant.

A POWER-BASED MODEL OF CHANGE

Further examples from the Aston case which may be grounded in the literature provide additional illustrations for the power-based model of change. Pettigrew (1985) and Pettigrew *et al.* (1987) note the analytical challenge of linking the three main components of change – context (internal and external), process and content. Process and context components have been considered in the foregoing analysis, and the remainder of this section presents illustrative content and further context examples.

Content of change

An instance of content, already referred to, is that of A level entry grades. The employment of these was fundamental to the change process at Aston. At the time of the 1981 UGC letter the Vice-Chancellor maintained that these were a prime criterion used by the UGC to rank universities for the purpose of resource distribution. The Vice-Chancellor mobilized the external context of the relevant UGC operational framework to identify for closure courses where A level entry grades were poor. Whether A level entry grades *per se* were at that time a prime UGC criterion is still uncertain. However, they provided a numerical tool which could not easily be challenged within the University. Course closures were achieved by a combination of the process of the formal committee structure and the use of channels through which departmental and faculty resources were allocated. For example, if the relevant university committee determined that the pool of applicants for a course was insufficiently large, then the course was deemed to be unviable. The appropriate course committee would then decide that the course should be closed. This meant that the department running the course would be deprived of the resources to support that course, making the department itself vulnerable to closure or to merger with another department.

Once data on Aston and all-university average A level grades were widely disseminated, the process became self-sustaining. Every Aston course came to be measured against these criteria – truly institutionalized assessment. Mobilization of the internal context took place as staff monitored their own and other courses to ensure that they were meeting the criteria, and to judge relative vulnerability of courses. Thus, A level entry grades remain important to restructuring in the internal context, although it is known that they are not now used in the external context of UFC decision-making.

Organizational size is another instance of content within Pettigrew's sense of the term. The reductions in staff and student numbers have already been mentioned. The process by which academic staff reductions were effected has already been alluded to, and offers a stark contrast to the cedures described by Lovelady (1984b). In place of the barng, project-based development and problem-solving strate X' (McGregor 1960) approach was evident in which the carrot of various mobility incentive schemes was reinforced by the stick of threats to starve groups and departments of resources, and to inform individual members of staff that they were no longer wanted at Aston.

Context for change

Mobilization of external context includes the organization/environment interface and the Vice-Chancellor's control over this. The Vice-Chancellor had privileged access to many sources of information outside Aston – as well as to the UGC and the CVCP,[7] he also had access to government ministers[8] and probably also to senior civil servants. It was observed by many that, early in 1981, departments and other groups had been set an exercise to plan for a reduction in resources almost identical to that which resulted from the July 1981 UGC letter. The UGC announcement provided the clear external context for the restructuring of departments and faculties which occurred. Further reductions in the number of departments continued at a much slower pace until 1989, concomitant with further external interventions by the UGC in respect of research selectivity.

Aston's crisis enabled the Vice-Chancellor to discredit the previous regime, for example by reference to statements made by eminent persons years before, and by invoking the spectre of an ailing institution, ill-adapted to the current era. Such images were important in developing an effective foundation for the legitimacy of many events which accompanied the change. Under their 'variety generation' phase heading, Doz and Prahalad (1987) note that in working towards a legitimation of their vision, new key executives sought to undermine the legitimacy of the prevalent conventional wisdom.

The Vice-Chancellor also was able to mobilize the internal context, because as well as rivalry between institutions, there is also rivalry within institutions – between departments and faculties. This feature of university life was used during the restructuring process by way of producing constantly changing staff ranges and age profiles for all departments, so that those which were identified as 'understaffed' could be encouraged to put pressure on those deemed to be 'overstaffed' (on the basis of student numbers). This ploy ultimately failed, once the superordinate issue of compulsory redundancies among academic staff gained salience. At this point, the academic staff closed ranks, and this was one of the issues over which the Vice-Chancellor's will did not prevail. Age profiles were also used at an individual level to put pressure on older staff to depart, in order to relieve the pressure of threatened redundancy on younger colleagues.

A further instance of context relates to rewards received by staff members. The external environment mobilized in this case was the wider academic community, which in various ways sets standards for institutions within it. This example illustrates Child's (1972) observation of the capacity of decision-makers not only to screen out environmental signals, but also to redefine the environment. It was argued that in order to achieve standing in the academic community, Aston should demonstrate certain academic 'spurs'. One of these was the proportion of staff with first class degrees, and this became a qualifying criterion for staff appointments.

Another component was the award of a DSc degree, and those who achieved this qualification were portrayed as role models for others to emulate.[9]

In a US Post Office case study, Biggart (1977) reports the dismantling of the former management recruitment system, for example through weakening the seniority system, and by imposing new criteria for promotions. At Aston there was an effective promotion blockage from lecturer to senior lecturer, while the DSc degree became recognized as a qualifying criterion for promotion to Reader. Mobilization of this aspect of the internal environment was to a large extent congruent with individual aspirations, as many, if not most, staff are highly motivated to achieve status and further qualifications in their field. Thus, this component of the reward system – when pay and morale were generally acknowledged to be low – provided the Vice-Chancellor with control over a vital context for change.

OVERVIEW

Of the two frames of reference considered, the pluralist, with its basis in bargaining through a heterogeneous distribution of power (see, for example, Towers *et al.* 1972, Walton and McKersie 1965, IRRR 1986) was argued to be inadequate for the analysis of change in this particular case example. This is not to imply that a pluralist analysis might not be adequate in other instances of organizational change. In a commentary on Doz and Prahalad (1987), Child suggests that a portfolio of models will be required as more sophisticated analyses develop, so that for example different models are required when radical organizational changes occur within a context of high perceived threat or survival.

A power-based model, involving imposed direction by a single key actor, was identified as the most appropriate diagnostic framework for this case. The top-down change strategy which the Vice-Chancellor was able to impose contrasts sharply with bottom-up strategies described, for example, by Ottaway (1976) and Auer (1985). An important aspect of this was the Vice-Chancellor's adroit management of 'crisis' in respect both of 'objective' indicators – particularly the 1981 cuts and the interpretations of this event by which he legitimized his effective hegemony of the change process. There are parallels with the observations of Doz and Prahalad (1987), who note the pressure which could be generated within organizations by the creation of a sense of impending crisis through emphasizing the risks of performance decline and comparative competitive weakness, as well as the (cognitive) legitimacy required for the new strategy to take root.

By controlling resources and information flows and by managing uncertainty for others (Pettigrew 1975) through imposing his construction of reality, the Vice-Chancellor effectively assumed an extremely powerful position, with a virtual power vacuum beneath him. His style is reminiscent of a description of Margaret Thatcher as Prime Minister, in a book which describes another organization undergoing radical change – taking every decision, everything had to be referred back to her, leaving ministers with little or no credibility (Edwardes 1983).

The case is an example of a severe external threat to an organization, driven both externally and internally by political considerations. The advent of a new Vice-Chancellor presented a severe challenge to the academic status quo, and the external threat served as a vehicle for far-reaching changes within the organization. The power 'balance' within the organization was fundamentally changed as a concomitant of the organizational changes.

The case also illustrates that while powerful parties are able to exert planning and controlling influences upon events, there are always likely to be limiting factors as less powerful participants are pushed to their tolerance limits. Finally, the case has revealed the importance of opportunist methodologies like participant observation as a valuable adjunct to more formalized methods.

NOTES

1 AUT – Association of University Teachers: principal trade union and collective professional association for academic and related staff (e.g. senior library staff, senior administrators, research staff) in UK universities. At Aston some 65 per cent of eligible staff are AUT members, while nationally the figure is 72 per cent. The percentage membership can vary widely between universities and departments.

2 It is instructive to compare these figures with those reported for ICI during roughly the same period. Pettigrew (1985: 377) reports staff losses from 89,400 in 1979 to 61,800 in 1983 – a 31 per cent reduction over a five-year period.

3 Vice-Chancellor: academic head of an English university (in other UK universities, the Principal). The Vice-Chancellor has overall responsibility for the management of a university, and wide executive powers (see Moodie and Eustace 1974, Walford 1987, and figure 3.7).

4 University Grants Committee: body responsible for allocating government university sector budget among UK universities. In 1989 the Universities Funding Council became the newly constituted body to carry out this function.

5   A level: UK school examinations. Grades obtained at A level are the principal determinant of entry to higher education.

6   Exceptional qualifications meant: a first class honours degree, publications, being under thirty years of age and having a doctorate (PhD or DPhil – equivalent to habilitus or Doctorat d'Etat). Departments able to recruit such paragons were at an advantage over those which found it difficult. Even then, appointments were made for only three years, with a possibility of a further three-year contract. This strategy is in line with that reported by Atkinson (1984) for increased organizational flexibility.

7   CVCP – Committee of Vice-Chancellors and Principals. This body is the forum for debate and strategic decision-making for heads of UK universities.

8   The University Secretary's brother was Secretary of State for Employment, at the time, and Aston was visited by a number of ministers and other Members of Parliament – including formal sessions with the Select Committee for Education. Notable visitors included the Prime Minister and other high-ranking cabinet ministers, including the Secretary of State for Education – who opened the Centre for Extension Education – as well as royalty. Aston had a high external profile.

9   Photographs and articles about staff who had recently been awarded DScs adorned the cover of at least one issue of *Aston Fortnight*, for example. (The DSc – Doctor Of Science – degree is a higher doctorate awarded by UK universities in recognition of outstanding research achievement.) Admissions tutors were also identified by the Vice-Chancellor at one meeting and were publicly applauded as Aston's average A level points entry began to outstrip the national average for the first time ever. The irony of this exercise is that at Aston, admissions tutors have minimal discretion in respect of candidate admissions, as criteria and targets are set centrally.

REFERENCES

Aston University (1985) *Planning for the Late 1980s: Response to the UGC from Aston University*, Aston University, November.

—— (1988a) *Rationalisation and Change at Aston: An Academic Planning Update* (2 vols), Aston University, June.

—— (1988b) *Visit of UGC Main Committee 23–24 November 1988*, Aston University.

—— *Aston Fortnight* (various issues).

Atkinson, J. (1984) 'Manpower strategies for flexible organisations', *Personnel Management* August: 28–31.

Auer, P. (1985) *Industrial relations, work organisation and new technology: the Volvo case*. Working Paper, Arbetslivcentrum, Stockholm.

Beckhard, R. and Harris, R.T. (1987) *Organisational Transitions: Managing Complex Change* (2nd edn), Reading Mass.: Addison-Wesley, (1st edn 1977).

Biggart, N.W. (1977) 'The creative-destructive process or organizational change: the case of the Post Office, *Administrative Science Quarterly* 22: 410–26.

Child, J. (1972) 'Organisational structure, environment and performance: the role of strategic choice', *Sociology* 6: 2–22.

Child, J. and Smith, C. (1987) 'The context and process of organisational transformation: Cadbury Limited in its sector', *Journal of Management Studies* 24: 565–93.

Clegg, H.A. (1979) *The Changing System of Industrial Relations in Great Britain*, Oxford: Blackwell.

Downs, A. (1967) *Inside Bureaucracy*, Boston: Little, Brown.

Doz, Y.L. and Prahalad, C.K. (1987) 'A process model of strategic redirection in large complex firms: the case of multinational corporations', in A. Pettigrew (ed.) *The Management of Strategic Change*, Oxford: Blackwell.

Dunlop, J. (1971) *Industrial Relations Systems*, Southern Illinois UP: Feffer and Simons.

Edwardes, M. (1984) *Back from the Brink*, London: Collins.

Flanders, A. (1965) *Industrial Relations: What is Wrong with the System? An essay on its theory and future*, London: Faber.

Fox, A. (1974) *Beyond Contract: Work, Power and Trust Relations*, London: Faber & Faber.

Freeman, J.H. and Hannan, M.T. (1975) 'Growth and decline processes in organisations', *American Sociological Review* 40: 215–28.

Glendon, A.I. (1977) 'The participant observer and groups in conflict: a case study from industry', PhD thesis, London University.

Gold, R.L. (1958) 'Roles in sociological field observations', *Social Forces* 36: 217–23.

Greiner, L. (1967) 'Patterns of organisational change', *Harvard Business Review* 45(3): 119–30.

Grinyer, P.H. Mayes, D.G. and McKiernan, P. (1987) *Sharpbenders*, Oxford: Blackwell.

Handy, C. (1986) *Understanding Organisations* (3rd edn), Harmondsworth: Penguin.

IRRR (1986) 'Change in a traditional environment – the CWS experience', *Industrial Relations Review and Report* 361, 4 Feb: 10–15.

Johnson, G. (1987) *Strategic Change and the Management Process*, Oxford: Blackwell.

Junker, B.H. (1960) *Field Work: An Introduction to the Social Sciences*, Chicago: The University of Chicago Press.

Levine, C.H. (1978) 'Organizational decline and cutback management', *Public Administration Review* 38: 316–25.

Lovelady, L. (1980) 'Evaluation of planned organisational change: issues of knowledge, context and politics', *Personnel Review* 9(4): 5–14.

—— (1984a) 'The process of organisation development: a reformulated model of the change process', *Personnel Review* 13(2): 2–11.

—— (1984b) 'Change strategies and the use of OD consultants to facilitate change', *Journal of Leadership and Organisation Development* 5(2): 3–10.

Lukes, S. (1974) *Power. A Radical View*, London: Macmillan.

McGregor, D. (1960) *The Human Side of Enterprise*, New York: McGraw-Hill.

Miller, D. and Friesen, P.H. (1984) *Organizations: A Quantum View*, Englewood Cliffs: Prentice-Hall.

Mintzberg, H. (1987) 'Crafting strategy', *Harvard Business Review*, 87(4): 66–75.

Moodie, G.C. and Eustace, R. (1974) *Power and Authority in British Universities*, London: Allen & Unwin.

Ottaway, R. (1976) 'A change strategy to implement new norms, new styles and new environment in the work organisation', *Personnel Review* 5(1): 13–18.

Pettigrew, A. (1972) 'Information control as a power resource', *Sociology* 6(2): 187–204.

—— (1973) *The Politics of Organisational Decision Making*, London: Tavistock.

—— (1985) *The Awakening Giant: Continuity and Change in ICI*, Oxford: Blackwell.

Pettigrew, A., McKee, L. and Ferlie, B. (1987) 'Understanding change in the NHS: a review and research agenda', Warwick University: CCSC Working Paper, June.

Pfeffer, J. (1981) *Power in Organisations*, London: Pitman.

Plant, R. (1987) *Managing Change and Making it Stick*, Aldershot: Gower.

Rainey, H.G. Backoff, R.W. and Levine, C.H. (1976) 'Comparing public and private organizations', *Public Administration Review* 36: 223–34.

Slatter, S. (1984) *Corporate Recovery*, Harmondsworth: Penguin.

Towers, B., Whittingham, T.G. and Gottschalk, A.W. (1972) *Bargaining for Change*, London: Allen & Unwin.

Walford, G. (1987) *Restructuring Universities: Politics and Power in the Management of Change*, Beckenham: Croom Helm.

Whetten, R.E. and McKersie, R.B. (1965) *A Behavioral Theory of Labor Negotiations: An Analysis of a Social Interaction System*, New York: McGraw-Hill.

Whetten, D.A. (1980a) 'Organisational decline: a neglected topic in organisational science', *Academy of Management Review*, October.

—— (1980b) 'Source, responses and effects of organisational decline', in J.R. Kimberley, R.H. Miles and associates *The Organizational Life Cycle: Issues in the Creation, Transformation, and Decline of Organizations*, San Francisco: Jossey-Bass: 342–74.

Yarmonlinksy, A. (1975) 'Institutional paralysis', *Daedalus* 104(1): 61–7.

4 Strategic decision making in organizations

A research model and some initial findings

J. Pool and P.L. Koopman

INTRODUCTION

Strategic decision making has long received the attention of the organizational sciences. Barnard (1938) worked on it before the Second World War, and later Simon (1947, 1957) and March and Simon (1958) published many books and articles. In the past twenty years, contributions have been made to the study of strategic decision making by many disciplines and from many points of view (e.g. Allison 1971; Cohen *et al.* 1972; Mintzberg *et al.* 1976), while recently a number of important books have been published (e.g. Heller *et al.* 1988; Hickson *et al.* 1986; Quinn *et al.* 1988; Schwenk, 1988). This activity, however, has not led to a generally accepted theory of strategic decision making. The works of such authors as Weick (1979) and Morgan (1986) even raise the question of whether such a theory can be found.

Undaunted by this, we present a new research model in which an attempt is made to integrate several elements of the models of the pioneers and later researchers. The model is aimed at clarifying the main possibilities for actors to control and influence the decision-making process. The model is psychological, in that it focuses on the individual choices decision makers can make. The primary attention is aimed at managerial choices. However, the model can be applied to different kinds of actors and participants. We describe this model below.

To illustrate the model, we go on to present two studies of strategic decisions. We regarded decisions as strategic, following the definition by Mintzberg *et al.* (1976), if they were of importance to the future of the organization, in the opinion of the main participants. For example, one can think of product-innovation, take-overs, reorganizations and cut-backs, or large-scale automation decisions. These kinds of decisions, when they are taken in the end, mostly imply a more or less fundamental innovation in organizational domain or practice.

After the case studies we compare the theoretical model to the empirically obtained cases. Conclusions are drawn about the model's usefulness for the study of decision making, innovation and change, and about the effectiveness of the qualitative research strategy we employed.

THEORY AND RESEARCH MODEL

In this section we present in brief some literature that has contributed to the development of the research model. Utilizing the results of previous studies, we first sketch the various elements of the model, and finally present the model as a whole.

Models and process dimensions of decision making

The most important point of entry to our model involves what we call the 'process dimensions' of decision making. For decades, researchers have endeavoured to bring into focus what strategic decision making really is. Their work often has resulted in typologies of the different courses strategic decision making processes can take. For instance, Mintzberg *et al.* (1976) presented seven process types, McMillan (1980) four types, Hickson *et al.* (1986) three types, Allison (1971) three as well, Nutt (1984) five types, Grandori (1984) six types, and Shrivastava and Grant (1985) four types.

In an attempt to discover some system to these typologies, we classified them into four decision-making models (Koopman and Pool, 1990a). Each model emphasizes a specific element of strategic decision making. For example, decision making in the 'bureaucratic model' is a process which is subject to rules, regulations and agreements; in the 'arena model' it is a process in which negotiations between various parties plays an important role.

In an earlier project we tried to develop more grip on the manageability of decision making and change processes (Koopman and Pool 1987). This study, in which three large-scale change processes in governmental departments were analysed, yielded a list of ten control options (or management dilemmas). Further analysis led to a reduction to four central dimensions on which decision-making processes can be controlled. The dimensions distinguished are: centralization, formalization, information, and confrontation. They are the indicators that describe the 'process' of decision making in our model.

Centralization

The amount of centralization reflects the extent to which top management keeps decision making to itself, or involves other groups, parties or hierarchical levels. Aspects of this concept are the openness with which the top approaches the rest of the organization, the extent to which parts of the decision-making process are delegated, and the way in which organizational members participate. An important measure for centralization is the influence distribution that comes about during the process. In some studies, this dimension is regarded as the main source of variance in decision processes (IDE 1981a; Heller *et al.* 1988). Although we consider centralization to be an important parameter, we also feel that processes can show important differences on other characteristics.

This indicator is a feature of models of decision making which emphasize power, power-sharing and influence relations (Bacharach and Lawler 1980; Heller *et al.* 1988; Mintzberg 1983; Pfeffer 1981).

Formalization

Decisions can be highly formalized in the sense that they are regulated by established procedure set down in advance (as in governmental decision making), or they can proceed more flexibly, according to informal considerations of what is appropriate. Other aspects of formalization are whether the decision takes place within the fixed communication and consultation structure, or whether a separate, temporary structure is set up, how many committees need to discuss the decision, and whether prescriptive contingencies (in terms of money or resources) are set in advance within which the process or the decision must remain. If this is the case, it is also important to what extent control is exercised over whether or not these contingencies are observed. Finally, in addition to formal consultation, the extent to which the decision is discussed informally ('off the record') is also an aspect of formalization.

This indicator is derived from previous studies of bureaucratic and organizational models of decision making (Allison 1971; Klootwijk and Wagenaar 1983; Lindblom 1959; Perrow 1972).

Information

Information is important in determining the way the substance of a decision comes about. On the basis of what information is a decision made? What alternatives are developed or sought, and where do they come from? Have important possibilities or consequences been overlooked? Aspects of this dimension are the number of alternatives that are considered, where the information is sought (internally or externally), whether the solution found can be implemented directly or whether further synthesis is needed, what confidence people have in it, and whether consultants are enlisted.

The information dimension comes from classical decision-making theory, in which it is assumed that decision makers not only have access to all necessary information, but can also process it (see e.g. Harrison 1981). In practice this is not feasible, and perhaps may even be undesirable (Janis 1982; Nutt 1984; O'Reilly 1983; Schwenk 1984, 1988; Simon 1947, 1957).

Confrontation

The fourth and final dimension is the extent to which there is confrontation and conflict in the decision-making process. Especially in strategic decisions, different parties often have different interests in certain outcomes. In order to articulate this, it must be possible to find some way to balance preferences. The amount of negotiation that turns out to be necessary to arrive at a decision gives an indication of the amount of confrontation. The way in which conflicts of interest are dealt with is also important. Negotiators may prefer a clash – followed by pushing through their own preference – or a compromise, in which a solution is found by consultation and negotiation; similarly, they may choose to convince the opposite party on the basis of arguments, or to postpone or sidestep the decision until the subject of conflict has died down or disappeared (Wrapp 1988).

This last dimension comes from models of decision making as a political process, in which parties try to achieve their own interests on the basis of their power positions (Allison 1971; Hickson *et al.* 1971; Mintzberg *et al.* 1976; Pettigrew 1973).

These dimensions are the basis for a description of the control exercised in decision-making processes over time. However, this does not take place in a vacuum, but in a specific context, and related to content of the decision under attention.

The context of decision making

Decision making does not take place in a vacuum, but in a social space. This space is filled at various levels by actors and parties. At the lowest level we find the individual decision maker. Depending on the present situation and the organization, the individual will sometimes be able to make decisions alone, but usually will have to take others into consideration. This brings us to the level of the group and the organization. However, particularly in strategic decisions, the boundaries of the organization are often exceeded, because the relationship of the organization to its environment is the very subject of decision making and change. The next level involves the question of what the environment is like, and how it reacts. We will briefly elaborate these context levels, from high to low.

Environment

The organization receives its most important information about its functioning and about the necessity of change from its particular environment. The environment can be described in terms of actors (other organizations, such as competitors, suppliers and purchasers, government agencies, customers) or in terms of other more general dimensions (threat, turbulence, complexity) (Porter 1988; Stein 1981).

Organization

The organizational context provides, as Hickson *et al.* (1986) put it, 'the rules of the game'. The more or less stable pattern of positions and communication channels largely determines how decision making should take place. In strategic decision making, however, elements of the structure are often under discussion, or the decisions are so important or new that the existing structure is inadequate (Wilson *et al.* 1986). Nevertheless, the organizational structure as it exists at the beginning of a decision-making process is a very important determinant for the further course of that process (Frederickson 1984, 1986; Horvath and McMillan 1979; Miller 1987).

The decision maker

Strategic decision making is a part of the job of top management. Within the boundaries of the environment and the organization, they can try to achieve their wishes and their visions. A number of personal characteristics and skills are of importance for the manner in which they go about this. One important characteristic is the reactivity versus proactivity of managers (Larson *et al.* 1986). Another is the extent to which managers are willing to take risks (Donaldson and Lorsch 1983; Singh 1986). Lastly, Miller and Toulouse (1986) named the flexibility of managers as a factor. In a field study, they found that all three personal characteristics showed a relationship to the decision-making method used.

These three context factors can be seen as constituting limits to the room to manoeuvre, or limits to the degree of freedom in the control and organization of decision-making processes. This space is further bounded by the subject on which a decision must be made.

The content of decision making

A decision-making process in the context of a drastic reorganization involving forced dismissals may take a different course from a process relating to automated communication with clients. In other words the content of the subject matter may affect the course of the decision-making process. Following Hickson *et al.* (1986) we distinguish two main characteristics, the 'complexity' of the subject matter and its 'political import'.

Complexity

Strategic decisions are often complex by definition; however, there are differences in the extent to which this is true. An important aspect of complexity is the newness of a problem. Decision makers, if they have had to deal with a problem previously, can use this experience the next time. A second aspect is the ambiguity. Some problems are fairly clear, others are vague and amorphous. A third factor is the importance of the decision, how basic it is to policy. The more basic a decision is to policy, the more relations there are to other fields. A fourth factor is the size or scope. As the size of a problem increases, so do the number of sub-aspects and angles of approach, and thus in a literal sense the complexity. The size of the change correlates with its magnitude, or the extent to which the situation to be achieved differs from the old one. Finally, the degree to which a decision is strategically embedded is a fifth aspect of complexity. If the decision is based within known policy, then uncertainty about it and thus complexity will not be so great. However, if a decision sets parameters for future decisions and changes, thus creating a precedent, then its importance will exceed that of the individual decision.

Political import

This arises in strategic decision making because often the structure of the organization or its relation with the environment changes. As a result, the positions of various parties in and around the organization may change and this can cause different preferences to arise about the decision to be made (Pettigrew 1986). This may involve conflicts of interest between internal parties, but it is equally conceivable that such tensions exist between the organization and external parties.

The outcomes of decision making

The question central to the study of decision making is how decision processes can be organized or structured so as to optimize their outcome. We distinguished two kinds of outcomes: first, the course the decision-making process follows in time, and second the way the decision and the decision-making process are evaluated.

Strategic decisions often take much time, during which they go through several phases (Witte 1972; Mintzberg *et al.* 1976). In addition, decision-making processes are often characterized by delays and by feedback loops to earlier phases. Decision-making processes that show much retracing and many delays become turbulent, or even chaotic, while other processes can remain more fluent. These descriptors refer to the manner in which processes run neatly and smoothly through a sequence of phases (first orientation, then development, choice and implementation), or – alternatively – are characterized by delays, stops, restarts and a disorderly attention to activities (development following choice, after blocking of an earlier solution).

As aspects of the outcome we distinguish: effectiveness, by which we refer to the quality of the decision made and the extent to which it is accepted; efficiency, the cost/benefit ratio – satisfaction with the decision and the way in which it came about; and lastly, the ease with which implementation takes place. These are troublesome qualities to measure, because it is anything but simple to find suitable criteria. It is not possible to compare the results of decision-making processes that treat different topics and take place in totally different contexts. In addition, the effects or results of such decisions often can only be assessed in the long run. It is for these reasons that, in our research, we asked for the opinions of respondents about the criteria distinguished.

Research model

The foregoing has given a description of the various parts of the research model we use. It has described what factors are of importance in the organization of decision-making processes, what context factors and content aspects influence the control dimensions, and finally, the course they take and how the processes are evaluated. All these elements are shown in the research model in Figure 4.1.

The four choice opportunities distinguished in the organization of decision-making processes (centralization, formalization, information and confrontation) are shown as independent variables.

The content (complexity and political import) and the context variables (environmental characteristics, organizational characteristics and personal characteristics) are shown in the model as moderating or intervening variables. This means that they influence the relationship between the choices that are made about the organization of the process and its results. For instance, the efficiency of a large-scale process can be increased by delegating authority and by formalizing the approach. Or its effectiveness can be increased by allowing existing conflicts to come to the surface.

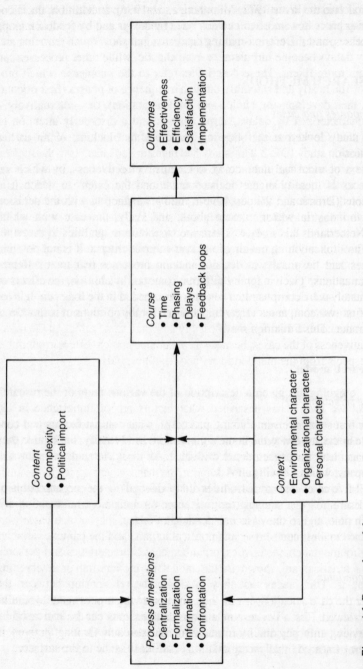

Figure 4.1 Research model
Source: Pool 1990a

The study of strategic decision making, as described above, is one approach to the investigation of organizational innovation and change. The main issue is how more effectively to organize strategic decision-making processes, and therefore, organizational change.

RESEARCH METHODS

Companies and cases

The study looked at the same organizations that had taken part in the replication study IDE-2. This study had investigated changes in the societal context of industrial democracy in Europe in the 1980s, and the consequences of these changes for the distribution of influence within organizations (Drenth and Wilpert 1990). The IDE-2 study had been conducted in two industrial sectors: the metal industry, and insurance companies. In the Netherlands this study was expanded to include hospitals (Pool 1990b).

The replication character of the study implied that the group of companies and hospitals was fixed, and contained a maximum of sixteen organizations. Twelve agreed to participate, and twenty-five case studies ultimately were completed.[1] The cases described in this chapter come from the first two companies to participate in the study. Both companies are in insurance. This limitation may possibly have had some effect on the representativeness of the cases, because the insurance branch differs in a number of respects from the metal industry and from hospitals.

Case selection

As a first step, an inventory was made of important decisions that had been made in the last few years in the organizations involved. In consultation with management, it was then decided which cases would be studied. In the first company, which we will call Assurance, the management agreed to the study of all five cases inventoried. The board of directors in the second company, Tradesure, felt that studying the four proposed decisions would take up too much time, and so one case was discarded. For this chapter, two cases were selected to illustrate the research model, one from each company.

Respondents

After the case selection, it was then discussed which informants would be interviewed. First a key respondent was decided upon per case; in an initial interview, this person informed us of the decision-making process in general lines. At this meeting it was also decided who would serve as further informants. It was attempted to achieve as good a coverage as possible of all viewpoints and aspects of the decision-making process. A minimum of three respondents per case was agreed upon, including one member of management or the board of directors, and one representative of the works council.[2] It was also agreed that, depending on the needs of the study, more people could be interviewed for each case. This possibility was frequently utilized, so that the number of respondents per case in these companies varied between three and eight.

Data

The primary source on which the analysis was performed was the interview material. The interviews were based on a semi-structured interview schedule taking about one-and-a-half hours on average. They served to obtain a chronological survey of the course of the decision-making process, and to sound out the opinions of the respondents on a number of relevant aspects (mainly the control dimensions and the subject aspects). The interviewees also completed a questionnaire in which they were asked for their opinion about the influence distribution during the various phases, as well as for a brief evaluation of the process.

In addition, relevant documentation was collected (minutes of management, works councils and other meetings, memos, reports, etc.) on each case, so far as it was (or was made) available. This written information was used to support, supplement and check the oral information (Schwenk, 1985).

Processing

Processing mainly qualitative information is difficult, and not without risks. Two of the inherent dangers are subjective influence by the researcher, and selective representation of the information. We tried to minimize these risks by the feedback of case information to the respondents. The revised case descriptions were then analysed by two researchers, and after intensive discussion a scoring was obtained for all process characteristics, context factors and content variables. Scores mostly ran from low to high, indicating a relative position on the aspects and dimensions evaluated. So the values attached to the data are not absolute measures of centralization, but should be interpreted with regard to the complete set of data in this study. These scores were given by the researchers, based on their intimate knowledge of the cases, and were 'fact based', as they were extracted from the validated case descriptions. For some of the process variables the scores given by a key respondent were used. For the evaluation of the outcomes and for the data on influence distribution per phase, aggregated data of all respondents per case were used.

Decision-making processes are often supposed to run through a sequence of phases: start up, development, choice and implementation (Mintzberg *et al.* 1976; Heller *et al.* 1988). In some cases, this sequence occurred, and distinct phases could be identified. In other cases, however, specifically the more complex ones, these distinctions were blurred: the order of appearance of phases was not as presupposed, and activities were more intertwined. This led us to identify phases by reference to specific activities and to time.

RESULTS

In this section, based on two case studies, we will assess the analytical value of the model. First the two cases will be briefly described: their course and the organizational contexts in which they took place will be outlined. After that we will systematically compare the two cases on the elements of the model.

Assurance: construction of new office

The first case concerned Assurance, a medium-sized insurance company which traditionally had had its offices in Amsterdam's old centre. After a turbulent period of search, the company moved in 1983 to one of the city's canals where it could rent a building on very favourable terms. By 1985, these premises had proved to be too small, and so the company rented two extra stories in the adjacent building (property of the same lessor) at the normal price. These contracts gave the company the first right to rent or purchase; they were due to expire in August 1988. At the end of 1985 the lessor contacted Assurance, because it had prospective tenants for the adjacent building. Assurance was offered the buildings for sale, but at a very high price. Further talks did not lead to a solution; the lessor decided to rent to new tenants. It thus became clear in early 1986 that Assurance would have to move into different premises in mid-1988.

The company started looking for possibilities through an estate agent. At first a location on one of the canals was sought. However, this had a number of disadvantages (the need for renovation; poor access). The agent made an inventory of the company's requirements, and they started looking for other possibilities. In spring 1986 this resulted in a list of alternatives; after a tour of the various locations, a large number were quickly eliminated because they did not meet the criteria.

Apart from this, the management received an offer from a property developer about a project to be developed on the IJ Boulevard (a new business district being created on the harbour front), following a magazine report that Assurance was looking for new office space. This project was very well received. Together with the possibilities suggested by the company's own agent, there were four alternatives in April 1986. All alternatives involved new construction, because no suitable premises were available to rent. Besides, investing in a building of their own was attractive to them at the time, so that purchase or new construction was a preferred option to renting.

One alternative was quickly eliminated because the new building would not be ready on time, due to the clearance activities it would entail. A closer study was made of the three remaining alternatives. Amsterdam South-East (a newly-built area south east of Amsterdam with several industrial estates) was financially attractive, but otherwise had almost nothing but disadvantages. Beside, the personnel showed emotional resistance to establishment on an industrial estate outside the city. Slotervaart (an area developing in the south west of Amsterdam) was felt to be attractive both in a financial and a practical sense (good access because of a new railway station and motorway, on a newly-developing industrial estate). The costs of the third alternative, the IJ Boulevard, came out high, but the site itself and possible future developments (upgrading of the IJ Boulevard by the city authorities) were rated highly.

These alternatives were presented to the works council in June, and together a tour was made of the three locations. The works council showed a clear preference for the IJ Boulevard. Then, in August, a housing report appeared for the board of supervisory directors[3] in which management expressed its preference for new construction on the IJ Boulevard. After touring the locations, the supervisory directors expressed themselves against Amsterdam South-East, leaving the other two possibilities undecided. This was taken by management as a green light to go ahead with the IJ Boulevard.

In spring there were further talks with the estate agent and the property developer. With the approval of the works council and the board of supervisory directors, this led to a draft agreement in October. After further talks, this was to result in a purchase and contracting agreement. There would also have to be talks with the city authorities about the land costs. A complication here was soil pollution which had since been discovered on the site. Partly because of this, contacts with the property developer deteriorated. He wanted to claim an item for extra work of 2 million guilders above and beyond the purchase price shown in the draft agreement. After prolonged discussions between Assurance, the property developer and the city authorities, some progress was made in the negotiations.

Nevertheless, a large area of disagreement between the developer and Assurance remained. At the end of December still no definitive agreement had been signed. Assurance was beginning to fear that the entire project would have to be abandoned, because time was beginning to press. Construction would have to be started by March at the latest in order to have the office ready on time. Starting at this point, a number of negotiating sessions were held. In eight sessions, the gap was finally bridged, thanks primarily to concessions on the part of the contractor. Assurance had threatened to withdraw if the extra work necessary did not remain within the limit of 500,000 guilders. Agreement was thus reached on financial and technical matters.

The definitive agreement was signed on 9 February. The decision was announced that same afternoon at a reception held for the personnel. Reaction was enthusiastic. After the soil cleaning in February and March, the first pile was driven by the Burgomaster on 1 April.

Tradesure: take-over of supplier

The second case took place in a larger Dutch company, Tradesure, that operated in a specialist area of insurance. Tradesure insures credit risks that companies run upon delivery of goods. The company therefore collects a very large and constant flow of information by which to assess the credit-worthiness of companies; they also buy supplementary information from a few credit agencies. In 1982 a discussion took place with one of these agencies at which the possibility of closer co-operation came up. At the time there was insufficient reason to consider it further.

Three years later, however, the idea seemed highly pertinent. The year before, Tradesure had considered opportunities for diversification, while the information agency was in urgent need of financial support to be able to keep up the pace of automation it considered necessary. Furthermore, in early 1985 it was rumoured that there were other potential buyers, which was the reason for Tradesure to make haste with the talks. If the supplier were to fall in the hands of a competitor, then the availability of the information, an essential 'resource', could be jeopardized, or at any rate the information would become more expensive. Two other considerations played a role as well. From a defensive point of view, it was reasoned that credit agencies, by supplying faster and more accurate information, would start to create more competition for credit insurance. Second, more offensively, it was thought that by offering more services than credit insurance alone, the position of the company would become more stable and less sensitive to economic cycles. In the long run, policy based on these considerations was to lead to a broad package of financial services and to provide access to the European market.

The first talks took place in the greatest secrecy – only the three top managers and the financial administrator knew about the developments. The diversification strategy was discussed in a general sense with the presidium of the board of supervisory directors in March, and reactions ranged from sceptical to negative. This, however, was no obstacle to management continuing the talks in the spring. They instructed their own accounting agency to make a financial analysis for this purpose. A number of alternative ways to tackle the perceived problems (starting their own information service, co-operating with banks, other take-over candidates) were explored, but not in earnest.

By summer the talks had progressed so far that the plans were announced publicly. A general strategy was adopted for this. All parties were informed almost simultaneously in a memo, in which the plans, considerations and alternatives were extensively described. The trade unions received a letter the day before the presentation to the board of supervisory directors in which the take-over was announced, while the works council and the entire staff were informed immediately after the meeting of the supervisory board. The board of supervisory directors felt acutely embarrassed. First of all, they were surprised, after their initial adverse reaction, to be confronted with a concrete take-over plan. In addition, the board members had had no opportunity to discuss the plans, and they felt they simply had no choice. Management defended its approach with the argument that the 'strategic initiative' had to be safeguarded, and that earlier reports would have jeopardized this. Despite its procedural objections, the board of supervisory directors gave the green light for the plans.

Initially the works council was overwhelmed by the plans, but after an explanation it was convinced of the necessity to go ahead. It asked questions about the plan's effects on employment opportunities, important primarily to the company's own information department, and about possible integration plans. These questions were answered adequately. After two meetings with the works council of the take-over candidate, at which some reciprocal agreements were made, the works council issued a positive recommendation. Following the approval of the board of supervisory directors, the negotiating results were quickly set down in a letter of intent. After the summer recess, this conditional agreement was converted into a firm agreement. Almost immediately after the conditional agreement was signed, it appeared that another credit agency had been taken over. The buyer of this agency, Vendex, contacted Tradesure to discuss future developments. One year later, this led to the establishment of a joint venture in which the two agencies would work together.

Comparison of the cases

Having described the two decision-making processes, we are in a position to make a systematic comparison. We start with the four dimensions along which decision-making processes can be classified: centralization, formalization, information and confrontation. Then we treat their contents and contexts. The comparison will be concluded with a discussion of the course the decision processes followed, and the evaluation data.

Centralization

This dimension involves the extent to which management keeps the reins in its hands, lets other parties, persons, or groups participate, or delegates part of the decision making, and the amount of openness it practises in the decision-making process (see Table 4.1). A division of influence results during the process, which we measured for each phase. From the point of view of the strategy or approach to centralization, the take-over of Tradesure was highly centralized. Prior to the announcement, only four persons knew about the plans. After that, the effective room to manoeuvre was essentially nil. Neither the board of supervisory directors nor the works council or trade unions could make any contribution. The trade unions were informed pro forma; later, they were involved in formulating the 'personnel plan'. This approach, which later had some repercussions, was defended on the grounds of the need for secrecy and the necessity to safeguard the 'strategic initiative'.

The new construction process in Assurance, on the other hand, was very participative and open. Both the board of supervisory directors and the works council could express themselves on the three serious options that existed in mid-1986. The notable participation by the works council was motivated by the importance that personnel attaches to the place of work and the influence this has on work satisfaction and motivation.

We also looked in more detail at the centralization (or participation) strategy adopted, in terms of perceived influence per phase for different internal and external parties; this gave a similar picture. The take-over case was highly centralized in all phases. The board of directors kept a maximum of influence on the process in all phases, involving the board of supervisory directors to a lesser extent. The works council was practically side-tracked. The other internal parties, except for the financial department for understandable reasons, had little to no influence. Externally, the start-up of the decision-making process was somewhat influenced by the competitive situation, but the influential position of consultants ranked highest. This strengthens the picture of centralized decision making, because the consultants stood by the board of directors in word and deed.

Table 4.1 Centralization characteristics

Aspects of centralization	Assurance (New Office)	Tradesure (Take-over)
Delegation	medium	low
• in what phase(s)	development	implementation
Participation strategy:	high	medium
• level/group	works council/board of supervisory directors	works council/trade unions
• in what phase(s)	development/choice/implementation	choice/implementation
Openness	high	low

Management also had a constant high influence in the new office case, which only diminished somewhat in the implementation phase; influence by the board of supervisory directors was also high. In contrast to the take-over case, however, the works council also had much influence, primarily in the initial phases and in the choice phase, where the works council's influence score was nearly maximal. The other internal parties in this case had little or no influence. External consultants had a clear contribution to make, primarily in the development phase. In addition, in this case local government had some influence in all phases, but its voice was heard most clearly in the central choice phase.

Formalization

Although the new office case was somewhat higher than the take-over process (see Table 4.2), neither case scored very high on this design aspect. This means that the decision making was highly informal in both cases. The higher formalization of the new office case was due to the clearly present prescriptive contingencies: the decision making had to be completed before March 1986, and the extra costs could be no higher than 500,000 guilders. Both elements played an important role in the ultimate decision making.

Time and money elements naturally played a role in the take-over (retention of the strategic initiative and the take-over price), but they did not act as formal limits to the decision-making process.

Information

The two cases studied differed substantially as to the information on the basis of which the decisions were made (Table 4.3).

Table 4.2 Formalization characteristics

Aspects of formalization	Assurance (New Office)	Tradesure (Take-over)
Structured process	medium	medium
• in what phase(s)	implementation	choice and implementation
Prescriptive contingencies: • time	high	low
• money	high	low
Control of contingencies: • time	high	N/A
• money	high	N/A
Separate structure	medium	low
Committees	low	low
Informal communication	high	high

Table 4.3 Information characteristics

Aspects of information processing	Assurance (New Office)	Tradesure (Take-over)
Number of alternatives	3	1
Search/develop	search	search
Internal/external	external	external
Confidence	medium	high
External consultants	yes	yes

In the take-over, both the company and the supplier felt the need for some form of co-operation. Other options were studied in theory, but were not considered serious alternatives. In the new office case, a large number of possibilities were considered via a convergent process until three serious alternatives remained, from which the choice was ultimately made. In both cases the information was sought externally, although in the take-over it can more properly be said that it was 'found'. Confidence in the information was greater in the take-over than in the new office case, in which there was some mistrust of the contractor, while internally, people ascribed different weights to the information. For instance, management assessed the location criteria differently from the works council, and one member of the board of supervisory directors wanted a closer analysis to be made of the financial consequences of the IJ Boulevard option. Lastly, management made use of external consultants in support of their own knowledge and skills in both cases.

Confrontation

The final design characteristic to be discussed deals with contrasting interests. Table 4.4 shows that the confrontation was mainly external in both cases.

Table 4.4 Confrontation characteristics

Aspects of confrontation	Assurance (New Office)	Tradesure (Take-over)
Negotiation	high	high
Conflict management	push through/ compromise	convince/ compromise
In what phase(s)	choice	development/ implementation
Internal/external	external	internal/external

The new office case showed no internal confrontation, nor did the take-over case, although the outcome of the decision was questioned by the supervisory directors and the works council. However, they allowed themselves to be persuaded by the board of directors. Externally, the start-up of the new office case was the result of a conflict of interests which was not resolved. Pressure was exerted during the decision-making process, and ultimately a compromise was reached. In the take-over case an external compromise was reached through negotiations.

Summarizing the above characteristics of the two cases on the main dimensions, we obtain the following picture (see Table 4.5). Both cases were controlled quite centrally by top management. For the new office case it was important that this approach was linked to a purposeful participation strategy. As a result, the overall score for centralization was set to medium. The level of formalization was very low in the take-over case. Only the final assessment was formal (by the board of supervisory directors, works council and unions).

The new office case, although rather informal, still had more formalization aspects. It also had a broadly convergent information strategy, while the take-over process aimed at one particular solution. Finally, external confrontation took place in the form of negotiations in both cases, while there were few internal problems.

Table 4.5 Summary of process dimensions

Process dimensions	Assurance (New Office)	Tradesure (Take-over)
Centralization	medium	high
Formalization	medium	low
Information	high	low
Confrontation (external)	high	high

So far we have only discussed how the cases took place and how they were structured. But this does not take place in a vacuum; the steps that must be taken are keyed to the context in which the decision is made, and to the content of the decision. We will now discuss these factors.

Context

In the context, we distinguished between characteristics of the environment, the organization and the decision maker (see Table 4.6). Assurance is a relatively small company, and in a threatening environment. Because of its limited size, the position of management is strong; Assurance can be characterized as an autocracy. In addition, the managing director had taken up his duties only recently, and he has pursued an energetic innovative policy with which he won the trust of the personnel. The autocratic nature is linked to a harmonious, informal participation philosophy, thus improving a sense of shared company identity. Policy is aimed at modernization and growth of market share, with the ultimate goal of surviving independently.

Although Tradesure is of medium size and its environment is less threatening (but changing), this company, too, can be characterized as an autocracy. The most important manager is a self-made man who rose up through the company. He, too, has pursued an active, innovative policy, enjoying much trust within the company. Policy is aimed at profit growth and diversification. A clear participation philosophy prevails, but it is strictly functional and highly formal.

Content

Although both the accommodation and the take-over topics can be called complex subjects, the latter nevertheless stands out above the new office case, on a number of points. Assurance had had recent experience in finding new premises, while Tradesure was making a take-over for the first time in

Table 4.6 Context factors

Aspects of context	Assurance (New Office)	Tradesure (Take-over)
Environment		
• stability	large	small
• complexity	limited	some
• hostility	some	little
Organization:		
• power system	autocracy	autocracy
• size	small	medium-sized
• participation philosophy	informal and strongly present	strictly functional and formal
• company identity	strong	strong
Decision maker:		
• proactive/reactive	proactive	proactive
• risk behaviour	moderate	bold

its history. In addition, the aspects of a take-over are difficult to assess and are ambiguous, while the pros and cons of a new office are more easily quantified. Taking the financial commitment as a yardstick for the size of the decision makes the new office decision more complex. The investment in a new office, in comparison to the turnover of Assurance, was much larger than the investment required for the take-over by Tradesure.

Table 4.7 Characteristics of the subject matter

Aspects of subject matter	Assurance (New Office)	Tradesure (Take-over)
Complexity:		
• new	no	yes
• ambiguity	small	large
• importance	great	very great
• size	large	average
• extent of change	great	limited
• embeddedness	somewhat	slight
• creation of precedent	small	large
Politicality:		
• power difference	large	large
• contention	external	external
• external influence	moderate	small

If we look at the extent of the change in terms of the percentage of staff members who would be affected by the consequences, then the new office decision clearly scores higher. As to importance, however, the scale tips to the other case. Although accommodation is an important issue, in the perception of work by the personnel, the take-over was surely of very great importance to Tradesure. This partly resulted from the fact that there was no firm policy on the issue, implying little possibility of advance control, while the decision set a great precedent. After all, the take-over was the first step on the way to an active diversification and take-over policy. The new office decision scored much lower on these aspects. The choice was circumscribed by the traditional establishment in the centre of Amsterdam, and it would hardly be taken as a precedent.

Choices about the design of decision-making processes are not separate from the context and the content. The fact that both organizations were autocratic increased their degrees of control. In Tradesure, the newness and the strategic nature of the decision gave rise to a centralized informal approach in which the opportunity that offered itself was seized with both hands. In Assurance, the consideration that the housing situation was of crucial importance to the work perception and the motivation of the personnel, led to a participative approach via the works council. This choice was perhaps facilitated by the previous experience and the slight ambiguity. The decision-making strategy could thus be geared to the nature of the situation and to the subject, with the goal of an optimal result.

Outcome data also were collected. We distinguished two classes of outcome: the course of the decision process and the evaluation.

Course

Both cases took a reasonably orderly course, from problem identification via development to decision making and implementation (see Table 4.8). In the new office case, there was a retracing cycle in the start-up phase when the purchase option fell through. What had started as a question of accommodation changed into a question of removal, ultimately to end as a question of new construction. The nature of the decision-making process thus altered during the process, influenced by the possibilities encountered. The take-over was started and completed more unambiguously, although an important adjustment had to be made immediately after the implementation.

As to delays, the new office case also scored highest. Because of the need for more information and the exploration of possibilities and alternatives, primarily in the development phase, and because of the problematic

Table 4.8 Data on the course of the two cases

Course	Assurance (New Office)	Tradesure (Take-over)
Duration	22 months	6 + 12 months
Phasing/recycling	phases clearly represented, some recycling	initially compressed, later chaotic; in fact two processes
Delays	somewhat, because of information need and negotiations	in the latter part, because of conflict with trade unions and troublesome co-operation

negotiations with the contractor and the city authorities in the decision-making phase, some time was lost. The take-over had no significant delays. This means that the new office case, with its duration of twenty-two months, was a lengthy decision-making process. The take-over had a duration of six months as far as the take-over went, and eighteen months if the subsequent formation of the joint venture is included. There were several delaying factors in the latter part: difficulties in talks with the trade unions, and troublesome co-operation on the part of the new management. Because of this, the process, which started out as quite neat and 'fluid', became rather turbulent and chaotic.

Evaluation

In contrast to the scoring of the process, context and design characteristics, arrived at after analyses by the researchers (researcher as respondent), the data on results come direct from the interviewees. They were given a form at the end of the interview, and were asked to complete it. These data were aggregated per case.

From Table 4.9 it appears that the new office case was systematically assessed somewhat more positively by the respondents than the take-over. These figures should be taken with some reservations, however. The assessments come from two different groups of informants, who may have used different frames of reference when answering the evaluation questions.

In addition, the evaluation of decision-making processes is in itself difficult. Often the results are only apparent in the long run, or they may be dependent on other events. So what initially looked like a good step to take may later turn out to be less fortunate; conversely, what seemed to be a foolish step may turn out to be wise. The wisdom of the take-over by Tradesure was borne out when immediately after the agreement it appeared that another credit agency had been taken over by another company.

Table 4.9 Evaluation data (scales 1–5, with the exception of resistance, –3 to +3)

Evaluated dimensions	Assurance (New Office)	Tradesure (Take-over)
Satisfaction with:		
• process	5.0	4.5
• decision	4.3	3.5
Quality of decision	4.7	4.0
Resistance	3.0	1.8
Efficiency	4.0	4.0
Ease of implementation	3.7	3.0

CONCLUSION

We have presented a model by which strategic decision-making processes can be described and charted. This model was illustrated by two case studies. What can we conclude about the model developed and its applicability to empirical material from this presentation? And what can we say about the research strategy chosen?

Using the model, it seems to be possible to make a more comprehensive analysis, in which attention is paid to four central dimensions available for the control of decision-making processes. This circumvents the limitation of studying only one dimension of decision making (such as the participation dimension, which has been central in a number of studies), without giving up the advantage of a dynamic temporal process analysis.

Additionally, viewing the process dimensions as basically free choices avoids a too determinist picture of strategic decision making (as is the case, for example, in Hickson *et al.* 1986). A comparison can be made with the 'strategic choice theory' of Child (1972). Child advocates a view of organizational structuring in which technological and environmental determinism are toned down in favour of the recognition of the choices management has in structuring its own organization. This can also be a fruitful way of looking at the structuring of strategic decision-making processes. Within the prescriptive contingencies, as set by the context and the subject, an approach can be chosen, whereby the total amount of leeway for choices can vary. This line of thought is shown schematically in Figure 4.2.

Describing decision-making processes opens up the way to analyse them in search of the ways control is exercised. The close examination and reconstruction of decision processes, as in this research project, seems the most feasible way to deal with the choices being made. Combining the

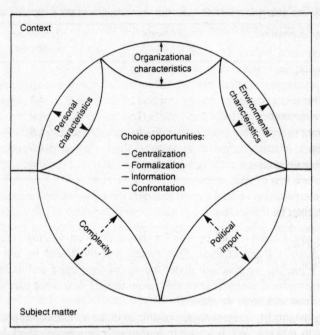

Figure 4.2 Schematic representation of opportunities and leeway for choice in the structuring of strategic decision making.

choices on the four dimensions leads to a profile which can be seen in terms of a decision-making strategy.[4] Such strategies have important consequences for the quality of the decision finally taken, and the way in which this decision is implemented. The study of innovation and change would be incomplete without firm knowledge of the decision-making processes which led to the innovations.

The material presented here is illustrative, not representative. This is not a drawback for the purposes of this chapter; it may even be an advantage. However, to arrive at a broader assessment of the model, more material is needed. Presently all twenty-five cases have been studied and described. Although this is still not many for statistical purposes, the total data set will give us firmer grounds for assessment of the model and the relations it assumes.

Finally, in reference to our experiences so far, we wish to make a number of methodological remarks. We will do this summarily and point by point, because a discussion of this problem would otherwise take an entire article. In this study of strategic decision-making processes based primarily on interviews with the persons involved and on document analysis, we encountered the following problems:

1 Participation policy of companies and selection of cases and respondents: the researcher is dependent on the benevolence of the company management, and has an informational handicap. Respondents have limited knowledge and perception of the events. Respondents no longer remember all facts and details (limited memory capacity) or do not want to remember them (rationalizing, colouring information).

2 Feedback is troublesome if there is no shared vision of events, or if respondents do not want to be reminded too sharply of unpleasant events (mistakes, loss of face, defeats).

3 The interpretation of data can be based on the views of the respondents, which may be limited but are reliable, or on the view of the researcher as respondent, who has a broader view but is open to the danger of subjectivity.

4 The intensity of the research strategy chosen is an obstacle to large-scale study, so that the number of cases will always remain relatively small.

Despite these remarks, the strength of the methodology used is that it provides insights to the fundamental choice process which lies at the heart of decision making. We have tried to minimize the weaknesses in the approach taken, by using a diverse and complementary set of methods, and by feeding back the results to the respondents.

The project described in this chapter is aimed at clarifying the ways decision situations can be handled. The description of control dimensions and the way these are linked to the topic under consideration and the context in which the decision takes place, provides a psychological frame of reference of decision making. The description of procedural choice options regarding the amount of centralization, formalization, the use of information and the handling of conflicts clarifies the behavioural repertoire of actors who participate in decision processes. Although the primary focus has been on top management, as the central body responsible for strategic decision making, the choice options can be used to describe the strategies chosen by other participants (e.g. the works council) as well. However, lower-level parties have less leeway than has management.

NOTES

1 The overall analyses of these data are presented in Pool (1990a).
2 Works councils in the Netherlands are the main bodies for employee representation, and are obligatory for all organizations larger than thirty-five employees. Also see IDE (1981).

3   Board of supervisory directors: this board is an obligatory council for private companies with assets above 20 million Dutch guilders. It is composed of advisors and executives of other companies. In most cases the board meets two to four times a year, and discusses company policies and results with executive management. Formally, they authorize substantial decisions, approve annual reports, and appoint chief executives.
4   A clear distinction in types of strategies should be based on more material than is being presented here. This also goes for the systematic analysis of effects of specific strategies on decision outcomes. A more comprehensive analysis of the material can be found in Pool and Koopman (1991). Prescriptive implications can be distilled from these empirical relationships, and will be formulated in a later stage.

REFERENCES

Allison, G.T. (1971) *Essence of Decision: Explaining the Cuban missile crisis*, Boston: Little, Brown.

Bacharach, S.B. and Lawler, E.J. (1980) *Power and Politics in Organizations*, San Francisco: Jossey Bass.

Barnard, C. (1938) *The Functions of the Executive*, Cambridge MA: Harvard University Press.

Child, J. (1972) 'Organizational structure, environment and performance: the role of strategic choice', *Sociology* 6: 1–22.

Cohen, M.D., March, J.G. and Olsen, J.P. (1972) 'A garbage can model of organizational choice', *Administrative Science Quarterly* 17: 1–25.

Donaldson, G. and Lorsch, J.W. (1983) *Decision Making at the Top: The Shaping of Strategic Direction*, New York: Basic Books.

Drenth, P.J.D. and Wilpert, B. (1990) 'Industrial democracy in Europe: cross-national comparisons', in P.J.D. Drenth, J. Sergeant and R.J. Takens (eds) *Advances in European Psychology* (vol. 3), Chichester: Wiley.

Fredrickson, J.W. (1984) 'The effect of structure on the strategic decision process', *Academy of Management Proceedings* 44: 12–16.

Fredrickson, J.W. (1986) 'The strategic decision process and organizational structure', *Academy of Management Review* 11; 280–97.

Grandori, A. (1984) 'A prescriptive contingency view of organizational decision making', *Administrative Science Quarterly* 29: 192–209.

Harrison, E.F. (1981) *The Managerial Decision-making Process*, Boston: Houghton Mifflin.

Heller, F.A., Drenth, P.J.D., Koopman, P.L. and Rus, V. (1988) *Decisions in Organizations: A three-country comparative study*, London: Sage.

Hickson, D.J., Butler, R.J., Cray, D., Mallory, G.R. and Wilson, D.C. (1986) *Top Decisions: Strategic Decision-Making in Organizations*, Oxford: Basil Blackwell.

Horvath, D. and McMillan, C.J. (1979) 'Strategic choice and the structure of decision processes', *International Studies of Management and Organization* 9, 3: 87–112.

IDE-International Research Group (1981) *Industrial Democracy in Europe*, Oxford: Clarendon Press.

Janis, I.L. (1982) *Groupthink* (2nd edn.), Boston: Houghton Mifflin.

Klootwijk, J.W. and Wagenaar, R.B. (1983), 'Veranderingsprocessen in bureaucratische organisaties: Varianten op een "traditioneel" model' ('Change processes in bureaucratic organizations: Variants of a traditional model'), *M & O Tijdschrift voor Organisatiekunde en Sociaal Beleid* 37: 402–15.

Koopman, P.L. and Pool, J. (1987) 'De bestuurbaarheid van besluitvormingsprocessen bij vernieuwing' ('The control of decision making in innovation'), in A.J. Cozijnsen and W.J. Vrakking (eds) *Handboek voor Strategisch innoveren*, Deventer: Kluwer/NIVE (pp. 178–93).

Koopman, P.L. and Pool, J. (1990a) 'Besluitvormingsmodellen' ('Decision-making models'), in J. von Grumbkow and J. van Hoof (eds), *Perspectieven Op Organisaties*, Heerlen: Open Universiteit, (chs 15–17).

Koopman, P.L. and Pool, J. (1990b) 'Decision making in organizations, in C.L. Cooper and I.T. Robertson (eds), *International Review of Industrial and Organizational Psychology*, New York: Wiley (pp. 101–48).

Larson, L.L., Bussom, R.S., Vicars, W. and Jauch, L. (1986) 'Proactive versus reactive manager: is the dichotomy realistic?' *Journal of Management Studies* 23: 385–400.

Lindblom, C.E. (1959) 'The science of "muddling through"', *Public Administration Review* 19: 79–99.

March, J.G. and Simon, H.A. (1958) *Organizations*, New York: Wiley.

McMillan, C.J. (1980) 'Qualitative models of organizational decision making', *Journal of General Management* 5: 22–39.

Miller, D. and Toulouse, J.M. (1986) 'CEO-personality and its relationship to strategy and structure', *Management Science* 32: 1398–1409.

Miller, D. (1987) 'Strategy making and structure: analysis and implications for performance', *Academy of Management Journal* 30: 7–32.

Mintzberg, H. (1983) *Power In and Around Organizations*, Englewood Cliffs, NJ: Prentice Hall.

Mintzberg, H., Raisinghani, D. and Théorêt, D. (1976) 'The structure of "unstructured" decision processes', *Administrative Science Quarterly* 21: 246–75.

Morgan, G. (1986) *Images of organization*, London: Sage.

Nutt, P.C. (1984) 'Types of organizational decision processes', *Administrative Science Quarterly* 29: 414–50.

O'Reilly, C.A. (1983) 'The use of information in organizational decision making: a model and some propositions', in L.L. Cummings and B.M. Shaw (eds) *Research in Organizational Behaviour* vol. 5, Greenwich, CN: JAI-Press, (pp. 103–39).

Perrow, C. (1972) *Complex Organizations: A Critical Essay*, Glenview, IL: Scott Foresman.

Pettigrew, A.M. (1973) *The Politics of Organizational Decision making*, London: Tavistock.

Pettigrew, A.M. (1986) 'Some limits of executive power in creating strategic change', in S. Shrivastva (ed.) *The Functioning of Executive Power*, London: Jossey Bass.

Pfeffer, J. (1981) *Power in Organizations*, Boston: Pitman.

Pool, J. (1990a) *Sturing van strategische besluitvorming: Mogelijkheden en grenzen (Control of strategic decision making: Possibilities and limits)*, Amsterdam: VU-Uitgeverij.

Pool, J. (1990b) 'Hospital management: integrating the dual hierarchy?' Paper presented at the 22nd International Congress of Applied Psychology, Kyoto, Japan.

Pool, J., Drenth, P.J.D., Koopman, P.L. and Lammers, C.J. (1988) 'De volwassenwording van de medezeggenschap: invloedsverhoudingen in de jaren '80' ('The maturation of participation: influence relations in the eighties'), *Gedrag en Organisatie* 1: 37–58.

Pool, J. and Koopman, P.L. (1991) 'Dimensions and types of strategic decision making: an empirical check of a typology', in S. Lindenberg and H. Schreuder, *International Perspectives on Organization Study*, Oxford: Pergamon Press (in press).

Pool, J., Koopman, P.L. and Kamerbeek, E. (1986) 'Veranderingsprocessen bij de rijksoverheid: cases en keuzemomenten' ('Change processes in government: cases and choices'), *M & O Tijdschrift voor Organisatiekunde en Sociaal Beleid* 40: 516–31.

Porter, M.E. (1988) 'How competitive forces shape strategy', in J.B. Quinn, H. Mintzberg and R.M. James (eds) *The Strategy Process: Concepts, Contexts and Cases*, London: Prentice-Hall.

Quinn, J.B. (1980) *Strategies for Change: Logical Incrementalism*, Homewood: Irwin.

Quinn, J.B., Mintzberg, H. and James, R.M. (eds) (1988) *The Strategy Process: Concepts, Contexts and Cases*, London: Prentice-Hall.

Schwenk, C.R. (1984) 'Cognitive simplification processes in strategic decision making', *Strategic Management Journal* 5: 111–28.

Schwenk, C.R. (1985) 'The use of participant recollection in the modelling of organizational decision processes', *Academy of Management Review* 10: 496–503.

Schwenk, C.R. (1988) *The Essence of Strategic Decision Making*, Massachusetts: D.C. Heath & Co.

Shrivastava, P. and Grant, J.H. (1985) 'Empirically derived models of strategic decision making processes', *Strategic Management Journal* 6: 97–113.

Simon, H.A. (1947) *Administrative behavior*, New York: Free Press.

Simon, H.A. (1957) *Models of Man*, New York: Wiley.

Singh, J.V. (1986) 'Performance, slack and risk-taking in organizational decision making', *Academy of Management Journal* 29: 562–85.

Stein, J. (1981) 'Contextual factors in the selection of strategic decision methods', *Human Relations* 34: 819–34.

Weick, K. (1979) *The Social Psychology of Organizing*, Reading, MA: Addison-Wesley.

Wilson, D.C., Butler, R.J., Cray, D., Hickson, D.J. and Mallory, G.R. (1986) 'Breaking the bounds of organization in decision making', *Human Relations* 39: 309–32.

Witte, E. (1972) 'Field research on complex decision making processes: the phase theorem', *International Studies of Management and Organization* 2: 156–82.

Wrapp, H.E. (1988) 'Good managers don't make policy decisions', in J.B. Quinn, H. Mintzberg and R.M. James (eds) *The Strategy Process: Concepts, Contexts, and Cases*, London: Prentice-Hall.

5 Towards a model of strike organization
Meanings and their management

David Waddington

INTRODUCTION

The outcome of the 1984–5 British coal dispute has been described as a 'heroic defeat' (Golden 1988) for the National Union of Mineworkers (NUM). The year-long dispute was undoubtedly a testimony to the spirit and fortitude of the thousands of mining families involved. However, despite the connotations of an orderly retreat, suggested by the miners' mass return to work without concession of the central issue of pit closures, 'the reality was a rapid implementation of closures and an equally rapid collapse of resistance to them' (McCabe and Wallington 1988: 107). By May 1990, no fewer than ninety-nine of the 172 collieries operating at the end of the dispute in March 1985 had closed; and the workforce had been reduced from 221,000 to 65,000 (The *Guardian*, 23 May 1990).

Several retrospective analyses of the dispute have been critical of the NUM's strategy (cf. Hain 1986; Hyman 1986; Francis 1985). Particular criticism has been made of its refusal to hold a national ballot – an issue which undermined the union's internal solidarity – and of its over-reliance on 'the very traditional, almost archaic, solely industrial strategy of mass and flying picketing' (Francis 1985: 31) as a means of invoking support and obstructing the transportation of coal, steel and other industrial products. In general terms, the NUM has been criticized for reapplying the strategy it used successfully in national stoppages in the 1970s, without sufficiently adapting it to the changed political context of the 1980s.

This chapter has two objectives. The first is to account for the lack of strategic innovation shown by the NUM, outlining the political and cultural obstacles to a more progressive strategic approach. The second is to build on recent psychological approaches to industrial conflict (Kelly and Nicholson 1980; Klandermans 1984; Waddington 1986, 1987), emphasizing the importance of socio-historical and cultural variables to our understanding of strike causation and development. These ideas are presented in the form of a case study, based on interview material collected as part of two recent research projects involving the strike (Waddington *et al.* 1989; Waddington *et al.* 1991).

SOCIAL PSYCHOLOGICAL APPROACHES TO STRIKES

Until recently, psychologists had made only the most tentative contributions to the strike literature (cf. Hartley 1984). This situation improved with the introduction of Kelly and Nicholson's (1980) integrated model of strike causation and process. Their model highlights the importance to strike mobilization of such key social variables as the actors' fundamental values (or 'frames of reference') and the influence on attitudes of the prevailing economic environment. However, the model contributes little to our understanding of the subjective processes of interpretation and decision making underlying strike action.

A more systematic explanation of the individual's decision to strike is provided by Klandermans (1984). His expectancy-value approach posits that the mobilization of workers for strike action is dependent on adequate knowledge of the goals of industrial action, a positive attitude to these goals, the expectation that sufficient people will take part to ensure the strike's success, and the anticipated costs and benefits of participating, e.g. winning a higher wage and maintaining the respect of one's colleagues, versus the risk of dismissal by the company, losing one's savings, or being arrested while picketing. These factors are held to be influenced, in turn, by a number of supplementary variables, notably the density and strength of trade union organization, the militancy of the proposed industrial action (e.g. whether it might involve confrontations with police or strike-breakers), the persuasiveness of the union's pre-strike mobilization campaign, and the 'demonstration effect' of previous actions by similar groups of workers.

In applying his theory to data from three empirical studies, Klandermans concluded that 'it is not the attitude towards the goals of action, but the costs and benefits of participation that determine the willingness to take action. The *attitude towards the goals of action* is indeed one of the factors which affect willingness to take action, but it is not the only one and as our research shows, it is far from being the most important' (Klandermans 1984: 119–20 emphasis added).

However, this conclusion is undermined by Keil's (1984) study of the mobilization of adolescent delivery, or 'carrier', boys in support of an American newspaper strike. The strike was precipitated when the employer, Capital Cities, tried to impose new working conditions on its reporting staff. The reporters reacted, first by striking, and then by setting

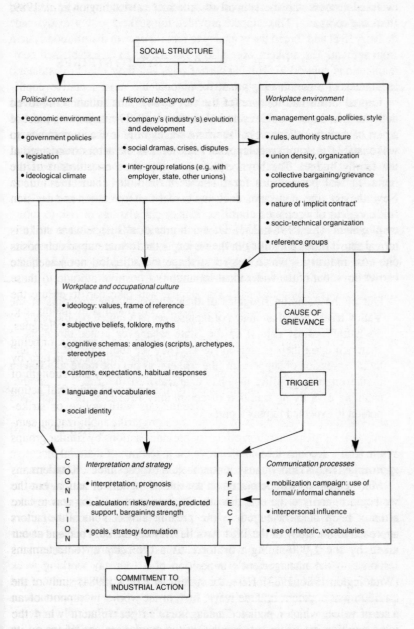

Figure 5.1 A social psychological model of strike commitment and organization

up their own newspaper in competition with the company. Crucial to their eventual success was the support of scores of carrier boys who defected from the company. This support provided the strikers with a ready-made delivery fleet and forced the company to rebuild its own distribution system from scratch. The strikers were also given access to an established communications network (involving carrier boys and their regular customers) as a means of disseminating pro-strike rationales.

Capital Cities had forewarned the carrier boys that failure to continue delivering its paper would result in their dismissal. The strike took place in a part of America (Pennsylvania) where wages were low and employment was unstable, making a regular paper route an 'indispensible component' of the family budget. The boys' decision to support the strikers therefore 'entailed real possibilities for financial misfortune' (Keil 1984: 336). Nevertheless, the collective decision to defect from the company was 'independent of economic considerations or calculations of risk to future employment' (Keil 1984: 337). Of much greater influence were the 'historical sensibilities prevailing in the region' – the former hub of the anthracite coal industry – which helped to shape the attitudes, not just of the carrier boys, but of the wider local community:

> Out of the common struggles of their ancestors, the residents of the Valley have created an image of themselves as a united people ready to do battle against capital or the State whenever either threatens to encroach upon their perceived rights. They see their present unity and their expression of support for [the strikers] as but one more stand taken in the ongoing conflict that has characterized the area . . . another example of a living tradition of community resistance in which each person is expected to play a part.
>
> (Keil 1984: 338)

While Keil's account does not disprove the assertions of material incentive approaches like Klandermans', it nonetheless exposes their limitations.

Much emphasis will be placed on the role of 'historical sensibilities' as we begin to analyse the coal dispute. The importance of the concept has already been acknowledged in the present author's social-cognitive approach to the study of the 1981 Ansells Brewery strike. This was undertaken by the 1,000-strong workforce as a typically uncompromising response to the management's imposition of a four-day working week (Waddington 1986; 1987). Here, the significance of workplace culture and tradition was apparent in three ways: first, in the workers' commitment to a set of values which repudiated management's right unilaterally to determine working arrangements; second, in the employees' belief (based on past experience) that strike action was the only language management was capable of understanding; and finally, in their knowledge of the company's tendency to yield to industrial action, because of the healthy market demand for its beers.

Some three weeks into the strike, management threatened the employees that, unless they agreed to a package of redundancies and revised working practices as a basis for an immediate return to work, they would be sacked and the brewery shut down. Far from intimidating the workers, this ultimatum merely strengthened their resolve. Management's objectives were understood in terms which characterized their behaviour as an attempt to emulate the type of strategy used by Sir Michael Edwardes to reduce trade union power at British Leyland (cf. Willman 1987). Seen in these terms, the strike represented a do-or-die struggle for the survival of the trade union organization.

The calculation of probable outcomes was evident in the application of scripts concerning closure: employees dismissed the threatened closure as a transparent coercive device, on the basis of two analogous situations where management had made similar threats which were later exposed as bluffs. Confidence in a successful outcome was further derived from the sense of solidarity existing between the workers: 'We are all in one union for a start' (i.e. a Transport and General Workers' Union closed shop), as a shop steward explained at the time: 'There is a tremendous family feeling. People know each other well and there is more solidarity than on the BL shop floor' (quoted in Waddington 1987: 86).

Finally, the Ansells workers pointed to their earlier participation in the infamous Fox and Goose Affair, between 1975 and 1977, as proof of their collective tenacity. Here, the refusal by Ansells delivery men to comply with a TUC (Trades Union Congress) instruction to lift their blacking of supplies to a West Midlands publican resulted in the TGWU's temporary suspension from the TUC. However, far from embarrassing the Ansells workers, the Fox and Goose Affair was mythically retained as evidence of their militancy and determination.

Ultimately, the six-month strike was defeated, resulting in Ansells' permanent closure. The strikers had overestimated their strength by failing to appreciate how important contextual factors (e.g. the serious decline in market demand for beer and the existence of excess production capacity at one of the parent company's neighbouring breweries) made the repetition of previously successful strategies – striking as a first response and calling the company's bluff – less reliable than before.

This study shows that models of strike commitment and organization must therefore be sensitive, not only to the rational-calculative aspects of the decision to go on strike (e.g. balancing possible costs and benefits, and predicting the likelihood of success) but equally to the more subjective and emotive sources of inspiration bound up in the ideology, myths and values comprising the workers' culture and traditions.

This point is now developed in relation to the year-long British coal dispute between the National Coal Board (NCB) (now British Coal), and the NUM. The decision to call the strike under conditions 'not propitious for the miners' (Saville 1986: 306) and the NUM's conservative strategic response are explained in terms of the constraining effects of culture and tradition. Research data are taken from two separate studies concerning the strike. The first study involved forty-two unstructured interviews with Yorkshire and Derbyshire miners between June and September 1984 (Waddington *et al.* 1989). The second incorporated eighty in-depth interviews with residents of three mining communities in Derbyshire, Nottinghamshire and Yorkshire between March 1987 and May 1988 (Waddington *et al.* 1991).

The case study begins with a brief overview of the main events of the strike, and a critique of the NUM's strategy. The next three sections analyse, in turn, the basis of commitment to the strike, the corresponding basis of opposition, and the NUM's strategic conduct. Finally, these ideas are summarized in the form of a tentative model of strike commitment and organization.

AN OVERVIEW OF THE STRIKE

The 1984–5 coal dispute was a defensive stoppage in opposition to the Conservative Government's policy of closing uneconomic collieries. The trigger for the strike was the National Coal Board's decision, announced on 1 March 1984, to close the Cortonwood colliery in South Yorkshire. The NUM was already engaged in a five-month overtime ban, commonly interpreted as an attempt to deplete national stockpiles of coal in readiness for a strike against pit closures later that winter (Wilsher *et al.* 1985: 39). It therefore seems conceivable, given its timing in the spring, and location in the union's militant heartland, that the closure of Cortonwood was a deliberate 'tactical provocation' by the NCB (Towers 1985: 15).

On 6 March, NUM officials learned of the Board's plan to close a further nineteen pits, and responded by calling out their members on an area-by-area basis, beginning with Yorkshire and Scotland. When miners in more moderate areas, notably Nottinghamshire, failed to join the strike, Yorkshire miners crossed the border intending to picket them out.

Politically, there was a great deal at stake for the Government. The NUM and its president, Arthur Scargill, were associated with events at Saltley in 1972, when a mass picket of miners and other trade unionists had enforced the closure of a crucial coke depot, and with the bringing down of the Heath

Government in 1974 (Crick 1985). The Prime Minister, Margaret Thatcher, had also been forced to climb down in the face of a threatened miners' strike over pit closures in 1981. The Government therefore was anxious to avoid a repetition of such events – or, perhaps, to avenge them (McIlroy 1985: 102).

The Government was well prepared for a confrontation. Ministers had followed the advice of the 1978 Ridley Report on how to deal with a miners' strike: by building up national stocks of coal, switching to the burning of oil at power stations, cutting social security payments to strikers, recruiting 'reliable', non-union lorry drivers to cross picket lines, and preparing large, mobile police squads to combat flying pickets (*The Economist*, 27 May 1978).

The appointment of Ian MacGregor as the NCB chairman in 1983 had been interpreted by the NUM as 'a certain sign that they would soon have a real fight on their hands'. MacGregor arrived at the NCB with a reputation for tough, anti-union style of management. During his three years as chairman of another nationalized industry, the British Steel Corporation, he had reduced that workforce by half (Wilsher *et al.* 1985: 27–8).

The NUM's efforts to win the strike were hamstrung by the recalcitrance of its Nottinghamshire members, who objected to their national officials' refusal to ballot the membership and to the allegedly intimidatory conduct of flying pickets. The union's picketing strategy was thwarted by the controversial deployment of hundreds of police riot squads, centrally co-ordinated by the National Reporting Centre (NRC) at Scotland Yard. Even where miners managed to penetrate an elaborate roadblock system, they were easily contained by the police, and generally kept well away from working miners and lorry drivers (Coulter *et al.* 1984). Picket-line confrontations between striking miners and police officers were a salient feature of media coverage of the strike, the dominant representation being that of the police reacting defensively in the face of violent provocation (Masterman 1985). Whilst this causal account is strongly disputed (Waddington *et al.* 1989), it helped to legitimize police aggression, and turned public opinion against the miners.

The NUM failed to gather the sympathetic support of strategically important groups of workers, such as the dockers and power workers. The NCB also managed to dissuade members of the pit deputies' union (NACODS) from joining the strike and bringing the industry to a standstill. The final blow to the NUM was delivered on 25 February 1985 when the Nottinghamshire Area NUM executive voted to call off their overtime ban, adding another 100,000 tonnes of coal per week to the national stockpiles. Thus, with the strikers seemingly facing defeat, on 3 March the NUM's national executive narrowly voted for an organized return to work of its members, without settlement of the strike.

Academic commentators have since doubted the wisdom of staging a strike (cf. Golden 1988). The NCB's timing of the closure of Cortonwood was finely calculated in its favour. Coal stocks were high, and consumer demand for heat and light was already tailing off as summer approached. The Government had also increased its oil imports in 1983, a crucial development, given that most power stations now had the flexibility to transfer from coal to oil, making them less prone to fuel starvation (Saville 1986: 306).

There had also been an important change in the political context since previous miners' strikes. The early 1980s was a period of 'coercive pacification', characterized by rising unemployment and economic policies which were 'deliberately intended to undermine workers' collective strength and confidence', as well as stringent anti-trade union legislation, and a 'strident ideological offensive against unions and strikes' (Hyman 1986: 199). The miners were therefore unable to rely on the level of sympathetic support they had received in 1972 and 1974.

The NUM also seemed ill-prepared for a struggle. Opposition to pit closures was liable to be undermined by the NCB's promise of attractive redundancy terms. (Carter 1985: 30), and the possibility that younger miners would 'never risk their cars and mortgages for a principle' (Field 1985: 13). The membership had voted against strike action in the three preceding ballots between 1981 and 1983 – another possible sign of their declining militancy (Samuel 1986: 13).

Finally, the late 1970s had supposedly heralded the 'bourgeoisification' of the Nottinghamshire and Midlands miners, something attributed to the larger productivity bonuses enjoyed by NUM members in geologically favoured areas (Francis 1985). Pits in these coalfields were also considered safe from the threat of closure, another reason for not counting on their support.

In addition to questioning the wisdom of undertaking strike action, some academic post-mortems have been critical of the union's strategy. There is general agreement on the following. First the failure to hold a ballot intensified internal divisions, undermined the strike's legitimacy, and provided workers in other industries with a pretext for withholding their support (Hain 1986: 229; Hyman 1986: 231). Second, there was too much reliance on mass and flying picketing, given policing developments since previous miners' strikes (Scraton 1985). Third, the miners lacked the imagination to adopt such non-confrontational tactics as national publicity campaigns and the type of 'passive' picketing pioneered by the Greenham Common women (Francis 1985). Last, the NUM leadership should have tried harder to sway public opinion in favour of the strike, by condemning picket-line violence, regardless of the focus of responsibility, and forging broad community alliances with the church, women's groups and peace organizations (Hain 1986; Round Table Discussion 1985; Saville 1986).

The above criticisms do not adequately explain three important issues: why there was such massive commitment to the strike despite apparent obstacles to its success; why the strike was just as strongly opposed by key sections of the union; and why the NUM's strategy was too predictable to be effective. These issues are now addressed in turn as we move on to consider the influence of culture and tradition on the formulation of definition and strategy.

COMMITMENT TO THE STRIKE

There are few workgroups so 'knowledgeable or obsessed' about their history as the miners (Hall 1981: 46). The danger and discomfort of working underground and the close-knit nature of mining communities encourages mutual sentiments of loyalty, comradeship and trust (Bulmer 1975; Pitt 1979). These conditions, combined with the earlier exploitative practices of the coal owners, engendered a strong commitment to the union (Hall 1981: 44), explaining why 'there can be no other group that would fight as hard for their traditions, collieries, colleagues and industry' (Hall 1981: 47).

Samuel (1986: 22) is therefore correct to identify the 'radical conservatism' of the mining families as the main 'animating spirit' of the strike. The strikers' principal objective was to guarantee:

Work for everybody for as long as they want it. More recruitment into the industry for the young lads – his lad and mine. No redundancies like they've had in the steel industry. Jobs for life. It's a matter of fighting for your industry, fighting for the community, fighting for a *future*.

(Interview, North Yorkshire miner 1984)

A powerful 'heredity principle' was invoked (Samuel 1986: 23), involving the belief that, morally at least, the mines belonged to the miners:

I can tell you what's going to happen if we lose this battle. You'll have so many pits – superpits, such as Selby and the Vale of Belvoir – and they'll be in private hands. You'll have the big businessman who comes along, puts seventy, eighty million quid into a pit and rakes in hundreds of millions of pounds' worth of profit at a stroke. It's not on. *Our forefathers* built that industry. You could say it's ours by right.

(Interview, South Yorkshire miner 1984)

The appointment of Ian MacGregor, followed by the closure of Cortonwood, underlined that the Government had an ulterior motive in mind:

I think that this government has got a vendetta against the miners because of the 1972 and 1974 strikes. She's out to smash the union.

She's appointed MacGregor as her agent. He's never been anything but a butcher; he butchered British Steel. She brought him in as a job jockey. It was done to provoke us, to clarify their intention.

(Interview, North Yorkshire miner 1984)

By extension, many strike supporters saw themselves as acting not just in their own interests, but on behalf of the wider working class:

The police have got their orders to suppress the NUM into the dust. No single union in history has had to take on what we're taking on now, because Maggie Thatcher has been planning for the last five years to take the miners on. Every working-class person in this country is looking at us and saying, 'If these miners go down, it's God help the rest of us'.

(Interview, South Yorkshire miner 1984)

Such people were proud of the miners' reputation as the 'shock troops' of the Labour Movement, the 'vanguard of the proletariat' (Adeney and Lloyd 1986: Hall 1981). The strike was a measure of their sense of responsibility to the wider working class.

OPPOSITION TO THE STRIKE

As we know, commitment to the strike was unevenly distributed. Thousands of NUM members, particularly in the strategically important Nottinghamshire Area, continued to work during the dispute, impeding its effectiveness. The reasons put forward for not striking by our Nottinghamshire interviewees reflected cynicism towards the NUM president ('He wanted to bring down the government') and indignation over the strike's conduct:

I honestly think if they'd allowed us to have a ballot, I'm sure we'd have been out. But the problem was that somebody in their wisdom – surely to God he wants hanging – decided to send in the flying pickets.

(Interview, Nottinghamshire miner 1987)

Gibbon (1988: 170–3) dismisses such rationales. He interprets this antipathy as a legacy of the old Nottinghamshire piece-rate approach to mineworking which encouraged 'a highly individualistic and incentive-oriented attitude to work, management and trade unionism' (Gibbon 1988: 175). This contrasted with the more collectivist attitudes prevailing in areas like Durham, Yorkshire and South Wales, where 'work group self regulation and restriction of output' were the norm.

In Yorkshire, this militant tradition was reinforced by major unofficial strikes in 1969 and 1970, and the emergence of a charismatic and well-educated left-wing leadership (including the NUM president, Arthur Scargill), which further radicalized the membership (cf. Allen 1981; Taylor 1984). Consequently, in two separate ballots on the issue of pit closures, in October 1982 and March 1983, Yorkshire miners voted for strike action, whereas Nottinghamshire miners voted overwhelmingly against (Callinicos and Simons 1985: 44). These contrasting traditions help to explain why the 1984–5 strike was well supported in Yorkshire, but not so by Nottinghamshire miners, who 'saw a strike over managerial prerogative as an irrelevant and essentially illegitimate exercise' (Gibbon 1988: 176).

Empirical evidence suggests that a large proportion of strike-breakers in areas of Yorkshire and North Derbyshire were people who lived outside the local pit village, or had no family tradition in mining (Coulter *et al.* 1984; Waddington *et al.* 1991; Winterton and Winterton 1989). Such factors as unusual working conditions, the idiosyncratic leadership styles of local management or branch officials (whether currently or in the recent past), or the influence of migrant labour, led to instances during the dispute where miners from two neighbouring collieries held fundamentally differing attitudes to the strike (Samuel *et al.* 1986: 86–92).

Finally, as this comment from a North Derbyshire miner emphasizes, financial commitments, family pressures, friendship networks and private principles all had a bearing on the decision to strike:

> You'd got people who'd got money and wanted to keep it; you'd got people who were big union men who'd die for their principles; you'd got people, same as me really, who couldn't really afford to go on strike, but who couldn't walk down the street and think, 'Well, he isn't working, and he isn't working'. You'd got to stick together, more or less. A lot of people believed in the action, but didn't want to go out on strike for it. I mean, our strike was split, fifty-fifty.
>
> (Interview, 1987)

Thus, whilst it is sensible to explain variations in strike support in terms of the different cultures and traditions of separate coalfields, and even of neighbouring collieries, this is not to deny the significance of the personal circumstances influencing individual responses (Klandermans 1984).

THE STRATEGIC CONDUCT OF THE STRIKE

Any decision to strike involves some calculation of relative bargaining strength and a choice of appropriate tactics. There is no doubt that mining families entered the 1984–5 strike in the knowledge that enormous odds were stacked against them. Many of them were already familiar with the implications of the Ridley Report. They knew that the winter months were behind them, and that coal stocks were high (Beynon 1985a: 107). However, calculations of relative strength were overshadowed by the need to make a stand: 'We had *no alternative*. It's like, if everybody had sat back when Hitler went into France, he'd have come into Britain next' (Interview, striking Nottinghamshire miner 1987)

Nevertheless, it was apparent that many participants drew inspiration from the miners' epic, though heavily mythologized, struggles of the past (Samuel 1986: 5). References were repeatedly made to the Battle of Saltley in 1972 (see earlier), to the bringing down of the Heath Government in 1974, and to the Thatcher climb-down of 1981. Younger men and women asked about the General Strike of 1926: 'How long did it last? When did it start? In all this they gained strength from the fact that they, or their parents and grandparents, had been through such a struggle before. It could be done again' (Beynon 1985b: 20).

Unfortunately, mining folklore tends to magnify the significance of these events. The closure of the Saltley coke depot had been achieved only with the assistance of 20,000 sympathetic West Midlands trade unionists (Callinicos and Simons 1985: 28). The downfall of the Heath Government had stemmed from its overconfidence in calling an election when threatened by a miners' strike (Beynon 1985b: 30). The earlier decision by Margaret Thatcher to withdraw from a confrontation with the miners had been an orderly retreat, to wait for more favourable circumstances (Beynon 1985b: 37). Finally, the General Strike had resulted, not in a glorious victory, but in a crushing defeat for the miners, stemming from the TUC General Council's hasty withdrawal of the support of the wider labour movement, and culminating in the formation of the breakaway Spencer Union in Nottinghamshire (Morris 1976: 272). This union was widely castigated by miners in other areas as a so-called bosses' union. It was not until the demise of the Spencer Union in the late 1930s that Nottinghamshire miners rejoined the national union.

It seems likely that, as with the Ansells workers, the miners were guilty of the tendency among decision makers to use their history badly. Previously successful strategies of the early 1970s were reimplemented without sufficient regard to important contextual changes, notably the 'coercive pacification' of the trade union movement. A second major problem for the NUM was that, in the words of one branch official, the government had 'learned from their mistakes and . . . corrected them; they consolidated their forces. We – because we were successful in 1972 and 1974 – didn't go through this examination' (quoted by Beynon and McMylor 1985: 43).

While the government's preparations included the setting up of a *de facto* national police force (McIlroy 1985: 106–7), the miners clung to a cardinal and time-honoured principle: 'the one comradeship that we have got left is that a miner won't cross a picket line' (quoted by Samuel 1986: 15). Those pickets who entered Nottinghamshire in the early weeks of the strike therefore were dismayed by the dismissive attitude of strike-breakers (Beynon 1985b: 6).

In earlier miners' strikes, notably 1972, picket-line behaviour had taken the form of a ritualized, largely symbolic, pushing and shoving between miners and the police (Geary 1985). The objectives of each side were tacitly approved of and legitimated in this pattern of accommodation (Waddington *et al.* 1989). In 1984, however, the police suppressed the pickets' 'customary right' to influence the behaviour and invoke the solidarity of working miners and lorry drivers. The resulting sense of powerlessness and indignation led to the type of violence which alienated public support for the miners (Waddington *et al.* 1989).

Claims that the premature picketing of the Nottinghamshire coalfield, and the NUM leaders' reluctance to hold a ballot, cost the union the vital support of its Nottinghamshire members have grown in credence since the strike. The emotive question of the ballot remains a powerful testimony of how 'archetypal images' structured people's perceptions (Samuel 1986: 5). Prominent among these archetypes was the spectre of the 'Spencerite' Nottinghamshire miner:

> They're lording it up down there. They haven't just got their fat bonuses to delude themselves with. There's millions of pounds in the old Spencer Union funds and Notts miners are drawing it off every week in pensions and holiday money. They have done ever since 1926. It's all wrong. They're class collaborators and always will be.
>
> (Interview, South Yorkshire miner 1984)

Jobs were reckoned to be more secure in the coal-rich Midlands areas. Strike activists in relatively disadvantaged areas therefore objected on the grounds that 'We're not letting those bastards in Notts vote our men out of a job' (Field 1985: 12). Nor could the strikers trust their Nottinghamshire counterparts to honour the result of a ballot, 'particularly after the experience in 1977–8 when a national membership ballot had voted to reject a productivity scheme, only to find Nottinghamshire, followed by other areas, agreeing to its introduction on a local basis' (Hain 1986: 228).

Other archetypal images – e.g. those of the unscrupulous trade union leader and the unprincipled 'sell out' – helped to maintain a distance between the NUM and potential support from the TUC, which the miners had still not forgiven for supposedly deserting them during the General Strike: 'Haunted by the memory of 1926 and understandably wary of allowing the "new realists" at the TUC to take over their strike, the NUM sought to maintain the General Council at arm's length while simultaneously blaming it for lack of support. This helped to marginalize sympathy for the miners in other trade unions' (Hain 1986: 236).

As stated earlier, retrospective analyses of the strike have been critical of the NUM leadership: firstly, for pre-empting the peaceful persuasion of the Nottinghamshire miners by prematurely deploying the flying pickets; and secondly, for doing too little to turn public opinion in favour of the miners. Such themes indicate a poor appreciation of the way that local culture and tradition had a constraining effect on the way that NUM leaders sought, but were sometimes unable, to influence their constituents.

Thus, the first of these criticisms underestimates the extent of rank-and-file autonomy traditionally exercised within the NUM. The Yorkshire Area has four regional sub-divisions, each of which is represented by a 'panel' of local lay officials who meet to discuss local and national NUM policy (Field 1985: 12). These panels – notably the historically militant Doncaster panel – played a key organizing role in 1984, just as they had done in a series of major unofficial disputes from 1955 to 1970, and in the national strikes of 1972 and 1974. Thus, whilst the Yorkshire Area executive initially determined on a policy of six miners picketing their own pits, local pickets 'surged over the borders into Notts', in defiance of these preliminary instructions (Field 1985).

After the strike, the NUM president was criticized for his uncompromising rhetoric, even from within his own union. Such criticism overlooks the important point that by softening his tone, Arthur Scargill would have risked alienating the activists, and diluting the principles on which the strike was based (Wilsher *et al.* 1985: 77). It was unfortunate for strike supporters that, while Scargill's rhetoric proved inspirational to miners from militant coalfields, it offended the sensibilities of the more moderate sections of his union.

SUMMARY

The above analysis emphasizes the need for social psychologists to go beyond rational-calculative models of strike mobilization and strategy to examine the influence of subjective and affective processes on the decision to engage in industrial action and which strategy to pursue. To this end, a working model is proposed (see Figure 5.1), which highlights the relationship between the cognitive and affective dimensions of the decision to strike, whilst emphasizing the mediating effects of culture.

Lack of space prohibits a systematic application of the model, but all the relevant terms, bar one, have either appeared in the context of previous discussion or will already be familiar to the reader. The one exception is the reference to the *implicit contract*, i.e. 'The tacit agreement between the employer and the individual employee about the amount of effort to be put into a job and the amount of control which an employee will accept in return for a certain level and mix of rewards (pay, status, job satisfaction, career potential, etc.)' (Watson 1987: 287). The model constitutes a dialectical approach to strike mobilization, emphasizing the 'dynamic interaction between structure and consciousness' (Hyman 1984: 76). Thus, processes of definition and strategic decision making are explained with due reference to the appropriate historical, political and socio-cultural variables.

The preceding discussion emphasizes how commitment to the strike had less to do with objective calculations of probable success or failure, than with the highly subjective, culturally mediated ideas of its participants – to the 'radical conservatism' embodied in their determination to protect the jobs, the trade union and the communities comprising their entire ancestral heritage. The strike's key aspects of definition and strategy were shaped by a rich cultural legacy of emotive parallels, ardent myths and prowling archetypes. Thus, timeless imagery – of the General Strike, Spencerism, flying pickets, Saltley, the collapse of the Heath Government, productivity bonuses and the climb-down of 1981 – was the principal guiding force.

Fox (1971: 128) is therefore justified in emphasizing that 'New interpretations and adaptations may prove difficult to achieve where tradition maintains habitual perceptions and responses generated in an earlier and different situation'. Looking back, it is difficult to imagine how the miners could have contemplated winning a strike against such a powerful and well-prepared adversary. At least part of the explanation lies in the possibility that they were 'snared' and 'deluded' by the lessons of their past (Morgan 1985: 283), taking too much encouragement from their famous victories of the 1970s and 1981, without sensing that changes in the political context called for a new, more innovative strategy.

Acknowledgements

This study was made possible by two research grants from the Economic and Social Research Council (grant numbers GO 225 0004 and GO 0232 311). The author wishes to thank the ESRC for the provision of this support.

REFERENCES

Adeney, M. and Lloyd, J. (1986) *Loss Without Limit: The Miners' Strike of 1984-5*, London: Routledge and Kegan Paul.
Allen, V.L. (1981) *The Militancy of British Miners*, Shipley: The Moor Press.
Beynon, H. (1985a) 'The Miners Strike in Easington', *New Left Review* 148: 104–15.
Beynon, H. (ed.) (1985b) *Digging Deeper: Issues in the Miners' Strike*, London: Verso.

Beynon, H. and McMylor, P. (1985) 'Decisive power: The new Tory state against the miners', in H. Beynon (ed.) *Digging Deeper: Issues in the Miners' Strike*, London: Verso.

Bulmer, M. (1975) 'Sociological models of the mining community', *Sociological Review* 23: 61–92.

Callinicos, A. and Simons, M. (1985) *The Great Strike: The Miners' Strike of 1984–5 and its Lessons*, London: Socialist Worker.

Carter, P. (1985) 'Striking the right note', *Marxism Today* March.

Coulter, J., Miller, S., and Walker, M. (1984) *State of Siege: Politics and Policing in the Coalfields*, London: Canary Press.

Crick, M. (1985) *Scargill and the Miners*, Harmondsworth: Penguin.

Field, J. (1985) 'Labour's Dunkirk', *New Socialist* April.

Fox, A. (1971) *A Sociology of Work in Industry*, London: Collier Macmillan.

Francis, H. (1985) 'NUM United: A team in disarray', *Marxism Today* April.

Geary, R. (1985) *Policing Industrial Disputes*, Cambridge: Cambridge University Press.

Gibbon, P. (1988) 'Analysing the British miners' strike of 1984–5', *Economy and Society* 17(2): 139–94.

Golden, M.A. (1988) 'Heroic defeats', paper presented at the Annual Meeting of the American Political Science Association, Washington D.C., 1–4 September.

Hain, P. (1986) *Political Strikes: The State and Trade Unionism in Britain*, New York: Viking.

Hall, T. (1981) *King Coal: Miners, Coal and Britain's Industrial Future*, Harmondsworth: Penguin.

Hartley, J. (1984) 'Industrial relations psychology: the case of industrial conflict', in M.M. Gruneberg and T.D. Wall (eds) *Social Psychology and Organisational Behaviour*, Chichester: Wiley.

Hyman, R. (1984) *Strikes*, (3rd edn) London: Fontana.

Hyman, R. (1986) 'Reflections on the miners' strike', *Socialist Register*, 1985/86: 330–354.

Keil, T.J. (1984) 'Mobilizing adolescent workers' support for an American newspaper strike: results from a case study', *Organization Studies* 5(4): 327–43.

Kelly, J. and Nicholson, N. (1980) 'The causation of strikes: a review of theoretical approaches and the potential contribution of social psychology', *Human Relations* 33(12): 853–83.

Kettle, M. (1985) 'The National Reporting Centre and the 1984 miners' strike', in B. Fine and R. Millar (eds) *Policing the Miners' Strike*, London: Lawrence and Wishart.

Klandermans, P.G. (1984) 'Mobilization and participation in trade union action: an expectancy-value approach', *Journal of Occupational Psychology*, 57: 107–20.

Krieger, J. (1983) *Undermining Capitalism*, London: Methuen.

McCabe, S. and Wallington, P. (1988) *The Police, Public Order and Civil Liberties*, London: Routledge.

McIlroy, J. (1985) 'Police and pickets: the law against the miners', in H. Beynon (ed.) *Digging Deeper: Issues in the Miners' Strike*, London: Verso.

Masterman, L. (1985) 'The battle of Orgreave', in L. Masterman (ed.) *Television Mythologies*, London: Comedia.

Morgan, K.O. (1985) 'A time for miners to forget history', *New Society*, 21 February.

Morris, M. (1976) *The General Strike*, Harmondsworth: Penguin.

People of Thurcroft (1986) *Thurcroft: A Village and the Miners' Strike*, Nottingham: Spokesman.

Pitt, M. (1979) *The World On Our Backs*, London: Lawrence and Wishart.

Round Table Discussion (1985) 'The miners' strike: a balance sheet', *Marxism Today*, April.

Samuel;, R. (1986) 'Introduction', in R. Samuel *et al.* (eds) *The Enemy Within: Pit Villages and the Miners' Strike of 1984–5*, London: Routledge and Kegan Paul.

Samuel, R., Bloomfield, B., and Boanas, G. (eds) (1986) *The Enemy Within: Pit Villages and the Miners' Strike of 1984–5*, London: Routledge and Kegan Paul.

Saville, J. (1986) 'An open conspiracy: conservative politics and the miners' strike 1984–5', *Socialist Register*, 1985/86: 295–329.

Scraton, P. (1985) *The State of the Police*, London: Pluto Press.

Taylor, A.J. (1984) *The Politics of the Yorkshire Miners*, London: Croom Helm.

Towers, B. (1985) 'Posing larger questions: the British miners' strike of 1984–5', *Industrial Relations Journal* 16(1): 8–25.

Waddington, D.P. (1986) 'The Ansells brewery dispute: A social-cognitive approach to the study of strikes', *Journal of Occupational Psychology* 59: 231–46.

Waddington, D.P. (1987) *Trouble Brewing: A Social Psychological Analysis of the Ansells Brewery Dispute*, Aldershot: Avebury.

Waddington, D.P., Jones, K., and Critcher, C. (1989) *Flashpoints: Studies in Public Disorder*, London: Routledge.

Waddington, D.P., Wykes, M., and Critcher, C. (1991) *Split At The Seams? Community, Continuity and Change After the 1984–5 Coal Dispute*, Milton Keynes: Open University Press.

Watson, T.J. (1987) *Sociology, Work and Industry*, London: Routledge and Kegan Paul.

Willman, P. (1987) 'Industrial relations issues in advanced manufacturing technology', in T.D. Wall, C.W. Clegg, and N.J. Kemp (eds) *The Human Side of Advanced Manufacturing Technology*, London: John Wiley.

Wilsher, P., Macintyre, D., and Jones, M. (1985) *Strike: A Battle of Ideologies: Thatcher, Scargill and the Miners*, London: Coronet.

Winterton, J. and Winterton, R. (1989) *Coal, Crisis and Conflict: The 1984–85 Miners' Strike in Yorkshire*, Manchester: Manchester University Press

Part II
Innovation and change

Introduction

Neil Anderson

What is meant by the concept of innovation? How does innovation differ from creativity and organizational change or development? What factors in the workplace influence the conceptualization and implementation of innovatory practices? Why should innovation constitute an imperative issue for organizational psychologists? And ultimately, what can organizational psychologists contribute towards a general understanding of innovation processes and outcomes?

These questions, and many others besides, have come to the fore as a result of a growing interest in issues of innovation and change at work. Judging by the prolific expansion over recent years in the numbers of textbooks and journal articles devoted to organizational innovation, the topic has emerged as a prevalent concern amongst social scientists and organizational psychologists alike. As a research domain, innovation may well have come of age, but it was only comparatively recently that organizational psychologists began to devote serious attention to innovation and creativity at work. One compelling explanation for this reticence to embrace innovation as a topic worthy of scientific research is that earlier work originated from academics in other social science sub-disciplines, whose approaches have proven problematic to integrate into the perspective of work and organizational psychologists.

Two distinct and largely disparate themes of enquiry are discernible: the development of creative talents within individuals, and the process of innovative product development within manufacturing organizations.

Studies within the first strand of research, concerned with the occurrence and development of creative talents, were rarely restricted to creativity in the workplace. Rather, much research effort was directed towards explicating the development of aptitudes and abilities in such domains as music, art, and educational attainment. Research in this tradition was clearly the preserve of child and developmental psychologists, whose primary goals were to explore the cognitive and cognitive-social dimensions of giftedness amongst a largely, but not exclusively, non-adult population (see for example, Albert 1990; Albert and Runco 1985; Cattell and Butcher 1968).

Studies by strategic management researchers into the conceptualization, development, and implementation of new product lines constitute the second strand of research, which pre-dates the recent attentions of organizational psychologists to innovation. Here the primary concerns were to delineate interactions between formal groups within the organization involved with the process of developing and manufacturing new product lines. Another concern was to examine the diffusion of innovations within industrial sectors, revealing patterns of uptake amongst competitor organizations of new technologies and production processes. Within individual organizations the objective was to chart patterns of interaction between functional groups over time as innovations were initiated and developed. For instance, the interaction between research and development departments responsible for developing prototype products, marketing departments charged with assessing their commercial viability and subsequently with promoting their sale, and production departments responsible for manufacturing and distribution (see, for example, Kanter 1983; Pettigrew 1985; Rosenfield and Servo 1991).

Organizational psychologists entering the innovation arena inherited a legacy of these two extensive but largely unrelated bodies of literature, both of which were only tangentially relevant to the issues which psychologists had uppermost on their research agendas. Akin to a developing third world country, sandwiched between the irreconcilable socio-economic strictures of the two superpowers, which was attempting to absorb the best of both systems, psychologists sought to pluck out appropriate concepts and methodologies from the creativity and strategic management literatures, and in so doing, to adapt and modify them to suit the needs of their particular research agendas.

This analogy begs the question of how successful have organizational psychologists been in assimilating and integrating these two disparate approaches into sensible research designs addressing psychological aspects of innovation in the workplace? Undoubtedly, in recent years considerable progress has been made toward integration, but in all fairness, this objective sets the sights very high indeed. More pragmatically we might expect to have to settle for psychological research which, whilst taking into account the previous research traditions and going some way toward integrating their distinct approaches, also superimposes its own research questions, methodologies, and agendas upon the existing body of knowledge.

Part II to some extent reflects these dilemmas. Just how original and innovatory its contents are is a judgement only the reader can make. It is certainly the case, however, that the three chapters in Part II are indicative of the developments in recent years made by organizational psychologists active in this area. The chapters reflect the three principal levels of analysis which have been pursued by organizational psychologists – the individual, the group, and the organization as a whole.

In Chapter 6 Bouwen, De Visch and Steyaert review innovation processes at the organizational level of analysis. Four in-depth case studies are presented which illustrate the paths of four quite different innovations: the implementation of an upgraded service ethos in a fast-food restaurant chain, a new client-rating system in a Belgian savings bank, an organization development and total quality management programme conducted in a subsidiary of an American insulation materials multinational, and the introduction of a CAD/CAM (computer assisted design/computer assisted manufacture) system in a Belgian consumer electronics manufacturing firm. The authors invoke the concepts of the 'dominant logic' and the 'innovation logic' to compare and contrast the different demands being experienced within each organization. Through a detailed presentation of their qualitative case study data the authors highlight the disruptive effects of the innovations upon organizational members, and in so doing, encapsulate the organizational learning that takes places throughout the progress of each innovation.

In Chapter 7 Anderson presents a state-of-the-art review of existing research into innovation which focuses specifically at the level of analysis of the work group or team. Conceptual and definitional issues are addressed initially, and existing results reviewed and critiqued under a three-fold typology: structural factors (group composition and development), psychological factors (group climate and social construction), and processual factors (process models and interpersonal interaction). The paucity of research at the group level is admonished and the need for future research strategies to envisage work group innovation as an emergent social process which reveals the groups on-going attempts to renegotiate social order is asserted in conclusion.

Chapter 8, by Jackson and Nicholson, is concerned with the individual level of analysis. Drawing from work role transition theory and from research into implicit knowledge in job performance, the authors describe a detailed experimental study into the individual transitions of UK police officers currently in the midst of being promoted. By presenting carefully constructed scenarios of work situations, Jackson and Nicholson explore marked differences between novice and experienced officers, concluding that the individuals' implicit knowledge of work role requirements may be a fundamental precursor to being able to innovate within a job role. Alternatively, the authors argue, work role innovations may simply be mistakes committed by individuals attempting to learn through trial and error the necessary implicit knowledge to perform their jobs.

REFERENCES

Albert, R.A. (1990) 'Identity, experiences and career choice among the exceptionally gifted and eminent', in M.A. Runco and R.S. Albert (eds) *Theories of Creativity*, London: Sage.

Albert, R.S. and Runco M.A. (1985) 'The achievement of eminence: A model of exceptionally gifted boys and their families', in J.R. Sterling and J.E. Davidson (eds) *Conception of Giftedness*, New York: Cambridge University Press.

Cattell, R.B. and Butcher, H.J. (1968) *The Prediction of Achievement and Creativity*, Indianapolis: Bobbs-Merril.

Kanter, R.M. (1983) *The Change Masters; Corporate Entrepreneurs at Work*, London: Allen & Unwin.

Pettegrew, A. (1985) *The Awakening Giant: Continuity and Change in ICI*, Oxford: Blackwell.

Rosenfield, R. and Servo, J.C. (1991) 'Facilitating innovation in large organizations', in J. Henry and D. Walker (eds) *Managing Innovation*, London: Sage.

6 Innovation projects in organizations
Complementing the dominant logic by organizational learning

René Bouwen, Jan De Visch and Chris Steyaert

INTRODUCTION

Innovation in an organization may seem a paradoxical process. Organizations that carefully plan for it are not at all assured of success, while organizations in adverse conditions sometimes succeed in making a major turnaround. Innovation creates a lot of tension in organizations, and is often experienced as both challenging and uncomfortable for those involved. During an innovative effort, organizations must be able to give attention to three behavioural tasks: dealing with continuity, thinking about new ideas or novelty, and going through the transition process itself (Bouwen and Fry 1988).

In four case studies of innovation projects in large organizations, we describe how the main actors construct the dominant logic or prevailing way of thinking and acting in their organizations. We analyse the extent to which the action logic demanded by innovation creates tensions between the parties involved and between the dominant and new action logics. The organizations concerned responded by using a set of action strategies to cope with those tensions. The strategies used and the outcomes attained allowed the researchers to check whether and what kind of organizational learning took place. Dominant action logic and organizational learning are introduced as basic concepts with which to frame the paradoxical experience of innovation and to understand how strategies can be guided toward specific outcomes.

THE EXPERIENCE OF INNOVATION

This broad definition of innovation is in line with the definition used in recent overviews of innovation studies, when the emphasis has been on the analysis of the behavioural aspects of the process (West and Farr 1990).

Organizational innovation here is considered to be any organizational or business change situation where disruption is experienced by those involved between the existing and the desired situation. The object of the innovation may be diversification through product, market, or technological innovation; it may be a process of managerial innovation, which often follows economic, technological, or cultural-political changes. The focus in this study is on the construction of the new shared organizational experience of all parties involved. How do we perceive the emergence of a new shared meaning, integrating the existing organization and the innovation project? How do people think and act in this innovation task?

Innovation is experienced as jumping from familiar ground into unknown, sometimes challenging domains. In the cases studied, people spoke often about a situation full of tensions, which were sometimes experienced as challenging or exciting. Many choices have to be made; problem definitions have to be exchanged, perspectives are confronted and involvement has to be created. Innovation is also often experienced as a paradoxical situation. Some organizations try to plan the process in a very logical and structured way, and yet the implementation itself may be disastrous. Other organizations muddle through a series of problems and crises and arrive at a new, shared organizational reality that could never have been foreseen.

It is the position of this paper that three behavioural processes have to be monitored simultaneously and continuously during the innovation effort: providing and maintaining continuity, introducing and shaping novelty into new and compelling ideas, and actually accomplishing the transition. These three foci have to be balanced and aligned with each other. This framework has proved to be useful in examining revival and innovation situations in general (Bouwen and Fry 1988). In this paper, four case studies will be used to illustrate the three elements of this triangle and the dynamics between them. The core objective of this study is to describe and conceptualize the dialectic process between 'old' and 'new'. This process is expressed in the way participants frame to each other 'old' and 'new' and how they incorporate these frames of reference into mutual action strategies. How they deal with these dualities or dilemmas, and whether they integrate the polarities, separate them, or avoid them etc. (Turner 1990) is the core question of this study.

The concept of dominant logic will be used to describe the core characteristics of how people frame the 'old' and 'new' situations. The difference in the mind-set provoked by the innovation project will be conceptualized as a difference in action logics. The tension experienced in an innovation situation will be conceived as the experienced opposition between the dominant, existing logic and the new, innovatory logic. This new action logic has to be added to, or must complement, the existing action logic to a new 'shared meaning', which is emergent among the different parties

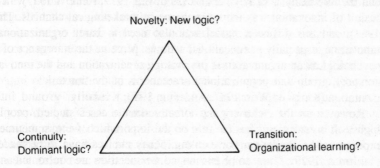

Figure 6.1 The three tasks of innovation management

involved. The transition as a third element of the scheme in Figure 6.1 will be conceptualized in terms of organizational learning. The action strategies used by the significant parties to deal with the existing tensions between the old and the new will determine what kind of dialectical processes are taking place and whether a new shared organizational meaning is going to emerge. A learning organization means that the actors involved transform the innovation situation into a self-monitoring process that enhances both the ability of the organization to steer itself and to improve its capacity for further innovations in the future.

A PROCESS-ORIENTED APPROACH TO INNOVATION

The focal attention of this study is directed towards understanding the process of conceiving the innovation project by the parties involved and the interaction among the parties to deal with the innovation task. There are excellent overviews of the ongoing research on innovation from various points of view: managerial (Tushman and More 1988); social psychological (West and Farr 1990); interdisciplinary (Grönhaug and Kaufmann 1988), and a more project-oriented point of view (Van de Ven, Angle and Poole 1989), which help to distinguish the process approach of this study. In research on business and management strategy there is a long tradition of studies on product/market innovation (Roberts 1977), mainly technological innovation (Maidique 1980). Entrepreneurship in starting business and new ventures has also received some attention.

After describing the elements of the strategic business situation, the attention of researchers focused more and more on the management process and the role analysis of key persons (Rothwell 1977; Roberts 1977). Diffusion of innovation was the main theme in marketing research (Rogers 1983), and this diffusion model was also used to study organizational innovation, especially in educational settings. Most research from a social psychological or organizational psychological viewpoint has focused on personal, group and organizational antecedents of the innovation implementation (King and West 1987; Anderson 1989; Kimberly 1990).

Research on the creativity and effectiveness of R&D departments in high-tech organizations has focused on the importance of communication processes to bridge the gap between disciplines and functional departments (Tushman 1979). This emphasis on communication and roles elicited predominantly process-oriented research work. Internal venturing processes (Burgelman and Sayles 1986) and entrepreneurial activities (Van de Ven 1986) are described in process terms. Burgelman (1986) distinguishes a 'variables approach' from a 'process approach'. The research reported in this paper has been based on this process approach. It emerges from the necessity to understand the interaction process among the parties in order to gain a more in-depth understanding and to gather knowledge usable to steer innovation processes in real time.

DOMINANT LOGIC AND ORGANIZATIONAL LEARNING MORE CLOSELY DEFINED

An organization cannot be everything at once. By acting on its environment, it creates a niche for itself. This framing and acting upon specific aspects of its internal and external environment can be called its dominant action logic (Prahalad and Bettis 1986). The concept of dominant logic enables us to understand the strategic 'focus' (or lack of focus) in the behaviour of management in more or less diversified corporations. The characteristics of the core business make some managerial tasks especially critical, and a mind-set or repertoire of tasks is developed that shapes the dominant logic of that organization. Prahalad and Bettis (1986: 491) define dominant logic as ' . . . a mind-set or a world view or conceptualization of the business and the administrative tools to accomplish goals and make decisions in that business'. In the first reported case study, for example, we could characterize the dominant logic as centralized and formalized managerial practices, quantitative control devices, standard operating procedures, etc. Globally we called this a 'distribution logic'.

The concept of 'dominant logic' has still to be defined in organizational psychological terms. In this study, concrete descriptions of behaviour and context will be used to typify the 'way of doing things'. The concept of dominant logic does not only cover cultural or structural aspects of the social network of the organization, but also task-oriented strategies to deal with the core business activities: e.g. distributing consumer goods using well organized, centralized, formalized procedures is characterized as a 'distribution logic'. One can talk about an 'academic logic' if that includes: reliance on research and abstract thought, looking for breakthroughs in knowledge, using experimental thinking. This is very different from a 'marketing logic', which means opportunistic orientation towards the environment, negotiating contacts with clients, being service-oriented, etc.

In this article we want to use the concept of dominant logic to describe the core characteristics of the existing mind-set and behaviour before an innovation occurs in an organization. We aim to illustrate that this can help to conceptualize the tensions and the change taking place in any innovative endeavour.

Prahalad and Bettis (1986) described the difference between a diversification and the related parent company in terms of core business characteristics. The quality of the business or pattern of diversification does not seem to determine success or failure so much, but the quality of management does. In this study, the focus of interest will be the interaction among the parties being an expression of managerial practices.

Related concepts in cognitive psychology are conceptual schemes or cognitive maps as an expression of how people frame their experiences and keep them in mind. Weick (1979) elaborated the cognitive map as an outcome of the behavioural sequence: selection–enactment–retention. These cognitive maps serve as schemas for negotiation among the parties involved to construct a shared social reality. Social constructionism (Gergen 1978) goes a step further by conceiving these cognitive maps as outcomes of interactions or qualities of relationships. Cognitive frames are considered as relational qualities of the interaction among the parties concerning the organizational activity around a task domain. Especially in an innovation situation, the social construction of a new shared image is actively in the making. The social negotiation is the organizing taking place around the existing and the emerging organization by opposing or integrating the framing of an innovation project. Following the growing paradigm awareness in organization theory (Morgan 1986), there is an explicit recognition of the viewpoint that people frame their social reality by relating to others concerning specific tasks or projects. An organization is conceived as a negotiated social reality with the intention of arriving at a satisfactory level of shared meaning, so that some common actions can be achieved (Gray *et al.* 1985). Gergen (1978) stresses the relational or interactional nature of cognitive frames. Conceived as purely individual characteristics, these cognitive frames or images are disparate; conceived as relational, they characterize the negotiation process among the parties involved.

The quality of the interaction processes among the parties involved, shaping the dialectic process between the 'old' and 'new' action logic, will be described in this paper in terms of organizational learning. Besides the content output of the dialogue, there is also a process output – this process output can be described by its organizational learning qualities (Argyris and Schon 1978; Hedberg 1981). Is the organization learning or improving its capacity to deal with innovation projects, and how is this expressed in the characteristics of the ongoing interaction? Is the capacity for innovation in the future increased or decreased? Is the organization gaining improved 'process knowledge' about 'how they do things over here without being forced to rely only on structural or personnel changes'? Can the organization improve its quality to integrate dualities and to cope more effectively with the dialectics of the innovation?

THE APPROACH OF THE STUDY

In an exploratory study focusing on organizational processes which hinder or stimulate the implementation of innovation projects in organizations, in-depth case studies were conducted in four organizations. Observational data were collected over periods from six to eighteen months to document over time the consecutive steps and the main behavioural strategies described by the key actors. The focus of this study is at the project level. The cognitive frames of the participants expressed through documents and interviews form the raw data which describe the development and the characteristics of the project in relation to the organization. The research heuristic we used consisted of three major questions:

1 What meaning do people attribute to the ongoing innovation tasks, and which similarities and tensions can be observed between these meanings of the actors?
2 What action strategies in behavioural patterns are used to deal with emerging meaning in an effort to come to shared meaning, enabling common action and progress of the project?
3 What organizational arrangements, procedures and forms emerge to anchor the results obtained?

These questions formed the basis of extensive interviewing of the key actors, co-inquiry through feedback of the interview protocols, participant observation of project group meetings, minutes of meetings and documents about the project, and in some cases organizational climate surveys. All verbal material formed the data base for applying a Glaser and Straus (1967) saturation approach, deriving concepts and interpretations, in which data from the different sources are collected and new concepts are derived until some convergence in meaning can be observed. A concept is considered then to be 'saturated' on the content level. This conceptual saturation is to this research approach what statistical representativeness is to the positivistic research paradigm. Concepts about meanings, actions, and outcomes were registered and documented through observable statements and events in vignette descriptions. The relationships between the emerging concepts were identified from those vignettes. Mental maps could be derived to picture patterns of meaning, tensions between meanings, and relations between meanings and actions.

The mental mapping of the dominant logic and tensions between logics during the process of analysis emerged from the concepts describing how people phrased their experience of the existing organization, of the evolving innovation project, and of the relations between both.

Organizational learning is described by the kind of actions that form the interaction patterns between the parties to deal with the innovation task and the resulting outcomes of progress, polarization and integration. We consider organizational learning to take place when we see progress being made in the direction of common action and higher commitment in such a way that further development is facilitated and further steps in the process are not jeopardized. To do this, we use internal process characteristics of effectiveness as indication of organizational learning. Two-sided communication process characteristics, expressions of involvement, and the generation of valid data are mentioned by Argyris and Schon (1978) as indications of organizational learning taking place.

FOUR CASE STUDIES

Four innovation projects in large organizations will be described and synthesized in a schematic form. First, the dominant logic will be described in the firm, then the tension between meanings created by the project and the main logic required by the innovation project. Then the action strategies to cope with the demands of the innovations are described, with special attention being given to the interactive character and the distribution of influence in the process. Finally the outcome for the project and the effects on learning are described.

Each case is a complex interaction of many influences. The description of the cases is focused on the main concepts. In each case, the connections between the concepts are stressed. As a conclusion, the four cases will be contrasted and compared.

Case A: A fast-food restaurant

'Food' started in 1976 as a fast-food restaurant diversification of a super-market distribution system. Over a period of ten years, three fast-food restaurant chains were developed. Standardization and structuring of the outlets (meals, menus) and internal processes (cooking, presentation, service) was the rule. The management system was very centralized and a dependency relationship between Food and the parent company was encouraged.

The innovation within Food studied here, a diversification of fast food towards a more traditional type of restaurant (so called 'theme' restaurants), was initiated and explored by the top management of the parent company. It was general practice that centralized staff services scanned the market and proposed changes in products and processes. There was a strong emphasis on quantitative indicators; financial results were the main subject of staff meetings.

The idea for the new diversification was picked up by a manager of the parent company during a visit abroad: the so-called 'beef formula', which can be considered as a form of franchising. The franchiser relied on Food for specialized services and administration. The role of the local manager was quite important in developing a homely style and being the host with his co-workers for a more sophisticated clientele.

The main decisions about start-ups, locations, and the timetable for introduction were made by the parent company. Staff did not expect more involvement, and were willing to implement the initiated plans. Co-workers were hired and trained in the new formula by the franchising partner. The scheme was met by an overwhelmingly positive reaction by the clientele, giving a positive feeling to staff and co-workers. One of the cooks expressed their experience as follows:

> You can't believe how good we felt when the service went well. We were screaming and yelling at each other and to the waiters but, with a drink, in the end everything was O.K.

After three weeks, there was a drop in the number of customers, followed by negative feedback from the parent company. An employee said:

> We lost 50 per cent of our clients. Morale was dropping. We all were very tired and the cohesion was gone. Added to this came the negative reactions from the parent company that our gross product decreased too much.

Figures, quantitative analyses and prognoses became the main theme of every meeting. Supervisory personnel were replaced and there was a strong pressure to reassess the situation. General management intervened to obtain quick returns on investment.

A clear difference between the 'retailing logic' of the mother parent company and the 'restaurant logic' of the diversification began to emerge. The new supervisor followed the restaurant concept: contact with clients, personal service, importance of training of personnel, shared problem-solving. A second location was started by the new co-ordinator, but the 'mentality gap' between the new diversification and Food was growing. This is how the co-ordinator, responsible for the new concept, described the differences with the parent company, especially for training practices:

> In the new concept the emphasis is on the creation of self-awareness and trust in the management system. In Food training is restricted to the days just before opening new outlets and to the training of supervisory personnel. In the new formula there is a regular performance consultation. The emphasis is on positive motivation and answering questions that can improve functioning. In the Food organization the base line is central. Budgets have to be met. Evaluations concentrate on criticism often about details. Controlling actions by the HRM of the parent company were very strict.

The team co-ordinator described his behaviour towards his employees as follows:

> The barometer of the performance of the group is the level of information among people. Everyone can put topics on the agenda. We sat together over a cup of coffee and discussed alternatives. We introduced a new work schedule on their proposal with very motivating outcomes.

Finally, after about two years, the decision was made to close the new restaurant and to sell the two new locations to the franchising company. One could say that the controlling actions of the parent company pushed the new business out of the Food organization. There was a growing gap between the work principles in the parent company and the new restaurants. Figure 6.2 synthesizes the characteristics of the dominant logic of the parent company, which we term a 'distribution logic'. The action logic of the innovation project was quite different. This was creating several dilemmas for the organization as a whole to deal with. The action strategies used by the parent company, Food, and the project co-ordinator were quite different and emerged from the two opposed action logics. There was no combination of principles or bridging of the dilemmas encountered, and the consequence was that the new venture and the parent company went different ways. The Food organization returned to 'business as usual', and the innovation could not be integrated. The social construction process

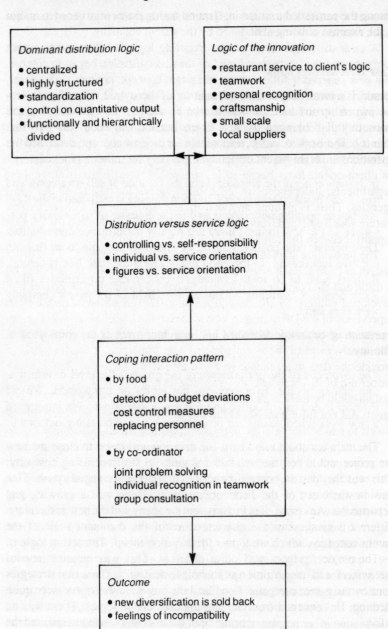

Figure 6.2 Interaction sequence dealing with the innovation project in 'Food'

among the parties led to some integration within the new project group, but at the expense of being abandoned by the parent company.

Case B: A savings bank

'Bank' is a local Belgian savings bank (with about 4,000 employees) with the ownership structure of a co-operative, with services from saving and loans to full banking activities. There are local agencies all over the country. The bank is independent from other financial organizations. Its operations are highly standardized, and it is only recently that the emphasis on client-orientedness began to be stressed. Several centralized support departments, independent of each other, serve the needs of the local agencies. There is a young and well-trained staff. The most characteristic feature which emerged from a survey of staff was the high score for 'mutual support' between the employees.

The innovation studied is the development and installation of a scoring system of clients. Each client is assigned a score indicating the services he is using and the commercial potential he has for the bank. The system was developed entirely by the data processing (DP) department under close supervision of the DP manager, who was also the leader of a project group representing central departments and representatives of the local offices. The involvement of those departments was important, since they had to provide the data in a reliable way and to understand the system to make proper use of it. There was also a feeling among the users that the scoring system could be used as an auditing device for the local agencies. The local agents did not fully understand the scoring weights used in the coding of clients to make manipulation in favour of certain clients impossible.

The main tension created by the innovation project centred around how the project could be made reliable and safe, yet still commercially useful. This was the tension between control and opportunity-orientedness. This tension was based on the different orientations between central and local departments. An issue related to this was the amount of participation by the different parties involved. Involvement was necessary, but the DP department wanted to retain control over the key elements of the scoring system.

The project leader played a crucial role in shaping the requirements of the system and the critical questions of the user group. His strategies continuously mediated between the tensions during the project group meeting. He concentrated on structuring and selecting the data processing information in such a way that the 'uniqueness' of the scoring system was emphasized: 'This is different but compatible with the existing systems, and it is really something new'. He guaranteed that he would take care of the 'technical matters', as he described the specificities of the project.

The project leader continuously emphasized that the comments of all parties would be heard and taken into account: 'the scoring is safe and commercial at the same time', was a recurring theme. The tension was not eliminated, but acknowledged and regulated without polarizing the interests of the different departments, as the following dialogue illustrates:

DISCUSSANT: When someone is withdrawing his money, even after two years, he gets a lower score.

PROJECT LEADER: Yes, but his score is increased, when he ties up his capital again.

DISCUSSANT: Precisely at the moment he has to make a choice. He is not by definition a bad client by taking out his money.

PROJECT LEADER: Maybe you have to become more cautious.

DISCUSSANT: At that moment exactly, you should be able to act very commercially.

REPRESENTATIVE OF INTERNAL AUDITING: But his money is still considered to be ordinary saving money.

PROJECT LEADER (closes the discussion): And this is not his only product. If it is indeed his only product, this client is a risk element.

Both polarities, 'safety' and 'being commercial', are dealt with, but it is the leader who was formulating the integration of the dilemma, and he was clearly persuading the discussant and closing the discussion.

A third strategy of the project leader was to emphasize the importance of the principle and to stress the importance of the work of the project group, asking for caution in extreme specific cases. 'This scoring system is a new way of thinking.' Again both aspects of the tension are integrated. But it is the project leader who is doing the work of combining and persuading people.

The outcome was a clear but rather narrow range of participation by the project group members. There was a benevolent acceptance and involvement by the departments. The importance of the group as a carrier of the innovation was emphasized by the establishment of a permanent work group around a new structure: a departmental 'organization'. The project leader became leader of this new section. This is clear evidence of organizational learning through institutionalization (see Figure 6.3).

Case C: A materials manufacturer

'Materials' was a subsidiary of a high-tech American multinational, and provided insulation materials for telecommunications and pipe protection. The growth rate was about 20 per cent in gross product during the 1970s. They had a very large range of specialized and customized products based

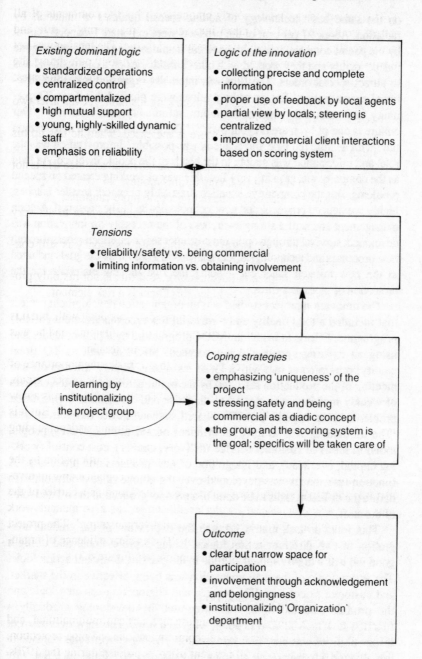

Figure 6.3 Interaction sequence dealing with the innovation project in 'Bank'

on the same basic technology of adding special qualities to materials by radiation. About 97 per cent of the products were exported. Financial control by the parent company was tight, but local manufacturing could operate quite independently and they worked with other subsidiaries on a competitive basis to attract special orders. The firm was internally organized following functional specialization. The prevailing values were phrased this way: 'Opportunity, technological progress, flexibility, informality, and creativity'. 'Our culture is one of "you are on your own"', 'The product has been delivered on time with as little red tape and beaucracy as possible.' Improvisation was the rule, and information was mainly in the heads of the people involved. As long as the company was growing very fast, this way of working created no special problems. But the competitive situation drastically changed: smaller batches, highly specialized products, and new technologies had to be produced. Among management and staff a strong awareness of the necessity for innovation was developed: survival through optimum customer services, effectiveness through new processes and technologies, and teamwork. These were the goals included in the new mission statement – being the first in new materials for the protection of pipes and wires.

The innovation project studied was an organization development project that included a total quality and a material resource management (MRM) programme. Efforts to install an MRM programme by a project leader and using an existing system did not succeed. MRM as well as TQ (total quality) programmes met with a lot of resistance. Finally, after an off-site meeting of the production staff, led by the manufacturing manager, a series of weekly meetings was started to diagnose and discuss the organization problems being experienced. The shared statement after this retreat was: 'The ultimate goal is to have an efficient organization (policies, people, tools) in terms of customer service (delivery, quality), cost control (working capital, overhead), and integration of new products and processes.' A function-task matrix was developed over the course of several months to define the different tasks to be done in a product group, and the related roles of the staff.

This function-task matrix became the expression of the gradual integration of two different action logics. Being a professional and doing a good job was a highly valued attitude in the existing dominant action logic. The action logic of the new orientation was being effective in the market, and customer orientation. The process and engineering-oriented logic and the product-oriented logic was integrated by developing gradually a function-task matrix: who is doing what and how? This new definition of responsibilities was very time consuming. The big concern was phrased in this way (on a transparency during a long discussion): 'Final question: why did it take so long?'

The next step was the growing awareness that only a total reorganization could implement the function-task analysis. Using the focused factory concept, a plan for redesigning the work floor and integrating staff departments was gradually developed. The implementation took several months, but the crucial decision about creating five integrated product groups was very stimulating. The third phase concerned the relationship to other departments and the maintenance of the involvement of the shop-floor staff. These efforts and actions are ongoing.

The main tension between the existing dominant logic and the innovation logic can be seen on two levels. The approach to problems was mainly opportunistic and power-seeking, individualistic, and boundary-setting. The development project asked for integrated action and inter-dependency of the departments.

The project group went through several cycles of redefining the problem and working on the moving target in the mean time. There was continuous criticism and open evaluation, which was perceived as very demanding in terms of personal tolerance for criticism and ambivalence. The role of the project leader was one of facilitating confrontation, developing proposals, and eliciting involvement in the decisions made (see Figure 6.4).

Case D: A communications company

'Communications' started in 1934 as a family firm producing radio receivers. They were the first firm in Belgium to produce a TV set, and in 1967 they produced the first multi-standard colour TV set in the world, built from multi-purpose modules. In 1980–1 Communications went through a serious crisis because of technological and market factors. The ownership changed, and new management was appointed after a sharp reduction in the range of activities. They began to specialize in specific niches in the consumer and industrial market (visual projection systems, TV and PC monitors). They saw themselves as aiming to be the first in a specific application and serving several groups of clients at the same time. Delivering high-quality products in consumer and industrial markets was their goal. They had a strong R&D department, and the manufacturing process involved a semi-automated assembly line. There was still a strong reliance on an authority relationship, dating back to the period of being a family-run business, but the new general manager was definitely changing this. Since they could overcome the crisis, there was a strong feeling of common interest among the personnel. The core characteristic of this firm was certainly the structuring along functional specialization. The products and process development department was also functionally-structured in terms of specific technical competencies (measuring instruments, projection, direct view, mechanical development).

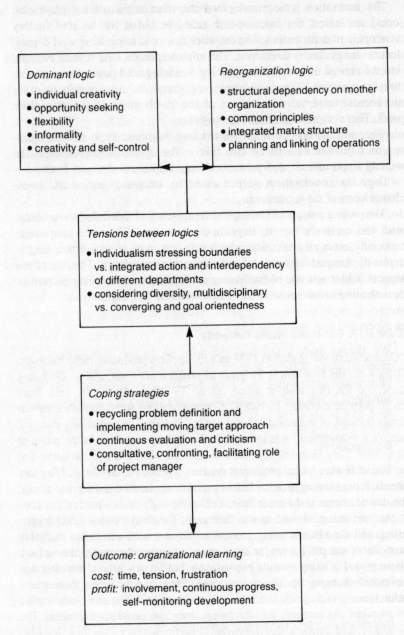

Figure 6.4 Interaction sequence dealing with the innovation project in 'Materials'

The innovation project concerned the introduction of a CAD/CAM (computer aided design/computer aided manufacture) system in the development departments. The requirement of shorter design and production times forced them to consider introducing a CAD/CAM system, which had been tried unsuccessfully five years before. Because the research director considered the new systems to be 'more than just commercial talk', and because he perceived the new possibilities for an integrated design and production system in the future, a project manager was hired. This project manager worked mainly in accordance with two principles: an integrated approach (different functions have to be included) and strong participation with all levels of staff, directors as well as designers.

The main tensions the project encountered concerned, first, resistance to change versus exaggerated expectations and, second, how and by whom the decision was going to be made. The designers had had a bad experience with the earlier effort to introduce computers, and the older ones, especially, were reluctant. Here the choice was made by the project leader explicitly for participation and open information-sharing of all technical aspects. Choices over whether the operation was to be a centralized or decentralized system were taken by the project leader in the same involving–explaining–listening mode. The project leader described his role as expert and educator in the following terms:

> We always made a proposal and went to discuss it with them. My proposal was a 200-dot drawing table. We showed the different possibilities and gave examples. What was the most appropriate for their situation? If you just ask for proposals, they cannot give an answer. You have to talk about the possibilities before they can give their opinion. When we made the decision, the 200-dot system was no longer among the alternatives.

The staff were included for two reasons: to get their involvement and to benefit from their experience. Managerial staff were kept informed about the developments and the actions taken.

At a critical point two options about the CAD/CAM system emerged: using individual PCs or using interconnected screens and a central unit. The proposal of the project leader in this case was very clearly for the second alternative. Based on his own expertise he took a particular standpoint, but nevertheless kept the discussion open. This is how he explained his behaviour:

> Individual PCs give developers a feeling of being their own boss. They can choose work methods and regulate the work themselves. With a central unit there is a stronger dependency and also uniformity in work

methods. The discussions are sometimes very sharp but I believe in the power of the over-arching system and I go in discussion for it. My hope is that the developers will appreciate the advantages during the implementation by concrete experience. I don't allow the discussion to escalate but I don't reject either the PC idea.

The project leader clearly acted as an 'expert' and a 'teacher', but the involvement and continuing dialogue with the users was his main mode of operating. He involved those who wanted to change to the new system, kept talking to the others and hoped they would be influenced by the success of the new system among the first users. Towards the managing director he acted as a co-worker, consulting him and following his main strategies.

Internal decision making on the project was shared, but based on technical principles. External decision making, towards possible vendors and suppliers, was done for this project by the general manager, who received full authorization from the steering committee. The project leader saw a shift towards external decision making. 'Everyone said the decision is going to be made on technical grounds. Now we are moving toward a political decision. The general manager will play the suppliers off against each other.'

The action strategies used throughout the project by the project leader are summarized in Figure 6.5. On the content level there is logical reduction of uncertainty based on functional specialization. Procedures and role distribution are very specific and on the relational level there is an emphasis on continuous contact and interaction. The process was clearly structured and guided by the project leader on logical rules and technical arguments. He invested a lot in permanent contact and open information sharing. Only towards outside agents did the project shift to political decision making and reliance on personal influence strategies.

COMPARISON OF CASES

In each case there is a coherent pattern of relationships between the tension of the logics involved and the strategies used to deal with these tensions. Table 6.1 gives an overview of the tension between dominant logic and innovation logic followed by action strategies and outcomes in all four cases. The outcomes are quite different. The four cases are not representative, but each illustrates a sequence of related processes that are helpful in understanding the specific development of different innovation projects over time.

The action strategies are the easiest subject for direct observation, and the distinction between the four innovation paths will be based on those

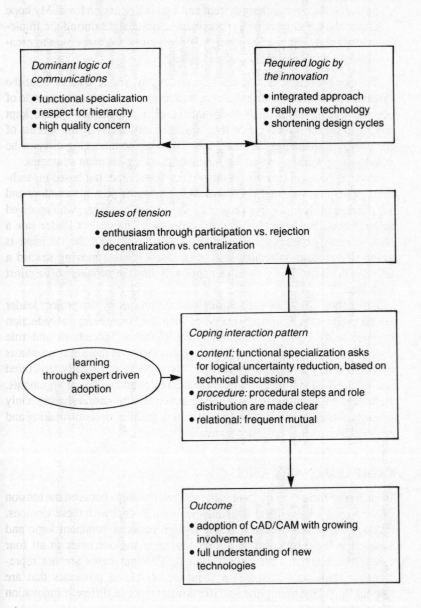

Figure 6.5 Interaction sequence dealing with the innovation project in 'Communications'

Table 6.1 Overview of analysis of four cases

	Dominant logic	Logic of innovation	Tensions among logics	Action strategies to cope with	Outcomes
Food	• standardized • centralized • quantitative control • functional and hierarchical	• service orientation • craftmanship • personal recognition	• distribution vs. service logic	• cost control on quantitative base • group consultation by project leader: 'influence-mode'	• new diversification sold back • incompatibility • rejection (or compliance)
Bank	• standardized • centralized • emphasis on reliability	• involvement and precise information	• reliability/safety vs. being commercial • limiting info vs. obtaining involvement	• stressing – uniqueness – being both safe and commercial – group involvement • benevolent authoritarian role of leader: 'selling mode'	• clear but narrow space for participation • institutionalizing 'organization' department • adoption
Materials	• individualism • opportunistic	• interdependency • planning	• individualism vs. interdependency • considering perspectives vs. converging	• recycling problem definition and action • confrontative role of leader: 'confrontation-mode'	• self-monitored organizational learning • high level of tension • involvement
Communications	• functional • respect for hierarchy	• integrated approach • shortening design cycles	• centralization vs. decentralization • participation vs. rejection	• logical uncertainty reduction • frequent contact: 'expert mode'	• step-by-step problem solving approach • undersanding

observable characteristics. Differences between the action strategies are particularly striking. We have called them an influence model, a selling model, a confrontation model and an expert model.

The influence model is mainly top-down and one-sided. The organization tries to steer the innovation using existing control mechanisms. In the case of Food the outcome was rejection. The selling model fits the benevolent authoritarian approach, and the outcome is adoption. The confrontation model fits the open critical approach in the Materials case, and leads to a high involvement, but is also very demanding. In this pattern the characteristics of a real long-term organizational learning process are realized most of all in these cases. In the Communication case, we see a high level of understanding as an outcome, but the role of the expert was very explicit and some dependency on his expertise will remain; we call it an expert model.

The important lesson to draw is the distinction between the different innovation paths. Even more important is that each of those paths lead to a very different outcome. The characteristics of these action strategies, and the contingencies of their appearance and respective outcomes, are discussed more in detail elsewhere (Bouwen and Fry 1991). Existing innovation process models concentrate on the innovation task, or content development over time. Rogers' (1983) innovation-diffusion model is typical of this tradition. Problem solving or organizational decision making models often describe the different steps of internally generated innovation projects from a project management point of view (Mintzberg 1981). Typologies of innovations rely more on the antecedent characteristics (Zaltman *et al.* 1973) than on the quality of the interactions among the parties. The advantage of this approach is that it combines several new research demands in this field, as argued by King (1990: 54): emphasis on internal development, describing cultural dimensions among the antecedent factors (e.g. dominant logic), interaction process orientation, and taking into account a multiplicity of perspectives rather than just that of management. Besides the diffusion model of Rogers, the process consultation model of Schein (1987) has been a source of inspiration for this typology. The focus on observable interaction patterns allows close contact of the researcher and practitioner with ongoing events. Outcomes and antecedent conditions can be related to the quality of the dialogue among the parties.

Finally, a note of caution. The set of cases presented here does not allow for definitive conclusions, and other alternative outcomes are also probable. But the observed relationships are worth further testing and may be able to be used as guiding principle in organizational practice.

Another important conclusion is about the differences between the existing dominant logic and the required logic of the innovation. A general hypothesis can be formulated. When the difference between both action logics is quite large, as in the Food case, then the innovation task is demanding, and chances of coping successfully are low. The differences between dominant and new logics can be described along several dimensions. The 'newer' the innovation is for the existing organization, the larger the possible distance. Is a new technology or new discipline involved in it? Is a new way of organizational functioning required? To what extent is the implementation irreversible? To what extent are new attitudes and behavioural values required from the employees? How much do all these aspects require a reconstruction of schemas of action? The distance between the dominant logic and the innovation logic is an indication of the novelty of the innovation, and therefore an estimation of the effort required to bridge the innovation gap.

The action strategy that is to be selected to work on the innovation gap will emerge from the existing dominant logic, and this can either impede or facilitate even further the possible outcomes. The organizational culture can be considered as part of the dominant logic action. How change is going to be handled is an aspect of organizational values. In a situation of innovation one can say that culture is in a transitory stage. In the four cases described, one can see that the dominant logic indeed has an important influence on the prevailing action strategy. This leads to the paradoxical situation in which the organization is least able to produce a 'path-breaking' action strategy (as in the Food case). In the case where the organization is able to produce an interactive and facilitating action strategy (as in the Materials case) the innovation task looks more attainable, although for more bureaucratic organizations this innovation task would be inseparable. (See also Glendon's analysis of these tensions between existing logics and the logic required by new procedures, presented in Chapter 3.)

The desired outcome will further define the appropriateness of a certain action strategy. In the Bank case, there was also a distance between the action logics, but the desired outcomes allowed a selling model to be sufficiently successful. Partial involvement was the desired outcome and a certain level of one-sidedness could be allowed. In the Communication case, the differences between the dominant logic and the required logic were not very great, and the action strategy emerging from that dominant logic fitted the expected outcome quite well.

One may speculate over combinations of logics, strategies, and outcomes. Further research is certainly required, but careful observation of action sequences in practice can help to make more informed choices about feasible innovation projects and appropriate steering strategies.

IMPLICATIONS FOR PRACTICE

From the sequential analysis and the comparison of the cases, some useful conclusions can be derived for practice. A situation of innovation is often experienced as chaotic by the actors involved. To help them map the existing dilemmas, the continuity–novelty–transition triangle is useful. Further specification is possible in terms of the dominant logic to understand the strength of continuity, and to estimate the 'distance' or the 'newness' from the introduced new logic. Tensions have to be understood as naturally linked with the innovation process, and an estimate of the extent of disruption can help to point out the most feasible and applicable action strategy.

If the capabilities, skills, and resources of the existing organization are taken into account, the appropriate path to innovation can be selected. Of course the desired outcome is also a possible guideline, but one can only stretch so far the possibilities of the available logics and the requirements of the innovation path selected.

FURTHER RESEARCH

Further research requires a more specific definition of what dominant logic exactly encompasses. Three main characteristics can be defined: cognitive schemas, structural implications, and value orientation. Cognitive schemas are related to ways of thinking and dealing with problems. Different scientific disciplines and different departments work with different schemas to formulate problems. Cognitive style (Kolb 1976) certainly has something to do with it. Structural implications can be understood in terms of the configuration qualities of Mintzberg (1979), and value orientation can be related to values in an organizational culture framework (Schein 1985). A more precise description of the dominant logic from the perspective of all significant parties is possible. Multi-perspective views and comparisons over time for the same organization are more important than inter-organizational studies.

The concept of organizational learning also needs further operationalization in other studies. This concept is useful in the comparison of the cases to characterize outcomes and their implications in the long run. In the Food case there was probably very little learning taking place, except about what not to do in the future. In the Bank case there was limited organizational learning when the criteria of Argyris and Schon (1978) – valid information and informed committed choice – are used. The learning effect was larger in Communications and probably largest in the Material case.

The framework derived from separate cases has to be tested further on a larger scale to come to general conclusions. The operationalization of the concepts of dominant logic and organizational learning, which proved to be useful, have to be developed further for inter-organizational comparison. The most important conclusion is probably the outlook offered on how an organization can be helped to develop 'process knowledge' while in a changing or innovative situation. The set of questions asked seems to be useful for each case to understand its own development. The only valid test for a certain approach is probably whether or not it helps an organization to increase its potential for common action in the future.

This study suggests a way to develop research projects for gathering 'process knowledge'. It is the understanding of the ongoing interaction process at a given moment in time. This kind of knowledge is always context bounded, and can be made available only when a given context is aroused and experienced. Process principles can be derived which serve as heuristic devices to orient the actor in the complexity of influences. This kind of research has to be practice-bounded to be useful. The actor or the consultant organizational psychologist can use general principles to 'read' the situation he is involved in and to serve as design guidelines to frame a desired future state in the relational context.

This study finally illustrates how a new organizational reality is being constructed (see also Anderson 1989, and Chapter 8, for a discussion of the constructivist stance to organizational innovation). The relations among the parties involved are expressed in the action strategies. The organ- izational capacity to produce the appropriate quality of dialogue or action strategy will define which innovation tasks can be accomplished. If co- ownership and shared competence is a condition for the emergence of a new organization then only an organization which is skilled in organ- izational learning will be able to construct the proper answer. If passive following and compliance can suffice to implement an innovation, then a one-sided organizational construction process can do the work. Further studies from a social constructionist paradigm can illustrate the validity of these construction rules.

REFERENCES

Anderson, N.R. (1989) 'Work group innovation: current research concerns and future directions', paper presented as part of a symposium at the Fourth West European Congress on the Psychology of Work and Organization, Cambridge, UK, April.

Argyris, C. and Schon, D.A. (1978) *Organizational Learning: A Theory of Action Perspective*, Reading, MA: Addison-Wesley.

Bouwen, R. and Fry, R. (1988) 'An agenda for managing organizational innovation and development in the 1990s', in M. Lambrecht (ed.) *Corporate Revival*, Leuven: University Press.

Bouwen, R. and Fry, R. (1991) 'Organizational innovation and learning. Four patterns of dialogue between the dominant logic and the new logic', *International Studies in Management and Organization*.

Burgelman, R.A. and Sayles, L.R. (1986) *Inside Corporate Innovation: Strategy, Structure and Managerial Skills*, New York: Free Press.

Gergen, K. (1978) 'Toward Generative Theory', *Journal of Personal and Social Psychology* 36(11): 1344–60.

Glaser, B. and Strauss, A. (1967) *The Discovery of Grounded Theory*, Chicago: Aldine.

Gray, B., Bougon, M. and Donnellon, A. (1985) 'Organizations as constructions and destructions of meaning', *Journal of Management* 11(2): 77–92.

Grönhaug, K. and Kaufman, G. (1988) *Innovation: A Cross-Disciplinary Perspective*, Oxford: Oxford University Press.

Hampden-Turner, C. (1990) *Charting the Corporate Mind. From Dilemma to Strategy*, Oxford: The Free Press.

Hedberg, B. (1981) 'How organizations learn and unlearn', in P.C. Nystrom and W.H. Starbuck (eds) *Handbook of Organizational Design*, Oxford: Oxford University Press.

Kimberly, J.R. *et al.* (1990) 'Rethinking organizational innovation', in M.A. West and J.L. Farr (eds) *Innovation and Creativity at Work*, New York: John Wiley: 163–78.

King, N. (1990) 'Innovation at work: the research literature', in M.A. West and J.L. Farr (eds) *Innovation and Creativity at work*, New York: John Wiley: 15–60.

King, N. and West, M.A. (1987) 'Experiences of Innovation at Work', *Journal of Managerial Psychology* 2: 6–10.

Kolb, D.A. (1976) *Learning Style Inventory: technical manual*, McBer & Company.

Maidique, M.A. (1980) 'Entrepreneurs, champions and technological innovation', *Sloan Management Review* Winter: 59–76.

Mintzberg, H. (1979) *The Structuring of Organization*, Prentice-Hall.

Mintzberg, H. (1981) 'Organization Design: fashion or fit?', *Harvard Business Review* Jan–Feb. 103–16.

Morgan, G. (1986) *Images of Organization*, London: Jossey-Bass.

Mulder, M. (1977) *The Daily Power Game*, Leiden: Martinus Nijhoff.

Prahalad, C.K. and Bettis (1986) 'The dominant logic: a new linkage between diversity and performance', *Strategic Management Journal* 7: 485–501.

Roberts, E.B. (1977) 'Generating Effective Corporate Innovation', *Technology Review* October–November: 27–33.

Rogers, E.M. (1983) *Diffusion of Innovations* (3rd edn), New York: The Free Press.

Rothwell, R. (1977) 'Generating Effective Corporate Innovation', *Technology Review* October–November: 27–33.

Schein, E. (1985) *Organisational Culture and Leadership*, Jossey Bass: London.

Schein, E. (1987) 'Lessons for managers and consultants', *Process Consultation*, vol. II, Reading, MA: Addison-Wesley.

Sexton, D.L. and Smilor, R.W. (eds) (1986) *The Art and Science of Entrepreneurship*, Cambridge, MA: Battinger.

Tushman, M.L. (1979) 'Managing Communication Networks in R&D Laboratories', *Sloan Management Review* Winter: 37–49.

Van De Ven, A.H. (1986) 'Central problems in the management of innovation', *Management Science* 32: 590–607.

Van De Ven, A.H., Angle, H.L. and Poole, M.S. (1989) *Research on the Management of Innovation*, New York: Harper & Row.

Weick, K.E. (1979) *The Social Psychology of Organizing*, Reading, MA: Addison-Wesley.

West, M.A. and Farr, J.L. (1990) *Innovation and Creativity at Work*, New York: John Wiley.

Zaltman, G., Duncan, R. and Holbek, J. (1973) *Innovation and Organizations*, New York: John Wiley.

7 Work group innovation

A state-of-the-art review

Neil Anderson

PLETHORA AND PAUCITY

Recent decades have witnessed a burgeoning academic literature by applied psychologists on organizational innovation and individual creativity at work (Kimberley 1981; Pierce and Delbecq 1977; Van de Ven 1986; Van de Ven *et al.* 1989; West and Farr 1990). At the same time exponential rates of environmental change affecting many organizations have generated considerable interest among practising managers in innovation. This has fuelled a resurgence of popular prescriptive texts on how to manage innovation processes (e.g. Kanter 1983, Peters and Waterman 1982; Peters 1985). Innovation has thus been portrayed as a critical business response strategy for coping with environmental change. As Zaltman *et al.* (1973) assert: 'The importance of new ideas cannot be understated. Ideas and their manifestations as practices or products are at the core of social change.'

In view of the growing body of research into organizational change and innovation, this topic looks set to become a central part of the organizational psychology research agenda well into the 1990s.

In direct contrast to the plethora of research focusing upon organizational innovation and individual work role creativity, however, there is a paucity of studies examining innovation processes at the level of the work group. Paradoxically, the implementation of many innovations necessarily involves group discussions, negotiations, and reaching consensus over plans to implement modified work practices or procedures. For example, an organizations' strategic plans will be discussed and implemented by its management team; R&D teams will be responsible for generating new product lines to replace obsolete ones; *ad hoc* project teams will be convened to perform specific tasks, and so forth.

This chapter argues for the utility of research focusing specifically at the level of the work group, and calls for additional research to address fundamental gaps in the existing research base. Initially, however, it is necessary to tackle intractable problems of defining exactly what is meant by the term 'work group innovation'.

Towards Definitional Specificity

Difficulties with defining terminology have plagued researchers in this field for some years. Distinguishing innovation from creativity and separating purposive innovation attempts from surrendipitous organizational change have been perhaps the two most tenacious conundrums. Nevertheless, considerable advances in definitional clarity have been made in recent years, principally through researchers becoming more explicit about the organizational processes under scrutiny in their work. Thus, Nicholson (1984) defines individual work-role innovation, and Anderson (1990) work group innovation, as follows:

> changes in task objectives, methods, materials, scheduling and in the interpersonal relationships integral to role performance.
>
> (Nicholson 1984: 175)

> Group innovation is the emergence, import, or imposition of new ideas which are pursued towards implementation by the group through interpersonal discussions and successive re-mouldings of the original proposal over time.
>
> (Anderson 1990: 3)

Both definitions are processual in orientation, emphasizing the symbiotic relation between tasks and interpersonal processes underlying innovation. This contrasts with earlier work by strategic management specialists (e.g. Kimberley 1981; Nyström 1979) which tended to treat innovation as an end product rather than as an ongoing process of accommodating task requirements within acceptable social structures. These more recent definitions by organizational psychologists are significant developments in framing the terms of reference for innovation research, since they hold innovation processes to be quintessentially social-psychological in nature. Indeed, the present author would contend that innovation can only sensibly be conceptualized as an emergent social process, not as a tangible product or outcome; and moreover, that innovation processes are not manifest as periodic disjunctures to normal group processes, but are symptomatic of groups' continual and ongoing renegotiation of social order (Anderson 1990).

Examining the different types of group innovation within organizations clarifies further any residual difficulties in defining this concept. King and Anderson (1990) expand upon the definition of work group innovation cited above, by suggesting three distinct types of innovation:

1 Emergent Where novel, unproven ideas and proposals are developed and implemented uniquely to a particular group or organizational sub-unit (e.g. the implementation of original information technology systems unique to the organization).

2 Imported Where systems and procedures already in use within comparator organizations are replicated and introduced into the organization by the group (e.g. replicating production processes used by competitors).

3 Imposed Where environmental changes force the group to modify its procedures or work practices (e.g. shifts in consumer demand or changes in industry regulatory frameworks).

Despite these advances in definitional specificity, there remains a comparative absence of studies examining the processual dynamics of work group innovation. In recent years, however, there has emerged a growing number of published studies which illustrate the influence of different factors upon innovation. Turning to these studies it is useful to sectionalize existing research under three categories:

1 Structural factors (sub-divided into group composition and group development factors);

2 Psychological factors (sub-divided into climatic and social construction factors);

3 Processual factors (sub-divided into process models and interpersonal interactions approaches).

Structural factors

Composition

The influence of team size, member characteristics, leadership style, and group structure are all variables which have been hypothesized to influence innovation and which have been examined by organizational psychologists to a greater or lesser extent. Payne (1990) reviews earlier work by Stankiewicz (1979) into the innovativeness and productivity of 172 Swedish academic groups. If groups were highly cohesive, larger groups tended to be more productive. However, if cohesiveness was low, groups with less than seven members performed better. In terms of group composition, avoiding excessive homogeneity of experience and training of individual members has been advocated by some authors as a necessary condition for securing a diversity of views, and hence innovation (Geschka 1983; Kanter 1983). Popular prescriptive models of team constitution and team building go further by suggesting that effective and innovative teams are composed of individuals matching specific role types (e.g. Belbin 1981; Margerison and McCann 1986), but it should be noted that little published research supports this assertion.

King (1989) reviews many of the studies into the effects of leadership style on innovation, and concludes that the general consensus supports a democratic-participative style as being a facilitator of innovativeness in work groups (cf. Nyström 1979; Coopey 1987; Wallace and West 1988). Manz *et al.* (1989) advocate more of a contingency approach, arguing that 'multiple leadership approaches appear to be appropriate in varying innovation contexts and at different stages of the innovation process'. Certainly a model of leadership moving from nurturing behaviours at the early stages of group innovation to stimulate and support ideas, through consensus-seeking behaviours during the middle stages of the proposal, to delegation and checking behaviours during and after innovation implementation, is intuitively appealing as a pragmatic leadership styles algorithm (Anderson and King 1991). But additional research is called for to examine in greater depth the relation between leadership styles and the development of innovations over time.

Development

A few studies have addressed the influence of group longevity upon innovativeness. Katz (1982) investigated the performance of fifty R&D teams over several years. An inverse relationship between longevity and innovativeness was reported: the longer groups had been in existence, the less innovative they became. Other authors have, on the basis of these findings, argued for restricting the active lifespan of groups, as a means for maximizing innovativeness (Nyström 1979; Payne 1990).

Recent work by applied psychologists into group development and task performance sheds more light upon the relationship between group innovation and development over time. In initial experimental studies Gersick (1989) presented groups of subjects with a simulated project task of one hour's duration, informing subjects in advance of this time limitation. Groups were videotaped and their interpersonal behaviour subsequently analysed. The results show an unequivocal change in subjects' task orientation at roughly the midpoint of the lifespan of the group (i.e. after 30 minutes), whereby individuals reappraised their approach to the task, developed new ideas, and initiated modified work practices. Gersick concludes that groups adhered to a 'punctuated equilibrium model of group development' (see also Gersick 1988), instituting a quantum leap in their work styles at the known midpoint of the group's lifespan. Subsequent field studies of this effect, e.g. Gersick 1989, have confirmed the salience of the punctuated equilibrium model in naturally occurring work groups, and thus hint at the applicability of this model to innovation processes in real-life task groups of fixed-term tenure.

Psychological factors

Climate

Group cohesiveness has constituted the primary focus for studies examining the effects of group climate upon innovativeness. Wallace and West (1988), for instance, found cohesiveness to be the principal discriminating variable between high and low innovative healthcare teams. As King and Anderson (1990) point out, an important component of group cohesiveness is homogeneity, which has already been noted as an inhibitor of divergent, radical innovation. In keeping with recent debates in the organizational climate literature (Rousseau 1988; George 1990), some research has adopted a more sophisticated, multidimensional, and 'facet-specific' approach (Rousseau 1988) towards the influence of group climate upon innovation (West and Anderson 1991). It is hoped that these studies will inform our understanding of this issue, and thus allow empirically grounded recommendations for practising managers and team leaders.

Social construction

The work of Bouwen and his co-workers (described in detail in Chapter 6) provides rich qualitative data on the social construction of innovation processes. Defining innovation as the 'ongoing construction and reconstruction of shared meaning' (Bouwen 1988: 1) this perspective has elicited detailed descriptions of the disruptive psychological consequences of innovations for individuals and work groups across a variety of organizational contexts (Bouwen 1988; Bouwen and Fry 1987; Bouwen and De Visch 1989). The comparative case studies of technical and administrative innovations presented in this volume highlight the conflict inherent in innovatory change for individuals as existing cognitive schemas (the 'dominant logic') are challenged and eventually replaced by new perspectives (the 'innovation logic').

Processual factors

Process models

Numerous models of the process of innovation at the organizational level and the process of creativity at the individual level are to be found in the literature, but basic similarities are discernible across most models. At the individual level, Nyström (1979), for example, proposes a four-stage model of innovation: preparation, incubation, illumination (insight), and verification. At the organizational level, representative of many other process models is that proposed by Hage and Aiken (1970), again comprising four stages: evaluation, initiation, implementation, and routinization. Fewer models have been developed at the group level, but West (1990) advocates a cyclical model based on the premise that group innovations proceed through four discrete stages – recognition, initiation, implementation, and stabilization – which then generate subsequent cycles of secondary innovations as a result of this process. Other findings, however, cast pertinent doubts on the validity of these neat, linear models of process, suggesting instead that innovations progress in more haphazard ways, often veering between quantum leaps forward and regression to previous phases of development (King 1989; Angle and Van de Ven 1989).

Interpersonal interactions

It is surprising that although group innovation as a process clearly involves interpersonal negotiations and the reaching of agreements for implementation, little applied research has examined the behavioural influence and persuasion patterns at different stages in the process. Nonetheless, the need for an individual within the group to champion any idea has been emphasized by several authors (Kanter 1983; Peters and Waterman 1982; Van de Ven *et al.* 1989). In contrast to these assertions, Gersick and Hackman (1990) present compelling evidence of the susceptibility of groups to becoming locked into habitual routines of behaviour, in spite of fundamental changes in their environment which should dictate modifications to their established work practices. As the counter-pressure against group innovation, more research is called for by organizational psychologists into the circumstances within which habitual behavioural routines restrict flexible and appropriate responses being instigated by groups to changing circumstances.

To overview and summarize the group level innovation literature, it is apparent that although three distinct categories of studies can be distinguished (structural factors, psychological factors and processual factors), group level innovation research remains at an embryonic stage of development. The restricted coverage of existing research, due mainly to the limited number of studies into innovation at the level of the work group, presents researchers in this area with a limited body of empirical study findings. On the other hand, there remains an expansive range of potentially useful directions for future research. So, where should these research efforts be concentrated? What types of studies into the processual dynamics of group innovation and influences upon innovativeness are called for? It is to these questions that the following sections are addressed.

A BRIEF CRITIQUE OF EXISTING RESEARCH

In addition to the criticism that organizational psychologists have paid sparse attention to the process of work group innovation, a number of methodological and conceptual shortcomings in the limited range of existing studies need to be acknowledged.

Dealing with methodological weaknesses first, a fundamental flaw in several studies is their use of a univariate design, wherein the relationship between a single independent variable (e.g. cohesiveness, leadership style) and innovativeness as the hypothesized dependent variable (e.g. frequency of innovation, radicalness of innovation) is evaluated. Even where significant results are reported, pertinent doubts remain that other unmeasured independent variables could have influenced the outcome measure. Indeed, in complex organizational settings it is difficult to envisage circumstances where the multiple and diverse factors of group composition, structure, and dynamics were not effecting innovations under progress. In accordance with the operational definition of innovation postulated earlier in this chapter, studies adopting multivariate designs are called for in future, to assess the influence of combinations of structural, psychological, and processual factors upon emergent, imported and imposed group innovations.

Conceptual weaknesses in existing research stem from the failure of researchers to specify explicitly the notion of innovation as a *group* activity. Of paramount importance is the basic theoretical premise upon which much of the research has been conducted. Two alternative perspectives are discernible: the consensus perspective and the conflict perspective.

In the first, innovation is viewed as a process which is both desirable as a means towards change, and a relatively trouble-free process in terms of interpersonal conflict and dysfunctional intragroup relations. The managerial literature on innovation, particularly popular texts, abounds with such 'pro-innovation bias' (e.g. Kanter 1983; Peters and Waterman 1982; Peters 1985). That is, any innovation is seen as good for all members of the organization, and the more innovation can be encouraged, the better (see Kimberley 1981 and King and Anderson 1990 for detailed criticisms of this bias). Here, innovation is seen as a desirable outcome to be stimulated and maximized by the introduction of appropriate organizational structures, communication networks, and styles of leadership. The conflict perspective, on the other hand, highlights the disruptive consequences of any attempt to innovate. The ethnographic case studies described by Bouwen, De Visch and Steyaert in this volume in chapter 6 show the extent to which innovations are perceived as disjunctive and conflictual processes by those involved. Far from the innovation process being experienced as a smooth transition through discrete phases or stages over time, these studies illustrate the iterative, disjunctive, and at times, conflictual nature of innovation at work. Considerably more studies have adopted the consensus perspective rather than the conflict perspective, although usually this has been implicit rather than explicit in the rationale given by researchers for investigating innovation processes. Such a pervasive pro-innovation bias is unfortunate, since increasing disquiet has been voiced about the presumption that innovation is a social process amenable to being initiated or controlled by managers (see Chapter 1 for a review of this 'illusion of manageability' bias). It was argued earlier in this chapter that group innovations are more sensibly researched, not as interruptions to routine group processes to be stimulated as beneficial to organizational profitability, but as manifestations of ongoing renegotiations of social order. In essence, the superordinate research question needs to move from being 'what makes groups more or less innovative?' to 'how is social order renegotiated in groups through emergent processes of innovation?'

FUTURE CONDITIONAL: STRATEGIES FOR GROUP LEVEL INNOVATION RESEARCH

Where should researchers go from here? Specific recommendations for developing understanding of innovation processes have been made throughout this chapter. In overview, two parallel and interdependent research strategies are called for:

1 the 'antecedent factors' approach;
2 the 'longitudinal process' approach.

Figure 7.1 summarizes the methodological characteristics and likely contributions of each approach. Multivariate antecedent factors studies are necessary to examine the influence of multiple group characteristics upon innovation processes. In particular, validated scale measures of both independent variables and outcome variables need to be developed. The publication of these measures is essential, and will contribute towards establishing a generally accessible item-bank of validated work group innovation measures.

Table 7.1 Approaches to group level innovation research

	Antecedent factors study designs	Longitudinal process study designs
Epistemological objectives	To quantify the relative influence of different group characteristics upon innovativeness	To study the development of innovation over time to delineate stages and processes of progression
Predominant methodology	Administration of validated attitude scale measures and open-response reports of innovation	In-depth case studies utilizing 'non-participant' observation, semi-structured interviewing, and in-company experiential data collection
Sample survey characteristics	Sufficient numbers of participants to ensure external validity	Small number of cases to ensure internal validity and depth of coverage
Contribution to innovation research	Identification of group characteristics associated with innovativeness	Generation of a rich seam of qualitative case study data
	Quantification of the relative impact of group characteristics	Publication of experiential accounts of the innovation process over time
	Publication of validated scale measures of independent and dependent variables	Development of *de facto* staging models of group innovation
Typical studies	Katz 1982 Nyström 1979 Wallace and West 1988	Angle and Van de Ven 1989 This volume, Chapter 6 King 1989 Schroeder *et al.* 1989

More importantly, research is needed which adopts a longitudinal process approach to studying innovation and which is sensitive to the social negotiation stance advocated in this chapter. Case study methodology is appropriate, using observational and ethnographic techniques to follow innovations as they develop over time, and to reveal the dynamics of intra-group processes as they mediate and realign the negotiated social order which accommodates task performance. In addition, retrospective reconstructions of innovation histories can make an important contribution by revealing inter-group and intra-group differences in perceptions of how innovations resulted in particular outcomes.

A complementary relationship should exist between the two research orientations: antecedent factors studies revealing important determinants of the development of the innovation process, while longitudinal and retrospective case studies should identify likely antecedents of innovation which had previously been overlooked.

CONCLUSION

This chapter has argued for the practical utility of research into work group innovation. Too few studies have addressed this level of analysis in the past, particularly given the importance of work groups as the medium for instigating and implementing organizational change from within. Future research adopting a processual and social negotiation perspective is called for to redress the restricted coverage and conceptual shortcomings of the existing body of studies into work group innovation.

REFERENCES

Anderson, N.R. (1990) 'Innovation in work groups: current research concerns and future directions', paper presented at the Fourth West European Congress on Work and Organizational Psychology, Cambridge, UK, March 1989, MRC/ ESRC Social and Applied Psychology Unit internal memo.

Anderson, N.R. and King, N. (1991) 'Managing innovation in organizations', *Leadership and Organization Development Journal* 12(4): 17–24.

Angle, H.L. and Van de Ven, A.H. (1989) 'Suggestions for managing the innovation journey', in A.H. Van de Ven, H.L. Angle and M.S. Poole (eds) *Research on the Management of Innovation*, Cambridge, MA: Ballinger.

Belbin, R.M. (1981) *Management Teams: Why They Succeed or Fail*, London: Heinemann.

Bouwen, R. (1988) 'Management of innovation', paper presented as part of symposium on 'Interpretive Approaches to Occupational Psychology' at the Annual Occupational Psychology Conference of the British Psychological Society, University of Manchester, January 1988.

Bouwen, R. and De Visch, J. (1989) 'Innovation projects in organizations: Complementing the dominant logic by organizational learning', paper presented at the Fourth West European Congress of Work and Organizational Psychology, Cambridge, April 1989.

Bouwen, R. and Fry, R. (1987) 'An agenda for managing organization innovation and development in the 1990s', in M. Lambrecht (ed.) *Corporate Revival*, Leuven: Katholic University.

Coopey, J. (1987) 'Creativity in complex organizations', paper presented at the Annual Occupational Psychology Conference of the British Psychological Society, University of Hull, January.

George, J.M. (1990) 'Personality, affect, and behavior in groups', *Journal of Applied Psychology* 75(2): 107–16.

Gersick, C.J.G. (1988) 'Time and transition in work teams: Towards a new model of group development', *Academy of Management Journal* 31: 9–41.

Gersick, C.J.G. (1989) 'Marking time: predictable transitions in task groups', *Academy of Management Journal* 32: 274–309.

Gersick, C.J.G. and Hackman, J.R. (1990) 'Habitual routines in task-performing groups', *Organizational Behavior and Human Decision Processes* 47: 65–97.

Geschka, H. (1983) 'Creativity techniques in product planning and development: a view from West Germany', *R&D Management* 13: 169–83.

Hage, J. and Aiken, M. (1970) *Social Change in Complex Organizations*, New York: Random House.

Kanter, R.M. (1983) *The Change Masters: Corporate Entrepreneurs at Work*, London: Allen & Unwin.

Katz, R. (1982) 'The effects of group longevity on project communication and performance', *Administrative Science Quarterly* 27: 81–104.

Kimberley, J.R. (1981) 'Managerial innovation', in P.C. Nyström and W.H. Starbuck (eds) *Handbook of Organizational Design* (Vol 1), Oxford: Oxford University Press.

King, N. (1989) 'Innovation in elderly care organizations: process and attitudes', unpublished PhD Thesis, MRC/ESRC Social and Applied Psychology Unit, University of Sheffield, UK.

King, N. and Anderson, N.R. (1990) 'Work group innovation', in M.A. West and J.L. Farr (eds), *Innovation and Creativity at Work*, Chichester: Wiley.

Manz, C.C., Bastien, D.T., Hostager, T.J. and Shapiro, G.L. (1989) 'Leadership and innovation: A longitudinal process view', in A.H. Van de Ven, H. Angle, M.S. Poole (eds) *Research on the Management of Innovation: 'The Minnesota Studies'*, New York: Harper & Row.

Margerison, C. and McCann, D. (1986) 'Applications of the Team Management Resource', *International Journal of Manpower* 7(2): 18–25.

Nicholson, N. (1984) 'A Theory of Work Role Innovation', *Administrative Science Quarterly* 29: 172–91.

Nicholson, N. (1990) 'The cultural deconstruction of innovation', in M.A. West and J.L. Farr (eds) *Innovation and Creativity at Work: Psychological Approaches*, Chichester: Wiley.

Nyström, H. (19179) *Creativity and Innovation*, Chichester: Wiley.

Payne, R. (1990) 'The effectiveness of research teams: A review', in M.A. West and J.L. Farr (eds) *Innovation and Creativity at Work*, Chichester: Wiley.

Peters, T. (1985) *A Passion for Excellence: The Leadership Difference*, London: Collins.

Peters, T.J. and Waterman, R.H. Jnr. (1982) *In Search of Excellence: Lessons from America's Best-Run Companies*, New York: Warner.

Pierce, J.L. and Delbecq, A.L. (1977) 'Organizational structure, individual attitudes and innovation', *Academy of Management Review* 77: 27–37.

Rousseau, D.M. (1988) 'The construction of climate in organizational research', in C.L. Cooper and I. Robertson (eds) *International Review of Industrial and Organizational Psychology*, London: Wiley.

Schroeder, R.G., Van de Ven, A.H., Scudder, G.D. and Polley, D. (1989) 'The development of innovation ideas', in A.H. Van de Ven, H.L. Angle, and M.S. Poole (eds) *Research in the Management of Innovations: The Minnesota Studies*, New York: Harper & Row.

Stankiewicz, R. (1979) 'The age and size of Swedish academic research groups and their scientific performance', in F.M. Andrews (ed.) *Scientific Productivity*, Cambridge: Cambridge University Press.

Van de Ven, A.H. (1986) 'Central problems in the management of innovation', *Management Science* 32: 590–607.

Van de Ven, A.H. Angle, H.L. and Poole, M.S. (1989) (eds) *Research on the Management of Innovation: The Minnesota Studies*, New York: Harper & Row.

Wallace, M. and West, M.A. (1988) 'Innovation in primary health care teams: The effects of roles and climate', paper presented at the Annual Occupational Psychology Conference of the British Psychological Society, University of Manchester, January 1988.

West, M.A. (1990) 'Innovation in groups at work', in M.A. West and J.L. Farr (eds) *Innovation and Creativity at Work: Psychological and Organizational Strategies*, Chichester: Wiley.

West, M.A. and Anderson, N.R. (1991) 'Innovation in management teams in the NHS', paper presented at the British Psychological Society Annual Occupational Conference, Cardiff, January 1991.

West, M.A. and Farr, J.L. (eds) (1990) *Innovation and Creativity at Work: Psychological and Organizational Strategies*, Chichester: Wiley.

Zaltman, G., Duncan, R. and Holbek, J. (1973) *Innovations and Organizations*, New York: Wiley.

8 Individual transitions, role learning and innovation

Georgina M. Jackson and Nigel Nicholson

INTRODUCTION

This chapter addresses the question of how people change as a consequence of occupational experience. We are concerned specifically with the impact of changes in work role on individuals. Role change is a characteristic feature of organizational life. At any point in time many individuals will be in the process of changing their job, moving either between or within the same organization. This is not a new phenomenon, although, arguably, the rate of change in working lives has been accelerating steadily in recent decades (Alban-Metcalfe 1984; Nicholson 1984). In view of its importance both for the people who move and for the organizations within and between which mobility occurs, it is surprising that only in the 1980s has the study of career transitions come of age as a field of inquiry (Allen and Van de Vliert 1984). This status can be claimed for the area because it raises distinctive theoretical and practical questions that do not figure in the related literatures on turnover, vocational choice, or lifelong career development which hitherto have dominated the literature on occupational mobility. These questions arise when one shifts the focus down from the level of the lifespan of the organization, to scrutinize the particular qualities of individual experience of change. This opens up the way for theory building about how consequences of job change may depend on identifiable features of the transition.

The research programme into work-role transitions at the Sheffield University Social and Applied Psychology Unit has sought for nearly a decade to build theory and a reliable corpus of empirical data on the causes, conditions and outcomes of various kinds of transition. The overall conclusion of this work can be summarized as follows. Transitions have important outcomes, including psychological change in the person, role innovation behaviours, and varying degrees of stress and strain (Brett 1982; Frese 1982; Nicholson 1984; Latack 1989). Predictors of these outcomes come from interactions of measurable influences from among four groups (Nicholson 1990): the nature of the transition (i.e. qualities of the roles between which movement takes place), the dispositions and characteristics of the person moving (e.g. motives and tolerance of change), the nature of the setting (e.g. occupational and organizational norms and structures), and the quality of the experience (e.g. the way the experience is resourced or handled by local agents).

Research has begun to map these relationships, but many issues remain unaddressed. This chapter is concerned with one of the most important: what consequences does changing jobs have on an individual's work performance? We know that it is common for movers to report a heightened sense of challenge and personal effectiveness (Krau 1983; Latack 1984; Nicholson and West 1988), but so far researchers have not identified the cognitive and behavioural consequences of transition in relation to primary work tasks. This is a question that has absorbed job redesign researchers, but their findings have limited generalizability to the transitions field, for three reasons. First, the nature of the role change in job redesign is highly circumscribed, usually involving a limited reconfiguration of tasks and their ambient social relations. Second, job design methodologies generally focus on aggregate sample shifts in parameters, not individual differences. Third, the dependent variables of studies of job characteristics tend to concentrate on measurable output and work attitudes, not cognition.

The present research examines what changes in knowledge and skills occur when an individual begins a new job and gains experience in performing it. This chapter argues for the need to address these issues through the development of measures which are sensitive to the qualitative changes in performance which accompany job change. We describe the development and use of one such technique for investigating changes in implicit knowledge. Although changes in performance are important both theoretically, in terms of understanding how work skills develop, and practically, in terms of facilitating skill acquisition, empirically this variable has been unexplored within the job-change literature. Where studies have included measures of performance, these have focused on global outcome criteria, relying on rating measures obtained either from individuals themselves, or their peers or supervisors. They have demonstrated significant differences in the performance of individuals undergoing a job change, compared with equivalent groups not undergoing change (Keller and Holland 1981; Kirjonen and Hanninen 1986; West and Nicholson 1989). These findings, though pointing out the generally favourable impact of job change, do not explain why performance can increase after a job change, nor do they address the part played by other factors such as motivation. Moreover, research has shed no light on the critical intervening function of alterations in job changers' skills and knowledge. These are especially relevant to cases of radical shift between the role requirements of new and former jobs, and lead to the question of what should be the design features of appropriate training for new role encumbents.

Asking questions about overall changes in performance level is insufficient for these purposes, since the criteria for evaluating job performance may shift across the transition, and simple rating measures will not detect complex qualitative changes in job performance. This is because although individuals may be able to state what they do in order to carry out their job, i.e. the nature of the tasks they perform and the order in which they carry them out, they will find it much more difficult to comment on tacit aspects of their role.

The assumption that much of our performance knowledge is tacit and difficult to verbalize has received much empirical support. Many laboratory studies have demonstrated dissociations between how people perform complex tasks, and what they can say about their performance. For example Broadbent and his colleagues (Berry and Broadbent 1984, Hayes and Broadbent 1988) have shown that even where subjects are able to perform complex computer tasks at a high level of competence, their verbalizable knowledge of the tasks may not be equivalent. That is, although subjects can demonstrate, by their performance of a task, that they implicitly make use of its underlying structure, they may be unable to verbalize these rules, or even be aware that the task is rule-governed. Similar discrepancies between what subjects can say about a task and how they perform the task have been demonstrated on a variety of other laboratory tasks (Lewicki 1986).

All of these studies have involved looking at changes in the performance and verbal knowledge of individuals as they gain experience with a task. Although the tasks used are artificial, they do illustrate important features of the way we learn in complex situations. On the basis of this research Reber (1989) has argued that in complex settings our abstract knowledge about how variables are interrelated is acquired mainly implicitly, outside of conscious awareness. Although such implicit learning processes may operate independently of explicit processing, it is likely that for most tasks, at the same time, we do try consciously to learn the contingencies between variables. Given the independence of these processes it is likely, under certain conditions, that implicit and explicit learning may proceed at different rates, and recent evidence has shown this to be the case (Sanderson 1989). Also, implicit and explicit knowledge may be inconsistent (Lewicki 1986). While explicit or verbalizable understanding may only occur after much practice with a task, implicit understanding typically occurs much earlier. In the work environment new role incumbents are faced with a similar and often more complex situation.

They cannot, at a conscious level, make sense of all aspects of the new role at once, nor may they know which are the important aspects to focus on (Louis 1980). For this reason implicit processes may be particularly important in early role learning. Even when the individual is able to operate at an expert level, full verbalization of expertise may not be possible (Murphy and Wright 1984). This is not surprising if one accepts Reber's viewpoint that implicit and explicit knowledge may never be equivalent. Even if, with practice, there is congruence between performance and verbal understanding, implicit knowledge of a task will always be qualitatively different, and richer, than explicit knowledge (Reber 1989). This evidence strongly suggests that we should not rely solely on self-reports of performance, from either novices or experts. Even where self-reports are known or assumed to correspond to performance measures, they provide a rather limited picture of both performance and knowledge change.

Implicit knowledge has also been addressed, although in a rather different manner, by Wagner and Sternberg (1986). They have set out to identify differences in the tacit knowledge of experienced and novice role encumbents in the fields of academic psychology and business management. While the term 'tacit knowledge' has been used synonymously with unconscious knowledge by Reber (1989), Wagner and Sternberg's (1986) definition (under the somewhat misleadingly evaluative title of 'practical intelligence') is broader, including knowledge which is rarely stated but may be available to introspection. Their construction of the notion includes knowledge about how to manage tasks and interpersonal relationships, as well as knowledge about how best to organize and motivate one's own work performance. This type of knowledge, although rarely discussed, is likely to be vital to competent performance since it allows role encumbents 'to meet the often unwritten and unspoken demands of their jobs' (Wagner and Sternberg 1986: 3). Knowledge of these demands, and how best to address them, can be expected to be a notable deficiency in the cognitive resources of the new role incumbent, especially where there are major functional differences between the old and new roles. In these cases not only will they need to acquire the skills to meet the explicit demands of the role, but they will also need to learn the implicit rules of a new social system, of which, initially, they will be unaware. Tacit knowledge, since it is rarely expressed, is learnt mainly through experience, rather than through formal training. Wagner and Sternberg view their research on tacit knowledge as exploring what it is that experience of a role provides, and they assume that competent performance in work settings depends heavily on tacit knowledge.

Wagner and Sternberg have explored the structure of tacit knowledge by means of work-related scenarios which have first been generated from interviews with experienced role encumbents. Each scenario is accompanied by a number of solutions, which subjects are required to rate. Although the scenario approach to measuring performance does not eliminate the use of self-reports, insofar as individuals are required to decide what they would do in particular situations, it does provide a measure of what the individual views competent behaviour to be. How such judgements relate to actual behaviour has yet to be directly established, although Wagner and Sternberg have found strong correlations between subjects' scores and their level of professional advancement, suggesting that experienced subjects not only know what constitute good responses, but also how to execute them. This method of investigation has features in common with critical incident (Flanagan 1954; McClelland 1976) and job simulation (Fredricksen 1966) techniques. However, although the tasks or scenarios used in all these three techniques may be very similar, the method of their evaluation is rather different. Wagner and Sternberg evaluate a scenario's 'worth' in terms of whether it is able to differentiate between novice and experienced role performers. Critical incident and simulation methods select tasks and evaluate a subject's performance qualitatively in terms of what have been previously defined to be important aspects of the role and the criteria for good performance. These techniques do not therefore measure how experienced individuals actually perform the task, other than via the report of the individual generating the incident.

METHOD

For the present study we have developed the Wagner and Sternberg technique to explore both cross-sectional differences and longitudinal changes in the tacit knowledge of police officers. Using scenarios generated by experienced police officers, we have been able to examine how novice policeman differ from more experienced colleagues, and how, as they gain experience in a new role, they move towards becoming 'experts'. Since our primary aim here is to illustrate the technique and its possible usages, only the results of the cross-sectional studies will be reported.

The subjects chosen for this study were officers from a large urban police force. The group was selected as particularly suitable for looking at longitudinal changes in work performance, because they constituted a sizeable cohort, at the same point in their career, who could be simultaneously followed over time through an equivalent role change. The job change they were all undergoing was promotion from the rank of constable to sergeant. This transition involves a radical change in function, since the rank of sergeant represents the first level of management within the British police. Officers performing the role of sergeant are responsible for the day-to-day supervision of as many as forty constables, the training and appraisal of probationary officers, and a range of administrative duties necessary for the efficient running of the organization. Therefore officers promoted to sergeant, if they are to adapt successfully to their new role, need to acquire a range of new skills and knowledge not already required for the effective performance of the role of constable. It should also be noted that these officers, although inexperienced in the sergeant role, are not novices to the organization, having at least four years' experience within the force. During this time they will have been in daily contact with officers performing the sergeant's duties.

Officers are promoted to the rank of sergeant primarily on the basis of passing a written examination which assesses their knowledge of police regulations and procedure, not their managerial potential. Following the examination, officers who have passed are promoted after they have attended a pre-promotion course designed to introduce them to managerial skills as well as task-based (legal and administrative) aspects of the new role.

A random sample of twenty-four officers[1] who had passed the sergeant's examination, and were awaiting promotion, was selected to make up the novice group. The expert group was randomly selected from a group of experienced officers, all with at least four years' experience in the role of sergeant. Both groups were asked to respond to seven work-related scenarios, representing actual situations which sergeants, in the development stage of the methodology (semi-structured interview accounts), had reported having encountered. Each of these situations could be considered typical of the kinds of open-ended problems – involving relationships with peers, subordinates or superordinates – which new sergeants are likely to confront. Each scenario was presented with an associated set of possible solutions, also previously generated from interviews with experienced sergeants. These scenarios differed from the kinds used by Wagner and Sternberg, in that ours described specific incidents rather than generic problems. In addition, our scenarios were designed to be contextually embedded in familiar police settings, and were worded in appropriate police terminology:[2]

Example of work-related scenario used in the study (scenario E)

Your relief Inspector is on annual leave and you are acting Duty Officer. One of your fellow Sergeant fails to turn up for early turn and on enquiring where he is you find that he has been shown annual leave by the night duty inspector because he arrived at the station unfit for duty through drink. Over the next two days you find on taking over from the night duty that this same sergeant has taken annual leave during the night. Finally, on the Sunday of your early turn week, you commence duty to find that this sergeant has not arrived for work you have no sergeants to fill the role of station sergeant, and that on this occasion he has not taken leave of any sort. During this time you, as acting duty officer, have not been contacted by the sergeant concerned.

Although, on first reading, such scenarios might be difficult to comprehend for individuals outside the police service, they are designed to embody interpersonal problems which are commonly faced by any manager.

Subjects were also asked, for each scenario, to appraise the situation on a number of dimensions; how difficult they thought the situation was, how much control they thought they had over the outcome, how important it was to achieve a successful outcome, how anxious the situation made them feel and how much prior experience they had of this type of situation. These questions were included so that we would not only have a measure of what experienced and novice officers might do if faced by these situations, but also how they might appraise the situations prior to any action. Because Wagner and Sternberg were primarily concerned with identifying the structure of tacit knowledge and developing a measure of tacit knowledge, they discarded any items which did not discriminate between experienced individuals and novices. Since our objective was rather different, to discover which aspects of judgemental cognition would not change during the transition from constable to sergeant, as well as those which would, no prior discrimination of this kind was applied to our scenarios. We wished to identify which aspects of tacit knowledge changed through role transition, and would be the most effective focus of training for people being promoted.

RESULTS AND DISCUSSION

Applying the scenario technique yielded quite clear differences between experienced and novice sergeants. First, when presented with a range of possible solutions to a scenario, and required to rank order them in terms of their acceptability as an adequate solution, the experienced group showed significantly more consensus over their choices, with most of the sample tending to converge on a small number of very similar solution orders. In contrast, the results for the novice group were much more heterogeneous, with almost no convergence on a consensual order across the group. This suggests that despite a minimum of four years' general police experience in the role of constable, with intensive preparation for, and subsequent success in the promotion examination, the actions taken by novice officers, if faced with problems such as those presented in the scenarios, might be more idiosyncratic and less predictable than those of the experienced group.

Second, the overall pattern of results on the various appraisal dimensions revealed qualitative differences in the way the two groups perceive and structure work-related problems (see Figures 8.1–8.3). The magnitude and direction of differences between the expert and novice groups on the various appraisal dimensions, as indicated by the interaction effects, was highly dependent on the nature of the problem presented in any particular scenario. Novice and experienced officers did not consistently rate all of the scenarios in the same direction. For example, the novice group showed an overall tendency to rate a successful outcome to the problems presented as less important than the expert group (Figure 8.1). However, for one scenario this overall trend showed a significant reversal, with the novice group overestimating the importance of a successful outcome compared to the expert group (scenario G). This scenario differed from others by representing the 'welfare' role of the sergeant, and concerned the personal relationship between two constables under the sergeant's supervision. As such it represents a situation outside the direct experience of the novice group, since officers at the constable level are not required to take responsibility over welfare matters.

One plausible explanation for these differences might be the degree to which experts, as a result of their greater experience in the role, make reasonable inferences beyond the details of the problem presented in the scenarios. In making their judgements, the experts seem to be considering what the problem might imply for parties or groups not mentioned in the scenario. A similar pattern of results was also found for the appraisal dimension asking officers to estimate how difficult they felt it would be to arrive at a solution to the problem presented (Figure 8.2). Although for several of the scenarios there was a consensual view, other scenarios showed significant differences between the groups. A typical example was the divergent views about what action should be taken over having to assume the duties of a new colleague (i.e. fellow sergeant) who was persistently late (scenario A). This was perceived to be more difficult by the novice group than by the experienced group. In contrast, the scenario of having to deal with a problematic colleague while performing the role of Duty Officer was rated as an easier problem to deal with by the novice group (scenario E). Performing the role of Duty Officer means that the sergeant is officially placed in a position of authority over fellow sergeants. Thus for the former scenario the sergeant was having to contemplate action against an errant officer of equal rank, while in the latter situation the position was one of temporary seniority.

Similar patterns of results, suggesting that the experienced group construe some problems differently from the novice group because they use a wider inferential knowledge base, were also found on many of the other

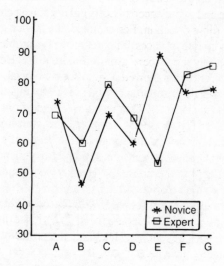

Expert at E significant at 0.05

Figure 8.1 Mean expertise differences in rated importance of outcome

appraisal dimensions. Some of these centred on group differences in ratings of the predicted impact of their chosen actions on a scenario's eventual outcome. In general it was found that the novice group underestimated the effect of their action, compared to the experienced group. However, for the 'welfare' scenario (scenario G) this pattern of results was reversed, with the novice group significantly overestimating the effect of their actions in this situation.

To the extent that these ratings can be assumed to be reliable indicators of behaviour, our results indicate that despite quite intensive preparation, novice officers had not acquired the range of skills necessary to go beyond routine problems for which explicit rules and procedures are provided. The

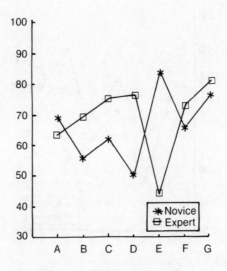

Expert at A, C and E significant at 0.05

Figure 8.2 Mean expertise differences in choice difficulty

scenario technique has shown that it is possible to identify qualitative differences in how work-related judgements are construed by experts and novices.

CONCLUSION

What we can infer from these data depends, in large part, upon the external validity of the method, i.e. what confidence we can have that responses to scenarios indicate what subjects might actually do in real life. In favour of this assumption is the high face validity of the scenarios, in the detailed representation they give of real problems faced by police officers.

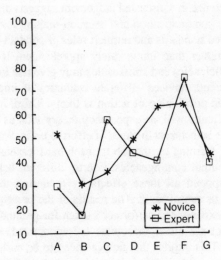

Expert at D and E significant at 0.05

Figure 8.3 Mean expertise differences in rated effect on outcome

Alternative solutions were similarly devised to represent the finite range of real options which would be open to them. It would be difficult, if not impossible, to test whether people would actually behave in accordance with their choices among these options, but it is reasonable to assume that they might do if unconstrained by other unstated influences.

But even without this assumption, the results still reveal sharp and important differences in how novice and experienced officers cognitively frame and evaluate common events. They do so in several ways. First, they differ in their consensus about possible courses of action. Second, they attach different importance to problems and solutions. Third, they differ in estimates of problem difficulty. Fourth, they assign different probabilities to the effects of their actions. These four differences have, potentially, a number of important implications for likely performance difficulties novices may encounter following promotion to positions of managerial responsibility, not just in the police, but in other kinds of organizations as well. Let us look at each in turn.

First, the difference in consensual judgement suggests that a greater load will be placed on communication and decision-making involving novices, for whom accepted standards and implicit rules of conduct have to be built up inductively, rather than immediately apprehended. It is not hard to imagine the inefficiencies and stresses this may give rise to while learning accumulates. Second, novices' different estimates of importance means that poor strategic prioritizing of action is likely. Third, incommensurate beliefs about difficulty will, as expectancy theory tells us (Lawler 1973), lead to inefficient or incorrect disposal of effort to tasks. We can expect the trial and error of learning on the job to teach hard lessons about the true nature of input-output contingencies. Fourth, different beliefs about outcomes will compound all these effects by rendering the task domain unpredictable in its causal logic. The results of the present study suggest that many of the experienced performer's taken-for-granted rules of judgement and conduct are either inaccurate or randomized, in the novice's cognitive frame. This implies that novices need to be cushioned from the worst consequences of their deficient tacit knowledge whilst they are in the process of acquiring it through experience.

But experience alone may not be enough, or may be slow and inefficient in establishing consistent and effective cognition. Training geared to an understanding of tacit knowledge requirements could support and accelerate role learning. This study offers guidance for this purpose in several ways. First, the methodology offers a more objective means of studying changes in performance than has been used in the past, and a diagnostic aid for uncovering the deeper and more intangible cognitive challenges of role change within organizational settings. Second, it offers guidance for the content of training programmes. Our results, and those of other scholars, demonstrate that much of the knowledge required for efficient performance of a role or task will not necessarily be verbalizable by 'experts', and that training programmes which rely exclusively on knowledge elicited from experienced performers will be unlikely to achieve many of the objectives set. For example, even where tacit knowledge is available to the 'expert', its very nature suggests that it is unlikely to be selected for inclusion in formal instruction. Moreover, even where it is possible to make explicit the role-specific knowledge used by experts, this offers no guarantee that novices will be able to utilize it. From the present study we would suggest that more objective techniques can be usefully used to gauge and explore qualitative differences in expert and novice performance, and to determine which aspects of performance need to be trained. Having identified gaps in the knowledge base of trainees, a variety of formal and informal methods will be needed to fill them. Although some aspects of a role, including tacit knowledge, may be appropriately taught using formal techniques, other aspects may best be acquired through the programmed scheduling of practical experience, under conditions of minimum risk and maximum feedback review.

These conditions may be difficult, it not impossible, to create in 'on-the-job' training programmes. The risks attendant upon police behaviour (i.e. the costs of error) may be irreducible, for obvious reasons, and similar constraints can be expected in many other positions of responsibility in other organizations. The common induction strategy of giving novices lightweight or makework tasks is no solution. It just postpones the important real learning, and besides creates corrosive feelings of underutilization and frustration in the novice (Hall 1976; Nicholson and Arnold 1989). In these cases practical experience, in some form, needs to be provided within the safety of a training setting. One way of providing this experience is through task simulation methods such as role enactment and computer-aided learning. The primary aims of these techniques should be to provide practice on the identified task (or in components of a task which are particularly problematic), enabling trainees to make explicit any limitations in their understanding about the role or task. A last practical implication of the method is its potential for assessing and evaluating the efficacy of different training programmes. It offers a way of quantifying changes in performance which do not depend on the verbal reports of either trainees or trainers.

Before concluding, brief comment is merited on the wider significance of tacit knowledge for our understanding of organizational functioning and role transitions. In relation to the former, it is clear that tacit knowledge is structured and normative among experienced organizational members. Our discussion has tended to imply that it is an accompaniment of effective performance. But we should also bear in mind that tacit knowledge of this kind can be dysfunctional. It may be erroneous and downright dangerous, such as when consensus forms around outdated, superstitious or deviant belief systems. Alternatively, in some circumstances the naivety of novices may be a refreshing source of diversity which is subsequently extinguished by the culture's convergent cognitions. These examples point out the principle that tacit knowledge is implicitly cultural, and is only as effective as the cognitive structure of the system from which it emanates. Although not directly concerned with innovation in organization, this last point also implies that role innovation may be an 'accidental' product, during early job tenure, of inexperience rather than intent. Before we assume that we want novices to acquire the tacit knowledge of 'experts' we should first question whether it is the cognitive universe of the experts' organizational culture which needs to be reformed. There is evidence that in some police organizations this may be the case (Glowinkowski and Nicholson 1986): 'pathological' misperceptions of role requirement, advancement criteria and organizational goals. From the organizational literature, there is good reason to expect similar pathologies to be endemic to many other kinds of organization, whose cognitive systems would benefit more from radical reform than from more efficient training (Brunsson 1985; Kets de Vries and Miller 1984; Morgan 1986). In short, before we evaluate training and knowledge needs, a more holistic organizational cultural analysis is necessary.

The implications for the analysis of transitions are less equivocal. The results identify a major lacunae in the literature, and illustrate its accessibility to systematic study. To date, theory and research has tended to concentrate on the effective dimensions of experience and outcomes. Even the extensive literature on socialization processes has much more to say about the agents, strategies and outcomes of learning, than about its content (Feldman 1976; Van Maanen and Schein 1979; Jones 1986). The concept of role has predominated, without detailing the cognitive substrata of role learning and performance. The present study has shown how changes in the structuring of tacit knowledge are an important aspect of role learning which raise fresh questions for transitions research. In particular, we need to investigate how cognitive change affects other outcomes, i.e. how does tacit knowledge insulate people against stress, or mediate coping strategies such as personal change and innovation? Investigation of the changing content of cognition also is necessary to understand the disjunctions and developments over time in the course of adjustment. This implies the need for longitudinal study, one of the main aims of the extension of the present research. Last, we need to know more about individual differences in tacit knowledge: the structure of its contents and its rate of acquisition. Results emerging from the present study indicate that some novices, independent of their previous experience, are more like experts in their cognitions than other novices. What is it that makes some novices call upon more sophisticated inferential knowledge systems than others? Personality and cognitive complexity may have an important bearing on this. Our current research is also investigating some of these avenues. Much remains to be done, but the prize is valuable: reliable knowledge and practical advice about which influences and resources can help what kinds of individuals to adapt constructively to the important changes which recur in all our working lives.

NOTES

1 These officers in fact form a sub-set of a much larger group who were participating in a longitudinal survey over the course of their transition from constable to sergeant.
2 In the police force studied, each shift is made up of a number of constables who are supervised by several sergeants. Overall, supervisory responsibility for the shift rests with the 'Duty Officer' who is an officer of Inspector rank. It frequently happens however than in this officer's absence a sergeant will deputize and perform the Duty Officer role, assuming the supervisory responsibilities which go with it.

REFERENCES

Alban-Metcalfe, B.M. (1984) 'Current career concerns of female and male managers and professionals: An analysis of free-response comments to a national survey', *Equal Opportunities International* 3: 11–18.

Allen, V.L. and Van de Vliert, E. (1984) *Role Transitions: Explorations and Explanations*, London: Plenum.

Berry, D.C., Broadbent, D.E. (1984) 'On the relationship between task performance and associated verbalizable knowledge', *Quarterly Journal of Experimental Psychology* 79: 251–72.

Brett, J.M. (1982) 'Job transfer and well-being', *Journal of Applied Psychology* 67: 450–63.

Brunsson, N. (1985) *The Irrational Organization*, Chichester: Wiley.

Feldman, D.C. (1976) 'A contingency theory of socialization', *Administrative Science Quarterly* 21: 433–52.

Flanagan, J.C. (1954) 'The critical incident technique', *Psychological Bulletin* 51: 327–58.

Frederiksen, N. (1966) 'Validation of a simulation technique', *Organizational Behaviour and Human Performance* 1: 87–109.

Frese, M. (1982) 'Occupational socialization and psychological development: An underdeveloped research perspective in industrial psychology', *Journal of Occupational Psychology* 55: 209–24.

Glowinkowski, S. and Nicholson, N. (1986) 'The promotion pathology: A study of British police inspectors', *Personnel Review* 15: 12–21.

Hall, D.T. (1976) *Careers in Organizations*, Pacific Palisades, CA: Goodyear.

Hayes, N.A. and Broadbent, D.E. 'Two modes of learning for interactive tasks', *Cognition* 28: 249–76.

Jones, G.R. (1986) 'Socialization tactics, self-efficacy, and newcomers' adjustments to organizations', *Academy of Management Review* 8: 262–79.

Keller, R.T. and Holland, W.E. (1981) 'Job change: A naturally occurring field experiment', *Human Relations* 34: 1053–67.

Kets de Vries, M. and Miller, D. (1984) *The Neurotic Organization*, San Francisco: Jossey-Bass.

Kirjonen, J. and Hanninen, V. (1986) 'Getting a better job: Antecedents and effects', *Human Relations* 39: 503–16.

Krau, E. (1983) 'The attitudes towards work in career transitions', *Journal of Vocational Behaviour* 23: 270–85.

Latack, J.C. (1984) 'Career transitions within organizations: An exploratory study of work, nonwork and coping strategies', *Organizational Behaviour and Human Performance* 34: 296–322.

Latack, J.C. (1989) 'Work, stress and careers: A preventative approach to maintaining organizational health', in M.B. Arthur, D.T. Hall and B.S. Lawrence (eds) *Handbook of career theory*, Cambridge: Cambridge University Press.

Lawler, E.E. (1973) *Motivation in Work Organization*, Monterey, CA: Brooks-Cole.

Lewicki, P. (1986) 'Processing information about covariations that cannot be articulated', *Journal of Experimental Psychology: Learning, Memory and Cognition* 12: 135–46.

Louis, M.R. (1980) 'Surprise and sense making: What newcomers experience in entering unfamiliar organizational settings', *Administrative Science Quarterly* 25: 226–51.

McClelland, D.C. (1976) *A Guide to Job Competency Assessment*, Boston: McBer.

Morgan, G. (1986) *Images of Organizations*, Beverly Hills: Sage.

Murphy, G.L. and Wright, J.C. (1984) 'Changes in conceptual structure with expertise: Differences between real-world experts and novices', *Journal of Experimental Psychology: Learning, Memory and Cognition* 10(1): 144–55.

Nicholson, N. (1984) 'A theory of work-role transitions', *Administrative Science Quarterly* 29: 172–91.

Nicholson, N. and Arnold, J. (1989) 'Graduate early experience in a multinational corporation', *Personnel Review* 18(4): 3–14.

Nicholson, N. and West, M. (1988) *Managerial Job Change*, Cambridge: Cambridge University Press.

Nicholson, N. and West, M.A. (1989) 'Transitions, work histories and careers', in M.B. Arthur, D.T. Hall and B.S. Lawrence (eds) *Handbook of Career Theory*, Cambridge: Cambridge University Press.

Pinder, C.C. and Schroeder, K.G. (1987) 'Time to proficiency following job transfers', *Academy of Management Journal* 30: 336–53.

Reber, A.S. (1989) 'Implicit learning and tacit knowledge', *Journal of Experimental Psychology: General* 118(3): 219–35.

Sanderson, P.M. (1989) 'Verbalizable knowledge and skilled task performance: Association, dissociation and mental models', *Journal of Experimental Psychology: Learning, Memory and Cognition* 15(4): 729–47.

Van Maanen, J. and Schein, E.H. (1979) 'Toward a theory of organizational socialization', in B.M. Staw (ed.) *Research in Organizational Behavior*, (Vol. 1) Greenwich, CT: JAI Press.

Wagner, R.K. and Sternberg, R.J. (1986) 'Tacit knowledge and intelligence in the everyday world', in R.J. Sternberg and R.K. Wagner (eds) (1989) *Practical intelligence: Nature and origins of competence in the everyday world*. Cambridge: Cambridge University Press.

West, M.A. and Nicholson, N. (1989) 'The outcomes of job change', *Journal of Vocational Behavior* 34: 335–49.

Zahrly, J. and Tosi, H. (1989) 'The differential effect of organizational induction process on early work role adjustment', *Journal of Organizational Behavior* 10: 59–74.

Part III
Technical change and work organization

Part III

Introduction

Robin Martin

The main stumbling blocks in the near future for the implementation of programmable automation technology are not technical, but rather are barriers of cost, organization of the factory, availability of appropriate skills and social effects of these technologies.

(Office of Technology Assessment, Washington DC, USA 1984: 92)

The above observations echo a long-held truism in organizational behaviour research, that the human aspects of work (such as job design and social relationships) are as important as the technical ones (such as design of machines and tools). The premise underlying this is that, since work involves the integration of people and technology, both these aspects need to be jointly considered in order to achieve optimum performance. Experience dictates that truisms need not equate with reality, however, and this is unfortunately true in this case. More often than not, organizations are 'technologically driven' such that there is a mismatch where a disproportionate amount of attention is given to the technical aspects, to the neglect of the human issues.

Part III addresses the above issues by examining the implications of technical change to the organization of work. The four chapters share the common perspective that the human aspects of work are as important as the technical ones, and that the full benefits of technology will only be realized when both aspects are considered together. This perspective thus clearly rejects a strict technological determinism stance, but argues for an integration of human and technological issues.

Each of the four chapters takes a different but complementary perspective of the relationship between technology and work organization. The first two chapters are related to recent theoretical developments in work organization, focusing upon the socio-technical systems approach to work design. This approach emphasizes the need to consider both the technical and human systems, in order to design an effective work organization. The remaining two chapters deal with one particular application of technological change, namely the implementation of computer aided manufacturing (CAM). Recent developments in information technology have made available a wide range of computer-controlled machines which can profoundly affect the nature of jobs, raising a number of important issues concerning work organization.

TECHNOLOGICAL CHANGE AND SOCIO-TECHNICAL SYSTEMS THEORY (STST)

One of the most pervasive theoretical approaches towards work organization was developed by a group of researchers at the Tavistock Institute (Trist and Bamforth 1951). Up until that time, approaches to work organization had concentrated almost exclusively upon technical considerations, with little regard to the people in the organization. By contrast, the approach adopted by STST proposed that an effective work organization depends upon the optimum integration of technical systems (equipment, procedures, etc.) and social systems (interpersonal relationships, interaction, etc.).

One of the central concepts of STST has been the development of autonomous work groups. These consist of groups of employees who have a high degree of self-determination over their work, with little or no direct supervision. Typically this involves collective control over the pace of work, distribution of tasks within the group, the timing and organization of breaks, and the training and recruitment of new members.

The STST approach to work organization has had considerable success in both Europe and North America. In the 1970s the Swedish car manufacturers Volvo and Saab rejected traditional manufacturing methods, and designed new car production plants which incorporated group working. Whilst there are many case studies illustrating the benefits of STST, there has been comparatively little research in developing the underlying theoretical concepts and in conducting empirical studies. Both these aspects are currently attracting attention, and the two chapters in this section each contribute to this debate.

Chapter 9, by Frans van Eijnatten, Christel Rutte and Annelies Hoevenaars considers recent developments to STST which have occurred in The Netherlands. The authors criticize the classical model of STST on a number of grounds, and offer a new variant which utilizes a multi-level approach. Their (re)design methodology is based on seventeen steps grouped into five diagnostic phases (identification of the problem, diagnosis, action planning, intervention and evaluation). Central to this model is the '(re)design interface' which draws upon three aspects: environmental issues (such as market requirements), knowledge issues (such as organizational theories and practices), and methodological issues (such as participative methods). A case study is used to highlight the (re)design process.

In Chapter 10, Wally Mueller and John Cordery present a planned change study involving the adoption of multi-skilled work teams, and thus provide a rare opportunity to examine the benefits of group working. The study takes place in a greenfield mining site where group work is introduced as a method of increasing internal labour flexibility. A particular strength of the study is that several waves of data are collected, using a variety of techniques (such as questionnaire, interviews and participant observation). The design of the study thus allows an understanding of the long-term effects of group working upon employees.

COMPUTER-BASED MANUFACTURING

While the relationship between technology and work organization has a long tradition, interest in the area has recently been rekindled due to advances in micro-electronics and information technology. This has led to the development of a wide variety of computer controlled and aided machines. The distinguishing characteristic of these machines is that they are able to conduct a number of different tasks under the control of a computer program, with little or no human support.

The arguments for investing in information technology are compelling, and thus indicate the increasing value they will have in manufacturing organizations. In the first instance, information technology offers the prospect of reducing the need for a skilled workforce, by allocating control of the work to the computer rather than the operator. In extreme cases, attempts have been made to replace humans with machines. While these strategies may lead to labour savings, increased costs are often incurred through the need for more specialized support staff (such as engineers, programmers, etc.). A more direct benefit of information technology is obtained through the ability to program the machines to conduct a wide range of tasks within precise production parameters. The speed and accuracy offered by these machines tends to be much greater than is possible by humans alone.

The potential of CAM to affect the nature of work raises a number of issues of concern to organizational behaviour in general, and to work organization in particular. Chapters 11 and 12 each deal with one of these issues. Chapter 11 examines current developments in incorporating human criteria into the design process of CAM, while the second chapter explores alternative ways of work organization for CAM.

In Chapter 11, Gillian Symon examines research focusing on the relationship between the design of the technology and its subsequent impact upon the operator. Typically, the design of CAM has been 'technologically driven', and little regard has been given to the users of such systems. The mismatch between technical and human criteria has led to a number of problems, and to many situations where CAM potential has not been fulfilled. An alternative approach to this can be identified, termed the 'human-centred approach', which advocates the need to consider jointly both human and technical criteria when designing CAM. Chapter 11 considers the underlying assumptions of the traditional technological and human-centred approaches to CAM design, arguing that the latter philosophy is the most appropriate. The author proposes a human-centred framework which incorporates a number of design criteria and human factor 'tools' which can be employed. The utility of the framework is demonstrated through a case study, with the aim of designing and implementing a computer integrated manufacturing (CIM) system.

Chapter 12, by Robin Martin and Keith Davids, examines research which has investigated the relationship between CAM and job design. The emerging literature examining this issue has been dominated by considerations of the skill requirements of those who operate such machines. A popular belief has been that CAM has the potential to diminish the skill level of shop-floor operators, reducing the role of such workers to that of 'machine minders'. In many cases this undoubtedly does occur, but such an effect is neither inevitable nor universal. In fact, a number of organizations have implemented CAM in such a way that jobs have been enriched, rather than deskilled, and consequently operators report positive well-being. It is thus clear that there is variation, thus choice, as to how organizations can design CAM jobs.

REFERENCE

Trist, E.L. and Bamforth, K.W. (1951) 'Some social and psychological consequences of the long-wall method of coal-getting', *Human Relations*, 4: 3–38.

9 Holistic and participative (re)design

Contemporary STSD modelling in The Netherlands

Frans M. van Eijnatten, Annelies M. Hoevenaars and Christel G. Rutte

INTRODUCTION

Socio-technical systems design (STSD) is again at a parting of ways. Some forty years have elapsed since its conception at the London Tavistock Institute (Trist and Bamforth 1951; Trist and Murray 1991). The classical STSD views and change methodologies, well documented in the literature, are becoming less and less popular. Conceptual inadequacies, restrictive emphasis on the work group level, and expert-led application scenarios have gradually been identified as the major weaknesses of the original approach (Van der Zwaan 1975; Emery, M. 1989; De Sitter *et al.* 1990). After four decades our models and methods are much more elaborated. Rapid technological and cultural change have called for further adjustments and regional developments of the socio-technical inheritance, and we now have more solidly anchored systems concepts, multi-level design options, and participative change procedures. In North America, Australia and Europe, new and innovative STSD approaches have been emerging, mainly on a local level.

This chapter is about contemporary STSD modelling in The Netherlands. It reports on developments of the approach to flexible productive systems (AFPS), a practical Dutch socio-technical systems variant which recently has evolved towards a multi-level method of integrating task design (Van Eijnatten 1986) and organization design (De Sitter *et al.* 1986). After discussing some relevant literature, the core of the chapter consists of a method for integral organizational (re)design, based on an analytical interface model and design-oriented methodology (Van Strien 1986; Den Hertog and Van Assen 1988). A short case illustration shows how the method is working.

STSD PARADIGM: SOME ESSENTIALS AND (PRE)JUDGEMENTS

STSD is an organization renewal paradigm aimed at supporting more integrated analysis and co-design of manufacturing process and work organization. It stresses the importance of 'joint optimization' or integration of social and technical aspects of production systems. Central to STSD is its method. Self-management and self-design are its ultimate goals.

The STSD paradigm, which is based on action research, has gone through a number of phases, as reported in the literature (Trist 1981; Emery, M. 1989; Van Eijnatten 1990, 1991). During the pioneering phase (1950–60) the semi-autonomous work group was emphasized (Trist and Bamforth 1951; Trist *et al.* 1963).

More elaborated concepts and expert methods were tested in the period of classical STSD (1960–75) – demonstration experiments in Scandinavia (Emery and Thorsrud 1964, 1975), work structuring experiments in The Netherlands (Van Beinum 1963; Van Beinum *et al.* 1968; Allegro 1973; Den Hertog 1977), and socio-technical consultancy practices in North America (Pasmore *et al.* 1982). From Australia, participative design first came to the fore (Emery and Emery 1974, 1975, 1976; Emery, M. 1982, 1989), giving birth to the phase of modern STSD (1972–89). Contemporary STSD is a mixture of classical concepts, local theories and participative methodologies. In Scandinavia currently a new phase is emerging, stressing democratic dialogue and large-scale change (Van Beinum 1986; Gustavsen 1985, 1988; Engelstad 1990).

In the literature, STSD is associated most often with the early Tavistock pioneering work. Several authors have criticized the initial conceptualizations, which indeed suffer from the growing pains of systems thinking in the 1950s and 1960s. The conceptual roots of the traditional STSD paradigm lay in biology, cybernetics and neurophysiology (Litterer 1963; Herbst 1974; Lilienfeld 1978). Although epoch-making insights, like the open-system conception, steady state, and equifinality (Von Bertalanffy 1950), the law of requisite variety (Ashby 1958), and learning in random networks (Beurle 1962) have had considerable impact on STSD scholars, an adequate translation and incorporation of these new concepts in early STSD models is problematic. In his commentary to the historical review by Trist (1981), Hackman (1981) has pointed to the elusive character of STSD's basic notions. According to Van der Zwaan (1975), in general the definition of concepts is poor. Also, the system-theoretical model has not been properly worked out. For instance, the vital concept of 'steady state' is not greatly elaborated. A main point of theoretical critique is that traditional STSD has not reached a satisfactory level of maturity. Conceptual clarity as well as coherence is especially criticized. Unfortunately, there is some degree of absurdity, even of logical inconsistency, in specifying coupled but independently-based social and technical systems which have to be jointly optimized (Emery, F. 1959, 1963). The brilliant idea of integral design which lay behind this, initially could not be sufficiently worked out theoretically, because the 'aspect-system' as a logical construct was not known at the time.

Socio-technical design principles have been borrowed mainly from 'naturally occurring field experiments'. Although Cherns (1976, 1987) did try twice to summarize those principles, the resulting theory has never been very coherent. According to Kuipers and Rutte (1987) the principles have not been clearly attributed to different kinds of organizational structure (production, control, preparation), while design application order has been totally neglected. Also, the scope of traditional STSD theory has been judged as too narrow. In addition, conventional STSD is not as integral as it claims to be. According to Van der Zwaan (1975) traditional STSD has occupied itself almost exclusively with psychological needs, resulting in unacceptable reductionism with respect to the social aspect of the system. Having reviewed thirty years of STSD, Pasmore *et al.* (1982) concluded that the contribution of the conventional STSD paradigm to technological innovation is very limited. According to Hackman (1981), surprisingly limited attention is given to the systematic multi-level evaluation of change attempts. More recently, one of the best-designed outcome evaluation studies on autonomous group functioning (Wall *et al.* 1986) failed to show any significant long-term effects on work motivation and performance whatsoever.

Criticizing complacency in traditional STSD, Pava (1986) complains that 'methodologically, little has been developed beyond the conventional "nine step method" forged by the pioneering efforts of Emery (1959, 1977) and of Day and Canter (1956) based on early change projects' (Pava 1986: 202). Indeed Hill (1971), Cummings (1976) and Cummings and Srivastva (1977) have made no substantial additions, merely reproducing the working drafts of the Tavistock's analytical models (Foster 1967). Pasmore and Sherwood (1978) reprinted the same text, citing Emery and Trist as its authors.

The basic problem with conventional STSD method is the lack of an explicit design orientation. Analytic activities dominate design activities. Because in the last decade the complexity of organization design activities has multiplied, there is a need for a new participative STSD method that encounters the action planning stage in a more appropriate way. From a methodological point of view Van der Zwaan (1975) argued that, because of an ill-developed analytical model, in practice there is a real risk of confusing system levels. Van der Zwaan found it difficult in conventional STSD paradigm to differentiate the analytical model from the action model. In a methodological critique of fifty-eight selected work experiments, Cummings *et al.* (1977) show that the majority of studies suffer from weaknesses concerning internal and external validity. Most selected studies score badly on minimum quality criteria of experimental design.

In the literature there seems to be only slow progress in system-theoretical, methodological and conceptual debates concerning what is generally known as core STSD. Probably one or more of the following circumstances are accountable for this:

- STSD key publications have been dispersed in heterogeneous volumes and in many international journals, while a number of conceptual papers have never reached these media at all. Prolonged difficulties in obtaining such documents have urged authors to copy older or non-original sources, resulting in inaccurate or incomplete discussion of the subject matter.
- STSD literature is very poorly organized with respect to the para-digmatic generations. Each author implicitly represents his or her own country with its idiosyncratic time schedule of STSD phases and local mixture of conceptual developments. STSD lacks a universal approach.
- STSD is mainly a strategy. Originally it was developed as a method, not as a theory. STSD method can produce a whole array of concrete, highly situation-specific end results which are not always reported as STSD-inspired endeavours.
- STSD has been strongly based on (a narrow version of) the open-systems concept. Early design principles lacked appropriate conceptual profundity. As stated earlier, part of the problem inevitably had to do with the immaturity of systems thinking in the 1950s and 1960s. It was not until the 1970s that more basic solutions were advanced. Para-doxically these new insights have not been picked up in STSD literature. During the same period, the STSD paradigm shifted gradually from an expert approach to a participative process. Because of this, further development of more specific and accurate structural design concepts faded, retreating more and more into the background.

It seems that after forty years the interest of the international academic world in STSD has largely vanished. But on a more local level, for instance in The Netherlands, the socio-technical inspiration is still very much alive. Although most problems concerning methodology and systems theory have been solved in the last two decades, international diffusion is hampered by the fact that a majority of studies are reported in Dutch.

DUTCH CONTRIBUTIONS TO STSD

Although its visibility in the international literature is minimal, the contribution on the part of Dutch researchers to the conceptual renewal of STSD has been quite significant, as we shall illustrate.

With respect to system-theoretical aspects, there have been two major developments. First, at the time that Ackoff and Emery (1972) published 'On purposeful systems', De Sitter (1973) presented an up-to-date system-theoretical paradigm of social interaction in which there is a systematic and thorough definition of systems concepts. Second, In 't Veld (1978) developed an elaborate analytical model of a system in steady state with equifinality, which has made it possible to differentiate systematically between succeeding systems levels in an ordered way. Both contributions can be characterized as 'empty cartridge' approaches, constituting some neutral system-theoretical framework on which a modern STSD view can be more firmly based.

With respect to methodological aspects there has been one significant Dutch contribution. In an attempt to support the process of giving full scientific status to the action model, Van Strien (1975) proposed the 'regulative cycle of diagnostic and consultative thinking'. This cycle contains five phases: identification of the problem, diagnosis, action planning, intervention, and evaluation. The unique aspect here is not the action cycle as such, but the epistemological and methodological treatment of action research as an equal alternative to the traditional scientific method (Van Strien 1986). Central to this is the 'theory of practice'. According to Van Strien (1975) 'the view of science as a system of statements is making room for a view of science as a set of conceptual and methodological tools in approaching reality' (p. 601). Modern STSD interventions can be methodologically treated as theories of practice.

With respect to design aspects, in The Netherlands during the last decade the STSD paradigm has moved towards a management science approach, covering more relevant systems aspects (production, control, information), including different levels of aggregation (micro, meso and macro level in the organization and its relevant environment) and at the same time combining design content (integration of tasks in self-controlled organizational units) and process (training for self-design, organizational learning).

Dutch STSD paradigm

Contemporary Dutch STDS can best be characterized as a mixture of up-to-date systems concepts and an integrated whole of various design aspects and management science techniques, applied in a participative design context. The modern Dutch STSD variant covers all necessary ingredients: basic socio-technical systems theory, including level-independent concepts (Van Assen 1980; De Sitter 1982, 1989; Van Assen and Van Eijnatten 1983; Van Eijnatten and Otten 1985; De Sitter *et al.* 1986; Van Amelsvoort 1989); an elaborated action methodology (Van Strien 1986; Den Hertog and Van Assen 1988; Van Eijnatten and Hoevenaars 1989); tailor-made research instruments (Van Eijnatten, 1985, 1986, 1987a; Pot *et al.* 1989a,b); and dedicated participative design strategies (Buyse and Van Eijnatten 1987; Den Hertog and Danklaar 1989). Dutch STSD uses a multi-level strategy, carefully combining task design (quality of work) with organization design (quality of organization). Semi-autonomous functioning has been generalized to departments, product lines and business units. The journal *Gedrag en Organisatie* (Behaviour and Organization) published a special issue on Dutch STDS in 1989. An English language monograph on the 'Dutch Variant' is also available (De Sitter *et al.* 1990).

NEW STSD METHOD

An analytical model for more integral organizational (re)design

In this chapter we will concentrate on the issue of a (re)design implementation logic. A multi-level model for more integral organizational (re)design is proposed, containing a mixture of (re)design ends, (re)design means and (re)design processes (see Figure 9.1). Central in the model is the so-called '(re)design interface' in which ends, means and processes are brought together to bring about the factual (re)design intervention. The model specifies three main entries to this (re)design interface: environment, knowledge and methodology.

- The environmental entry produces market requirements and functional claims to guide design ends for the (re)design intervention. These claims are normative in character.
- The knowledge entry specifies theories, practices and conceptual organizational paradigms to deliver design means for the (re)design intervention. These content theories are supportive in character.
- The methodology entry consists of action planning procedures and participative methods/techniques for (re)designing, in order to support the process of (re)design intervention.

Modern Dutch STSD method – here it is stressed again – is a mixture of content and process: it contains both rules and procedures based on structural paradigms arising from several key disciplines (including manage-

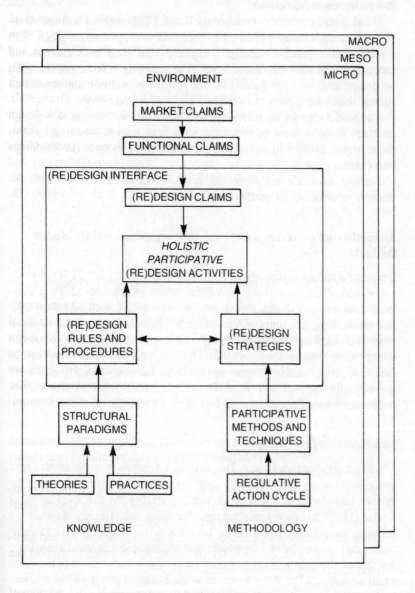

Figure 9.1 An analytical model for more integral organizational (re)design
Source: Van Eijnatten *et al.* (1988)

ment science, industrial engineering and accountancy), and (re)design strategies based on participative methods and techniques within a regulative action cycle framework.

What is really new in contemporary Dutch STSD method is the achievement of a proper balance of an up-to-date structural systems paradigm with a participative process paradigm, explicitly stressing both content and process on the same advanced level. The resulting holistic participative (re)design activities are guided by the normative multiple environmental claims, which have been analysed and given a concrete form.

The model stresses the multi-level quality of organization (re)design: the interface problem must be simultaneously dealt with at macro, meso and micro levels, in order to account for the actual complexity of the (re)design intervention.

Leaving aside the environmental and knowledge entries, we will continue by elaborating the methodological entry.

A tentative proposal for a more integral organizational (re)design method

Because of earlier-mentioned deficiencies in the traditional STSD method, a new method for integral organizational (re)design is proposed. To guarantee a more explicit design orientation, the new STSD method follows the five methodological steps of Van Strien's regulative cycle. Each of those steps is divided into smaller portions such that the new method contains a total of sixteen steps (see figure 9.2). The new method not only emphasizes the micro level, but also incorporates the meso and macro level to guarantee an integrative approach. It is also explicitly participative in character: a (re)design team of organizational members is trained to do the self-design.

Identification of the problem

1 Global strategic analysis The first step comprises a global strategic analysis of the system on a macro level. At this stage it is important that the system boundaries are widely chosen, preferably on the level of what Kotler (1988) has called the 'strategic business unit' (p. 39). Basically, a strategic business unit is a single business or collection of related businesses that can be planned separately and, in principle, can stand alone from the rest of the company. It has its own competitors which it is trying to equal or surpass. For the selected strategic business unit a global analysis has to be done with respect to environmental demands, and the consequences of these for the (re)design of the system. It is important during this stage to start specifying the environmental demands in terms of market

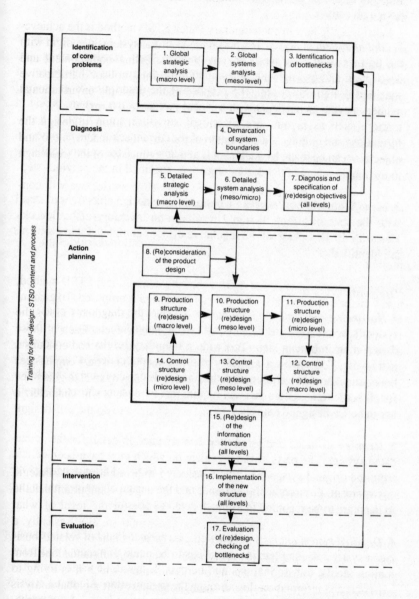

Figure 9.2 A tentative proposal for a more integral organizational (re)design method

claims with respect to controllability, flexibility and quality of work. In the succeeding phases of the regulative cycle these functional claims serve as design objectives.

2 Global system analysis The second step is a global system analysis of the business unit on a meso or departmental level, starting with a pure description and ending with an estimation of the current achievement in specified design objectives. The purpose of the description is to provide insiders as well as outsiders with a global picture of the system, taking in matters such as layout, organizational structure, main inputs, transformations and outputs. An estimation of the current achievement in design objectives can be made by analysing if and how much the system conforms to the requirements of the design objectives specified in the previous step.

3 Identification of bottlenecks Contrasting the design objectives of step 1 with the state of affairs in step 2 results in an inventory of bottlenecks. Herewith the first phase of the regulative cycle is completed: the problems are identified.

Diagnosis

4 Narrowing the system's boundaries To start the diagnostic phase, the system's boundaries are demarcated. Accurately demarcating the boundaries is an important step. Too wide a boundary results in unnecessary extra work. Too narrow a boundary results in incorrect design choices. The boundaries should be chosen such that the (re)design can provide a solution for all bottlenecks. Often this will require that the system chosen originally has to be (re)designed entirely.

5 Detailed strategic analysis Step 1 is repeated in detail for the demarcated system. The parts of the organization which may have been deleted from the original system are now considered to be additional parts of the environment. Environmental demands and the design objectives belonging to them are to be recorded in as much detail as possible.

6 Detailed system analysis Now step 2 is repeated in detail for the demarcated system. A complete inventory has to be made of material and information inputs, transformations and outputs. It has to be established how materials and information flow through the organization. All decision tasks have to be specified within the context of regulation loops. An inventory has to be made of all norms and of all supportive tasks. With the help of all these data it has to be established who performs what tasks. Finally a detailed description has to be made of layout, organizational structure and units, and product design.

7 Diagnosis and specification of (re)design objectives The data collected in step 6 are used to determine the exact causes of the bottlenecks specified in step 3. At this point the semi-autonomous (re)design team has detailed knowledge of the environmental demands (step 5) and of the causes of current problems. These insights into the system can be used to detail the (re)design objectives further. With this full description of the (re)design objectives the diagnostic phase is completed.

Action planning

8 Reconsideration of the product design A good, efficiently constructed product is of vital importance. In this step an attempt is made to reduce the number of components of the product and to minimize the number of manufacturing steps, to prepare for easier making (design for production).

9–11 Planning the (re)design of the production structure The (re)design of the production structure has to be done on all levels, planned in a top-down sequence. To start the planning of the action process, first the macro level has to be (re)designed (step 9). Next the production structure on the meso level is prepared for (re)construction (step 10). Finally the micro level production organization is (re)structured (step 11). In general the (re)design team will parallelize on the macro level, segmentize on the meso level, and build in operational flexibility on the micro level.

12–14 Planning the (re)design of the decision and control structure The (re)design of the decision and control structure is also done on all levels, but in reverse order (bottom-up). Starting on the micro level (step 12), the planning of the (re)design is continued on the meso level (step 13). The (re)design of the decision and control structure is completed on the macro level (step 14). In general the (re)design team will allocate decision powers as close as possible to the point where the problems originate.

15 Planning the (re)design of the information structure The (re)design of the information structure should not be started before the planning of the new production and control structure has been satisfactorily finished. How this can be done is still the subject of study (Van Eijnatten and Loeffen 1990). With this step, the action planning phase is completed.

Intervention

16 Implementing the plans This step has many facets. From a socio-technical point of view this step contains the actual building up of the planned production and decision (i.e. control) structures and information systems, in close co-operation with users and specialists.

Evaluation

17 Checking of bottlenecks After implementing the new system, an evaluation has to take place in terms of the (re)design objectives. If discrepancies are found, adjustments have to be made by starting a new regulative cycle.

A training programme to master modern STSD concepts, rules and procedures supports the (re)design team in the same way as used to occur in the participative design tradition. Training of process and content matter is seen as an essential condition for effective self-(re)design and organizational learning (De Sitter *et al.* 1990).

CASE ILLUSTRATION

To illustrate the first three phases of the method, a fictitious but as realistic as possible simulated model redesign is presented. The actual case (desk-chair production) is borrowed from a redesign exercise which arose in the context of an STSD training course (Van Amelsvoort and Vermeulen 1988). The case was originally developed by Van Amelsvoort and Vossen (1981). The stated problem is a cautious abstraction of a real-life project. The actual design solution was taken from a case study report of a student design team (Adams *et al.* 1988).

The redesign planning case concerns a small factory producing several kinds of chair in a rural production location employing some 130 workers, mainly local personnel. The original management team, members of the same family, had recently been replaced following amalgamation with a large office furniture manufacturer. The plant had been very unsuccessful, financially, in the past decade. The new management team wished to make a fresh start and called for an integral organizational renewal project. A company redesign team had been formed as a 'deep slice' (Emery and Emery 1974), containing members drawn from all levels of the manu-facturing plant. The redesign team had been thoroughly trained for self-design by an authorized external STSD training agency.

A global strategic analysis (step 1), carried out with some help from the senior consultant of a training agency, revealed that the production organization was confronted with rapidly changing product demands, such as customers' requirements for more product varieties, higher and more constant product quality, lower prices and earlier delivery times. Also the labour market had changed. More educated employees were presenting themselves, asking for more challenging jobs with 'whole' tasks, including all kinds of self-control and decentralized decision making. This multitude of environmental claims was operationalized by the redesign team as three basic functional requirements: higher flexibility in products and production process, higher controllability of the production process, and better quality of work. A flexible production process would enable the production departments to produce several product varieties, without taking too much time to change from one to another. A controllable production process would give the production department the capacity to control for variations in inputs, transformations and outputs. Quality of work would mean employees being offered work structures in which flexible allocation of individual tasks is possible, involving control of processes, and individual discretion.

The specification of the more concrete redesign parameters by the redesign team can be highlighted as follows. For our illustrative case a flexibility redesign parameter was, among other things, minimal throughput and delivery times for all product variants. A controllability redesign parameter included, a minimal number of hierarchical levels, and small units with appropriate decision facilities. A quality of work redesign parameter involved integration of non-decision and decision tasks, and loose co-ordination of people and machines.

After having translated the functional claims into more concrete redesign objectives for the organization, the redesign team continued with a global system analysis, which revealed a description of the existing design situation (step 2). The production process occurred in three shifts during a five-day cycle. Basic transformations were carried out in separate departments, involving sawing, bending, cleaning, welding, finishing, painting, varnishing, drying, assembling and packing. Some seventy-five workers were concerned with these basic transformations. Stocks of three days' work functioned as a buffer between the functional departments. Some fifty-five employees took charge of other functions: maintenance, planning and scheduling, buying, quality control, selling, marketing, developing new products and production methods, efficiency improvement, finance and administration, information services, personnel management, and physical distribution. Each staff member/department made decisions about only one aspect of the production organization. The organization chart showed six hierarchical layers, ranging from chief executive officer to the shop-floor workers.

The functioning of the production organization had been very disappointing. At the time the market was expanding, sales fell by some 10 per cent. Market share dropped from 11 to 6 per cent; costs rose more than 30 per cent. About 10 per cent of the previous year's production showed quality deficiencies, while only 25 per cent of the production orders could be delivered within two weeks. Most client orders had been delivered late, some more than five weeks after the due date. Personnel figures also scored badly: absenteeism had reached the astronomical level of some 11 per cent of total working time, 5 per cent being considered normal for the industry. A couple of interviews with production personnel revealed that employees took no pride in the job they had to perform. Needless to say, the plant eventually got into serious trouble: year after year, production suffered more severe losses. An amalgamation offer could no longer be resisted.

Summarizing, the global system analysis carried out by the redesign team revealed serious drawbacks on all specified parameters. Principal bottlenecks (step 3) included over-long feedback loops, too many hier-archical levels, over-long throughput and delivery times, too close integration of people and machines, and complete separation of decision and non-decision tasks. The symptoms described were indeed preventing the realization of a desired future, put forward in the requirements document of the redesign team, which was very much welcomed by the new executive management team.

The diagnostic phase consisted of the following. First, a re-examination of the selection of the system boundaries (step 4) did not result in any alterations. The chair production plant as a whole was selected for reorganization purposes. A detailed strategic analysis (step 5) gave the redesign team some additional insights in structural and functional deficiencies, as perceived by customers, for instance. Additional information on the position of the firm in the office chair market revealed that contemporary profit chances in upholstered chairs were far better than for plastic desk chairs. Other discussions with former customers ultimately showed that the firm's image suffered most because of unreliable delivery times and the absolutely impractical standard delivery quantity of six chairs.

During the detailed system analysis (step 6) the causes of insufficient flexibility, controllability and quality of work were pinpointed. The product apparently was built up from some nineteen parts. This observation prompted a closer look at the appropriateness of the design for production. The factory layout also called for reconsideration. Control requirements had been needlessly enlarged by creating small functional departments in separate rooms. The prevailing organization of the technical process obscured the picture of order status and drastically increased order throughput times.

With respect to ineffective control, the following causes were detected:

missing or over-extended feedforward, feedback and boundary transaction loops; missing or outdated production norms; too great a distance between operative employees and staff members; no decision power on the shop-floor; and too complex a layout. All product varieties had the same inconveniently arranged material flow, and boundaries of units were judged illogical: dependent employees had been allocated to different groups, and independent employees had been allocated to the same group. The separation of decision and non-decision tasks had led to a situation in which manufacturing employees were dependent on staff members who worked only on the day shift. During evening and night shifts this situation became especially problematic, because quality and order scheduling problems had to be tackled by the uninformed supervisors. This bottleneck added to further quality problems and increased throughput times.

Ending the diagnostic phase (step 7) the redesign team concluded that the way in which the product and production process structure was originally designed called for some extra control requirements. Intelligent redesign should make it possible to reduce those requirements. Concerning process redesign, order flow could be simplified by logical grouping. Concerning product redesign, design for production could lessen the total number of parts, while abandoning the unsaleable plastic models could further reduce control requirements.

The redesign team also came up with a number of ideas concerning the means of control. These means would be reallocated in such a way that all kinds of disturbances could be intercepted and controlled as close to their source as possible. Actual means of control could be increased by introducing an information supply system on the shop-floor, or by allocating more decision power to lower organizational levels. The redesign team developed and accepted the idea that by better balancing of the means of control with respect to control requirements, a better functioning organization results.

The action planning phase started with a reconsideration of product design (step 8). Although the modular design was appropriate for all product variants, minor construction changes could simplify assembly considerably. Bolts and nuts could be replaced by a clever design change; this innovation resulted in a reduction of eight out of nineteen parts! The action planning for the production process structure at a macro (or plant) level (step 9) resulted in no changes at all. On this level the organization of the technical processes was judged appropriate. The actual reorganization started at a meso (or departmental) level (step 10). The redesign team divided the system into two main segments: a components department and an assembly and packaging department. Within the latter, the team created two parallel flows: one for wooden chairs and the other for upholstered chairs. The reorganization of the production process structure was finished on a micro (or shop-floor) level (step 11) by tuning the individual tasks to the production means. Machines were grouped together in such a way that units were formed, combining several transformations, obviating the need for buffer stocks in the production of components. Individual tasks were grouped together in such a way that production units could function relatively autonomously. For instance one unit was planned to make black and grey frames, while another unit produced brown and white ones.

The planning of the decision and control structure redesign started on a micro (or shop-floor) level (step 12) by allocating operational flexibility to each process segment or unit. As much decision power as possible was allocated to this lowest organizational level, aimed at guaranteeing that workers within each segment would have the flexibility to solve as much production variance as possible. For example, for the 'black and grey unit' in the components department, this redesign measure resulted in 'whole tasks', where employees would not only produce black and grey frames, but would also control the amount of stock and decide when to replenish it. They would be equipped with simple repair tools in order to tackle small machine breakdowns, and would be made responsible for the quality of the frames. Clear targets were to be assigned to them with respect to the level of product quality and the quantity they had to reach. At the same time they would be set financial budgets, which should not be exceeded. All employees would receive tailor-made training.

The planning of the decision and control structure redesign on a meso (or department) level (step 13) resulted in an organization hierarchy with only four levels. The allocation of employees to staff functions was reduced, and separate staff departments were grouped together.

The planning of the decision and control structure redesign on a macro (or plant) level (step 14) resulted in allocating strategic decision power to the top level of the business unit. The executive management team should have one eye directed at the market and the other focused on the plant itself. It was ensured that the reorganization proposal should include a plan for up-to-date technical redesign of the information system (step 15), so that necessary information would reach those employees who had the decision power to act on that information.

The redesign plan was successfully implemented by the team in close collaboration with the workers involved (step 16).

In Table 9.1 some key attributes of the old and new structures are compared. It is predicted that the new system would function better in all sorts of ways (step 17). Evidence from similar real project evaluation studies is encouraging (Den Hertog *et al.* 1991).

Table 9.1 A comparison of some key attributes of the old and new structures of the desk-chair firm.

Key attributes	Old situation	New situation
number of product parts	19	11
type of process flow organization (production structure)	one flow for all orders (complex flow)	partly parallelized and segmented flow (simple flow)
buffer stocks between process steps	yes, many between each step	no, hardly any
type of work organization	functional structure	product structure
number of personnel	75 direct 55 indirect	90 direct 40 indirect
allocation of decision tasks (control structure)	no decision tasks allocated at the shop-floor level	quality and quantity decision tasks at the shop-floor
number of hierarchical levels	6	4
supply of information (information structure)	no information supply to the shop-floor	own information system at the shop-floor

DISCUSSION

The proposed method for modern STSD has been developed as a practical tool, which can be used in (re)design projects. As stated earlier, it is an intricate part of the Dutch STSD package, which also contains elaborated structural systems concepts, (re)design principles advocating more integration of aspects, and procedures supporting participative self-(re)design process.

At first sight the proposed method looks very much the same as its famous predecessors like the admired and abused 'nine-step method' (Foster 1967; Emery and Trist 1978). On closer inspection, however, there are some striking differences.

First, the proposed method for modern STSD clearly has an iterative character (see Figure 9.2). This is true for the cycle as a whole, as for the constituent phases. Therefore, in practice each project can have a unique intricate pattern of specific iterations of 'successive' steps and phases. In each stage techniques and instruments which are already available can be used and may improve the efficiency of the distinguished steps. We list some of them briefly for illustration purposes. System analysis (SA) can support the problem identification and diagnostic phase. A Dutch steady-state system model (In 't Veld 1978; Van Eijnatten 1987b) governs the descriptive and evaluative process on all the levels of aggregation (macro, meso, micro). Socio-technical process analysis (STPA) and socio-technical task analysis (STTA) can be used for task analysis at the micro level during diagnosis and evaluation (Van Eijnatten 1985, 1986). Recently, alternative Dutch task analysis instrumentation has become available (Pot *et al.* 1989a,b). Stream Analysis (Porras 1987) may be of great help in identifying core problems during the diagnostic phase, as well as in planning the (re)design actions and tracking the interventions in the action planning and intervention phase. TIED analysis may be very useful in the action planning stage (Schumacher 1975, 1979, 1983; Van Amelsvoort 1987). This (re)design technique governs segmentation of production flows, while controlling for machine interaction, process interaction and interference. Group technology is a similar technique for planning the parallelization of factory/ manufacturing flows (Burbidge 1975, 1979; Aguren and Egren 1980). Production flow analysis (Burbidge 1975; De Witte 1980) can be used to identify routes of production flows in the planning phase.

Second, we want to stress the importance of technical (re)design of the production process. Technical analysis once again has become vital in modern STSD. Of course, the whole array of OD techniques are good supporters of the diagnostic, action planning and intervention stages in the regulative design-oriented cycle, from process consultation (Harvey and Brown 1988) to user participation and quality cycle techniques (Juran 1978; Dewar 1980). These techniques include pareto analysis, Ishikawa's 'fishbone', and brainstorming. Soft systems methodology (Checkland 1979a,b, 1990a,b) can be used by all parties to organize and manage the process in each stage of the regulative cycle.

Third the proposed method for modern STSD basically promotes controllable organizations and democratic work structures at the same time. Although for traditional socio-technologists there is something of a paradox in this statement, we cannot elaborate on this here. Suffice it to say that Dutch STSD is trying to achieve a proper balance between variety *increasing* measures, like segmentation of flows constituting 'whole tasks', and variety *decreasing* measures, like inputs selection by means of parallelization of process flow. The argument is discussed in more detail in De Sitter *et al.* (1990).

Fourth the proposed method for modern STSD basically supports a multi-level approach. The parallelization of flows is advocated on the next higher level to segmentation. A strategic analysis of the system at a macro level may reveal the environmental demands of the near future. In this context we acknowledge the network approach of the Search Conference (Emery, M. 1989) as a means of achieving desirable outcomes under turbulent field conditions. In Holland an STSD (re)design tradition is gaining ground in which technological, social and organizational innovations go hand in hand. A series of more integral organizational renewal projects is being carried out along the theoretical and methodological lines of the approach to flexible productive systems (AFPS).

Fifth the proposed method for modern STSD is not necessarily linear in nature. The 'successive' steps do not prescribe a time order. They can also be used as a checklist to manage interconnections. The order of steps is indicative of available degrees of freedom for change. For instance, a change in production structure necessarily will urge forward changes in control and information structures, while a change in information structure is not expected to affect the production and control structure at all (see Figure 9.2). The steps stress dependencies in the (re)design process.

Finally, the proposed method for modern STSD is, of course, highly political in nature. Although it must be emphasized that different parties use it as a connecting and integrative device, insufficient control of that process can easily result in coalition formation. Also there will be some sort of paradoxical self-selection process among firms with respect to adoption. Because the method basically supports a democratic approach, organizations which want to adopt it will already feel sympathy for or will have invested in the type of change which modern STSD intends to accomplish.

In this chapter we have presented organizational (re)design methodology as explicitly advocating restructuring of construction at different levels of aggregation. The method to some extent supports 'manageable change and innovation', within the context of the integral organizational renewal of the total firm. The method is based on a socio-technical perspective which guarantees a better focus on the interactions between individual, group and organization in a highly automated work environment.

REFERENCES

Ackoff, R.L. and Emery, F.E. (1972) *On Purposeful Systems*, Chicago: Aldine-Atherton.

Adams, A., Hoevenaars, A.M., Nijnens, P. and Wierst, W. van (1988) *A Case Study Report of an Actual Redesign Solution for a New Production Organization*, Eindhoven: Eindhoven University of Technology, Faculty of Industrial Engineering and Management Science (Dutch Language).

Agurén, S. and Edgren, J. (1980) *New Factories: Job Design through Factory Planning in Sweden*, Stockholm: SAF Press.

Allegro, J.T. (1973) *Socio-Technical Organization Development*, Leiden: Stenfert Kroese (Dutch Language).

Allegro, J.T. and Vries, E. de (1979) *Project: Humanization of Work and Shared Control at Central Beheer*, Den Haag: COB/SER (Dutch Language).

Amelsvoort, P. van (1987) 'The Schumacher Approach to Integral Design of Flow Production Structures Starting from a Line Situation: A Revision and

Adjustment of the Original Schumacher Approach', Den Bosch: Koers B.V., internal paper (Dutch Language).

Amelsvoort, P. van (1989) 'A Sociotechnical Model for the Structure of Control: I'm a Genius, that's Why I am Working in the Production Group', *G&O: Dutch Journal of Behavior and Organization* 2(4/5): 253–67 (Dutch Language).

Amelsvoort, P. van and Vermeulen, A.A.M. (1988) *A Course of the Theory and Practice of Sociotechnical Design*, Eindhoven: Eindhoven University of Technology, Faculty of Industrial Engineering and Management Science (Dutch Language).

Amelsvoort, P. van and Vossen, H.P. (1981) *A Training Exercise in Sociotechnical Design*, Den Bosch: Koers, BV (Dutch Language).

Ashby, W.R. (1958) *An Introduction to Cybernetics*, London: Chapman and Hall.

Assen, A. van (1980) 'Organization Design: An Analytical Model for Job Consultation and Work Structuring', in A. van Assen, J.F. den Hertog and P.L. Koopman (eds) *Organizing on a Human Scale*, Alphen aan den Rijn: Samsom (Dutch Language).

Assen, A. van and Eijnatten, F.M. van (1983) 'A New Paradigm for Work Design', paper presented at the First West European Conference on the Psychology of Work and Organization, Nijmegen, The Netherlands, March 28.

Beinum, H.J.J. van (1963) *An Organization on the Move; A Social-psychological Field Experiment at Postcheque-en Girodienst*, Leiden: Stenfert Kroese (Dutch Language).

Beinum, H.J.J. van (1986) *The Warp and Weft of QWL*, Toronto: Ontario Quality of Working Life Centre.

Beinum, H.J.J. van, Gils, M.R. van and Verhagen, E.J. (1968) *Task Design and Work Organization: A Sociotechnical Field Experiment*, Den Haag: COP (Dutch Language).

Bertalanffy, L. von (1950) 'The Theory of Open Systems in Physics and Biology', *Science* 3 (3.1): 23–9.

Beurle, R.L. (1962) 'Functional Organization in Random Networks', in H.V. Foerster and G.W. Zopf (eds) *Principles of Self-organization*, Oxford: Pergamon.

Burbidge, J.L. (1975) *The Introduction of Group Technology*, London: Buttler and Tanner.

Burbidge, J.L. (1979) *Group Technology in the Engineering Industry*, London: Mechanical Engineering Publications.

Buyse, J.J. and Eijnatten, F.M. van (1986) 'Pseudo-autonomous Workgroups: The Challenge to improve the Quality of Work and Organization in Truck Assembly', paper presented at the Third West-European Conference on the Psychology of Work and Organization, Antwerp, Belgium, April 13–15.

Checkland, P.B. (1979a) 'Techniques in Soft Systems Practice. Part 1: Systems Diagrams – Some Tentative Guidelines', *Journal of Applied Systems Analysis* 6: 33–40.

Checkland, P.B. (1979b) 'Techniques in Soft Systems Practice. Part 2: Building Conceptual Models', *Journal of Applied Systems Analysis* 6: 41–9.

Checkland, P.B. (1990a) 'Techniques in Soft Systems Practice. Part 3: Monitoring and Control in Conceptual Models and in Evaluation Studies', *Journal of Applied Systems Analysis* 17: 29–37.

Checkland, P.B. (1990b) 'Techniques in Soft Systems Practice. Part 4: Conceptual Model Building Revisited', *Journal of Applied Systems Analysis* 17: 39–52.

Cherns, A.B. (1976) 'The Principles of Sociotechnical Design', *Human Relations* 29(8): 783–92.

Cherns, A.B. (1987) 'Principles of Sociotechnical Design Revisited', *Human Relations* 40(3): 153–62.

Cummings, T.G. (1976) 'Sociotechnical Systems: An Intervention Strategy', in W.W. Burke (ed.) *Current Issues and Strategies in Organization Development*, New York: Human Sciences Press: 187–213.

Cummings, T.G. and Srivastva, S. (1977) *Management of Work: A Sociotechnical Systems Approach*, Kent, OH: Kent University Press.

Cummings, T.G., Molloy, E.S. and Glen, R. (1977) 'A Methodological Critique of Fifty-Eight Selected Work Experiments', *Human Relations* 30(8): 675–708.

Davis, L.E. and Canter, R.R. (1956) 'Job Design', *Journal of Industrial Engineering* 6: 3–8.

Dewar, D.L. (1980) 'International Significance of the QC Circle Movement', *Quality Progress* 13(11): 18–22.

Eijnatten, F.M. van (1985) 'STTA: Towards a New Work Structuring Paradigm', Nijmegen, Catholic University, doctoral thesis (Dutch Language).

Eijnatten, F.M. van (1986) 'The Approach to Flexible Productive Systems (AFPS). Methods: 1. Design Philosophy; 2. System Analysis (SA): 3. Socio-technical Process Analysis (STPA); 4. Socio-technical Task Analysis (STTA); 5. Socio-technical Design (STD)', Nijmegen: Catholic University, internal paper (Dutch Language).

Eijnatten, F.M. van (1987a) 'The Approach to Flexible Productive Systems (AFPS): Design Philosophy', in A.L.M. Knaapen, W.J.M. Meekel, R.J. Tissen and R.H.W. Vinke (eds) *Handbook Methods, Techniques and Analyses*, Deventer: Kluwer (Dutch Language).

Eijnatten, F.M. van (1987b) 'System Analysis for the Personnel Manager' in A.L.M. Knappen, W.J.M. Meekel, R.J. Tissen and R.H.W. Vinke (eds) *Handbook Methods, Techniques and Analyses*, Deventer: Kluwer (Dutch Language).

Eijnatten, F.M. van (1989) 'What about Design-Oriented Research: A Methodological Reconnaissance', Eindhoven: Eindhoven University of Technology, Faculty of Industrial Engineering and Management Science, working paper (Dutch Language).

Eijnatten, F.M. van (1990a) 'Classical Socio-technical Systems Design: The Sociotechnical Design Paradigm of Organization', Eindhoven/Maastricht: Eindhoven University of Technology, Faculty of Industrial Engineering and Management Science, Monograph BDT/T&A 001; University of Limburg, Maastricht Economic Research Institute of Innovation and Technology, Research Memorandum 90-005.

Eijnatten, F.M. van (1990b) *A Bibliography of the Classical Sociotechnical Systems Paradigm*, Eindhoven: Eindhoven University of Technology, Faculty of Industrial Engineering and Management Science, report EUT/BDK/39.

Eijnatten, F.M. van (1990c) 'The End of the Labour Process Movement and the Sociotechnical Systems Approach: A Subject Matter Which Should be Disputed or Tried out in Practice?' *TVA: Dutch Journal of Labour Studies* 6(2): 46–61 (Dutch Language).

Eijnatten, F.M. van (1991) 'The Development of the Sociotechnical Paradigm: From Autonomous Workgroup towards Democratic Dialogue', in P.J.D. Drenth, H. Thierry and Ch.J. de Wolff (eds) *Handbook Work and Organizational Psychology*, Deventer: Van Loghum Slaterus.

Eijnatten, F.M. van Hoevenaars, A.M. (1989) 'Modern Sociotechnology in the Netherlands: Recent Methodology Developments on Behalf of Integral Organization Redesign', *G&O: Dutch Journal of Behavior and Organization* 2(4/5): 289–304 (Dutch Language).

Eijnatten, F.M. van and Loeffen, J.M.J. (1990) 'Some Comments about Information Systems Design for Production Control from the Perspective of an Integral Sociotechnical Organization Philosophy', paper presented at the International Conference 'Computer, Man and Organization', Nivelles, Belgium, May 9–11.

Eijnatten, F.M. van and Otten, J.H.M. (1985) 'Contributions to automation processes from the perspective of a Changing Work Structuring Paradigm', paper presented at the Second West European Conference on the Psychology of Work and Organization, Aachen, West Germany, April 1–3.

Eijnatten, F.M. van, Hoevenaars, A.M. and Rutte, C.G. (1990) 'Integral Designing of Organizations for New Technologies', in J.F. den Hertog and F.M. van Eijnatten (eds) *Managing Technological Innovation*, Assen: Van Gorcum (Dutch Language).

Eijnatten, F.M. van, Rutte, C.G. and Hoevenaars, A.M. (1989) 'The Approach to Flexible Productive Systems: Contemporary Developments towards a Multlevel Model for Design-oriented Research', paper presented at the Fourth West European Conference on the Psychology of Work and Organization, Cambridge, April 10.

Eijnatten, F.M. van, Keijsers, G.J., Otten, J.H.M. and Buyse, J.J. (1986) *Automation means Reorganizing: Lines of Sight for Personnel Management*, Deventer: Kluwer (Dutch Language).

Emery, F.E. (1959) *Characteristics of Sociotechnical Systems*, London: Tavistock Institute, document No. 527.

Emery, F.E. (1963) *Some Hypotheses about the Way in which Tasks may be more Effectively put together to make Jobs*, London: Tavistock Institute, document T.176.

Emery, F.E. (1977) 'The Emergence of a New Paradigm of Work', Canberra: Australian National University, Centre for Continuing Education, internal paper.

Emery, F.E. and Emery, M. (1974) *Participative Design: Work and Community Life*, Canberra: Australian National University, Centre for Continuing Education. Also published in Oslo: AFI (1975).

Emery, F.E. and Emery, M. (1975) 'Guts and Guidelines for raising the Quality of Work Life', in D. Gunzburg (ed.) *Bringing Work to Life: The Australian Experience*, Melbourne: Cheshire Publications.

Emery, F.E. and Emery, M. (1976) *A Choice of Futures: To Enlighten or Inform*, Leiden: Nijhoff.

Emery, F.E. and Thorsrud, E.L. (1964) *Form and Content of Industrial Democracy. Some Experiments from Norway and other European Countries*, Oslo: Oslo University Press. Also published in London: Tavistock (1969) and in Assen: Van Gorcum (1969).

Emery, F.E. and Thorsrud, E.L. (1976) *Democracy at Work. The Report of the Norwegian Industrial Democracy Program*, Leiden: Nijhoff. Also published in Canberra: Australian National University, Centre for Continuing Education (1975).

Emery, F.E. and Trist, E.L. (1978) 'Analytical Model for Sociotechnical Systems', in W.A. Pasmore and J.J.Sherwood (eds) *Sociotechnical Systems: a Sourcebook*, La Jolla, California: University Associates.

Emery, M. (1982) 'Searching: for New Directions, in New Ways, for New Times' (Revised edn), Canberra: Australian National University, Centre for Continuing Education, Occasional Paper No. 12. Also published in J.W. Sutherland (ed.) (1978) *A Management Handbook for Administrators*, New York: Van Nostrand.

Emery, M. (1989) *Participative Design for Participative Democracy*, Canberra: Australian National University, Centre for Continuing Education.

Engelstad, P.H. (1990) *The Evolution of Network Strategies in Action Research supported Sociotechnical Redesign Programs in Scandinavia*, Oslo: Work Research Institute/University of Karlstad, Sweden, Paper presented at the National Academy of Management Meeting, San Francisco, US, August 12–15.

Foster, M. (1967) 'Developing an Analytical Model for Socio-technical Analysis', London: Tavistock Institute, Document HRC7.

Gustavsen, B. (1985) 'Workplace Reform and Democratic Dialogue', *Economic and Industrial Democracy*, 6, London: Sage.

Gustavsen, B. (1988) *Creating Broad Changes in Working Life, The LOM Programme*, Toronto: Ontario QWL Centre.

Hackman, J.R. (1981) 'Sociotechnical Systems Theory: A Commentary' in A.H. van der Ven and W.F. Joyce (eds) *Perspectives on Organization Design and Behavior*, New York: Wiley: 76–87.

Harvey, D.F. and Brown, D.R. (1988) *An Experimental Approach to Organization Development*, Englewood Cliffs, NJ: Prentice Hall.

Herbst, P.G. (1974) *Sociotechnical Design: Strategies in Multidisciplinary Research*, London: Tavistock Publications.

Hertog, J.F. den (1977) *Work Structuring*, Groningen: Wolters Noordhof (Dutch Language).

Hertog, J.F. den and Assen, A. van (1988) 'The Methodology of Design-Oriented Research: A Reconnaissance on Behalf of the Research Promotion Programme Technology, Work and Organization', Maastricht: University of Limburg, Limburg Institute for Business and Economic Research, Internal Paper no. 4 (Dutch Language).

Hertog, J.F. den and Danklaar, B. (1989) 'The Sociotechnic Adjusted', *G&O: Dutch Journal of Behaviour and Organization* 2(4/5): 269–87.

Hertog, J.F. den *et al.* (1991) 'Integral Organizational Renewal: Cases Illustrating the Application of the Approach [working title]', Maastricht/Den Bosch, University of Limburg MERIT/Koers B.V., (Dutch Language, in press).

Hill, P. (1971) *Towards a New Philosophy of Management*, London: Gower Press.

Juran, J.M. (1978) 'International Significance of the QC Circle Movement: Can Non-Japanese Cultures apply this Concept of using Work Force Creativity to Improve Company Performance?', paper presented at the International QC Circle Convention, Tokyo, October 16.

Kotler, P. (1988) *Marketing Management: Analysis, Planning and Control*, Englewood Cliffs: Prentice-Hall.

Kuipers, H. and Amelsvoort, P. van (1990) *Organizing Quick repartee: Introduction to Sociotechnology as Integral Theory*, Deventer: Kluwer (Dutch Language).

Kuipers, H. and Rutte, C.G. (1987) 'Principles of Sociotechnical Design: An Analysis', in *Proceedings NOBO Conference on Industrial Engineering and Management Sciences*, Rotterdam (Dutch Language).

Lilienfeld, R. (1978) *The Rise of Systems Theory*: An Ideological Analysis, New York: Wiley.

Litterer, J.A. (ed.) (1963) *Organizations: Systems, Control and Adaptation, vols I and II*, New York: Wiley.

Pasmore, W., Francis, C., Haldeman, J. and Shani, A. (1982) 'Sociotechnical Systems: A North American Reflection on Empirical Studies of the Seventies', *Human Relations* 35(12): 1179–204.

Pasmore, W.A. and Sherwood, J.J. (eds) (1978) *Sociotechnical Systems: A Sourcebook*, La Jolla, California: University Associates.

Pava, C. (1986) 'Redesigning Sociotechnical Systems Design: Concepts and Methods for the 1990s', *Journal of Applied Behavioural Science* 22(3): 201–21.

Porras, J.I. (1987) *Stream Analysis: A Powerful Way to Diagnose and Manage Organizational Change*, Reading, MA: Addison-Wesley.

Pot, F.D., Peeters, M.H.H., Vaas, S., Christis, J.H.P., Middendorp, J., Fruytier, B.G.M. and Kommers, H. (1989a) 'Job Improvement and Working Environment Act', *G&O: Dutch Journal of Behaviour and Organization* 2(4/5): 361–82 (Dutch Language).

Pot, F.D., Christis, J.H.P., Fruytier, B.G.M., Kommers, H., Middendorp, J., Peeters, M.H.H. and Vaas, S. (1989b) *Job Improvement and the Organization of Work*, Voorburg: Directoraat Generaal van de Arbeid, Ministerie van Sociale Zaken en Werkgelegenheid, S71.

Schumacher, P.C. (1975) 'The Schumacher Work Structuring Method', London: Philips Electronics Industries, Central O&E Department, internal paper.

Schumacher, P.C. (1979) 'Principles of Work Organization', London: Philips Electronics Industries, Central O&E Department, internal paper.

Schumacher, P.C. (1983) *Manufacturing System Design: The Schumacher Work Structuring Methods, Steps I to VI*, Surrey/London: Philips Electronic Industries, Central O&E Department, training manual.

Sitter, L.U. de (1973) 'A System-theoretical Paradigm of Social Interaction: Towards a New Approach to Qualitative System Dynamics', *Annals of Systems Research* 3: 109–40.

Sitter, L.U. de (1982) *Towards New Factories and Offices: Production Organization and Labour Organization on a Cross-road*, Deventer: Kluwer (Dutch Language).

Sitter, L.U. de (1989) 'Modern Sociotechnology', *G&O: Dutch Journal of Behaviour and Organization* 2(4/5): 222–52.

Sitter, L.U. de and Hertog, J.F. den (1988) 'Integrated Organizational Innovation: A Structural and Strategic Framework', Maastricht: University of Limburg, MERIT, paper presented at the Conference on Technology, Organization, Job Design and Human Growth, Venice, October 10–14.

Sitter, L.U. de, Hertog, J.F. den and Eijnatten, F.M. van (1990) 'Simple Organizations, Complex Jobs: The Dutch Sociotechnical Approach', Maastricht: University of Limburg, MERIT, paper presented at the American Academy of Management Meeting, San Francisco, 12–15 August.

Sitter, L.U. de, Vermeulen, A.A.M., Amelsvoort, P. van, Geffen, L. van, Troost, P. and Verschuur, F.O. (1986) *The Flexible Business: An Integrated Approach of Flexibility, Controllability, Quality of Work and Production Automation*, Deventer: Kluwer (Dutch Language).

Sommerhoff, G. (1950) *Analytical Biology*, Oxford: Oxford University Press.

Strien, P.J. van (1975) 'Towards a Methodology of Consultative Thinking in the Social Sciences', *Dutch Journal of Psychology* 30: 601–19 (Dutch Language).

Strien, P.J. van (1986) *Practice as a Science: The Methodology of Social-scientific Actions*, Assen: Van Gorcum (Dutch Language).

Trist, E.L. (1976) 'Foreword', in G.I. Susman, *Autonomy at Work: A Sociotechnical Analysis of Participative Management*, New York: Praeger.

Trist, E.L. (1981) *The Evolution of Sociotechnical Systems: A Conceptual Framework and an Action Research Program*, Ontario: Quality of Working Life Centre/Ministry of Labour.

Trist, E.L. and Bamforth, K.W. (1951) 'Some Social and Psychological Consequences of the Longwall Method of Coal Getting', *Human Relations* 4: 3–38.

Trist, E.L., Higgin, G.W., Murray, H. and Pollock, A.B. (1963) *Organizational Choice: Capabilities of Groups at the Coal Face under Changing Technologies: the Loss, Re-discovery, and Transformation of a Work Tradition*, London: Tavistock Publications; reissued 1987, New York: Garland.

Trist, E.L. and Murray, H. (1991) *The Social Engagement of Social Science. A Tavistock Anthology, Volume II: The Socio-technical Perspective*, Philadelphia: The University of Pennsylvania Press.

Veld, J. in 't (1978) *Analysis of Organization Problems: An Application of Thinking in Terms of Systems and Processes*, Amsterdam: Elsevier (Dutch Language).

Wall, T.D., Kemp, N.J., Jackson, P.R. and Clegg, C.W. (1986) 'Outcomes of Autonomous Work Groups: A Long-term Field Experiment', *Academy of Management Journal* 29: 280–304.

Witte, J. de (1980) 'The Use of Similarity Coefficients in Production Flow Analysis', *International Journal of Production Research* 18(4): 503–14.

Zwaan, A.H. van der (1975) 'The Sociotechnical Systems Approach: A Critical Evaluation', *International Journal of Production Research* 13(2): 149–63.

NOTE

This study was partly sponsored by a grant from the Dutch Technology, Labour and Organization research promotion programme for the industrial sector.

10 The management of strategies for internal labour market flexibility

Walter S. Mueller and John L. Cordery

INTRODUCTION

Over recent years, pressure for increased flexibility within organizations has arisen from a range of factors. These include the structure of the labour market, changing attitudes towards work and productivity, new technology, and economic factors (Mueller 1991; OECD 1986; Walton and Susman 1987). Organizations have responded in part to such pressures by building flexibility into labour markets, using a variety of internal and external strategies (Curtain 1987).

Management strategies to achieve internal labour market flexibility, the focus of the current chapter, may include such initiatives as job rotation schemes, the creation of self-regulating work groups, and multi-skilling programmes (Cordery 1989). Such strategies, while improving internal labour flexibility, are also often linked to the humanization of work (Cordery 1985). For example, a common outcome of socio-technical systems approaches, which claim to balance technical and socio-psychological system needs, is the introduction of multi-skilled self-regulating teams (Cherns 1976; Cummings 1978; Wall *et al.* 1986). Given the inherent potential for conflict between organizational demands and human needs (Kelly 1978), it is important to study the implementation of such 'joint optimization' strategies. In particular, data concerning the degree of implementation of a negotiated socio-technical design may indicate the degree to which balance has been achieved, also providing clues as to the intent and realization of management strategy.

This chapter reports on a longitudinal study of the management of multi-skilled self-regulating teams within a greenfield minerals processing plant. It focuses on a combined skills development and work design initiative, which was intended to promote internal labour market flexibility while also promoting employees' quality of working life. The chapter describes why the programme was only partially implemented, and the consequences this had for the quality of working life outcomes.

THE SETTING

In this particular instance, a large multi-national corporation had sought to trial flexible internal labour market strategies within a small greenfield minerals processing site, with around 300 employees. Processing involved about twenty discrete stages. After mining, the mineral ore was brought to the site on a conveyor belt, and stockpiled for processing, which involved crushing, cleansing and chemical treatment. Each of the stages was accomplished within a self-contained, single-purpose building, connected to the others by a complex piping and pump system. Two or three production workers operated each building on a continuous shift system. At established sister sites, workers were assigned to each building by a first-line supervisor, often remaining attached to a single building for many years.

In contrast to the rigid job demarcation at these sister sites, the organization's stated aims for the greenfield site included the promotion of flexibility in the internal deployment of labour and skills, and the provision of more interesting and satisfying jobs. Following socio-technical systems analysis (Pasmore 1989) an approach to work organization and skills resource management, referred to internally as the 'team concept', was developed. Under this approach, production workers were organized into two functionally distinct teams, each responsible for separate halves of the process. Each team was to be afforded a high level of self-regulation for daily operating decisions, covering the elements listed in table 10.1.

In addition, members of each team were to be multi-skilled (trained across traditional job and craft boundaries) such that each member could perform all of the production tasks within each operating area, along with some ancillary maintenance tasks. As a strategy, multi-skilling provides functional flexibility in terms of the internal allocation of labour, work organization, and the potential to be more responsive to changing technological and environmental demands.

The multi-skilling was effected by means of a skills training system provided in two stages. First, the operator completed both general and specific training modules associated with the area for which credit was being sought. The modules were developed specifically for the organization and produced in book form, which an operator could sign for and take on to the job. The operator was then required to complete a written test, which would be administered by his first-line supervisor. The second part of the assessment involved a minimum period of time spent working on a given task or in a given operating area, and a practical assessment of

Table 10.1 Planned areas of work group autonomy

1	Allocating work (including work group administrative roles)
2	Maintaining safety and cleanliness standards
3	Maintaining a productive and healthy group climate
4	Setting work group objectives
5	Planning work priorities
6	Writing operating logs
7	Planning leave arrangements
8	Writing and approving work requests
9	Ordering operating supplies
10	Maintaining attendance and timekeeping records
11	Conducting safety meetings
12	Writing accident/incident reports
13	Reviewing technical data and solving local process problems
14	Reporting on work group performance
15	Isolating (tagging) equipment for maintenance
16	Planning and conducting training for work group members
17	Liaising directly with maintenance and other process work groups
18	Involvement in budget preparation, control and review
19	Counselling work group members on performance problems
20	Making recommendations about the hiring of new work group members

competence. This assessment was made by several part-time officers, who were usually operators nearing retirement age and who had specific expertise covering a group of areas.

Multi-skilling was rewarded by the adoption of a skills-linked reward and classification system. Instead of a number of distinct job titles linked to particular functions, a generic title of 'shift process worker' was created, with three levels defined in terms of the number of task competencies possessed. Movement between classification levels reflected an increase in the range of tasks able to be performed within the team, and was associated with an automatic pay increment. A points system was used to weight various tasks competencies, and to allow flexibility in terms of the degree of horizontal and vertical skills specialization achieved.

Within each team's area of responsibility, clusters of tasks were associated with particular physical locations. To ensure that flexibility in labour allocation could be maximized, shift process workers were to be required to rotate periodically through each of the geographic locations. Effectively, this amounted to a formal job rotation scheme, though distinct job titles were not associated with each area. Rotation ensured that employees picked up competencies through on-the-job training, that they maintained these skills, and that they could be allocated to areas according to varying operating requirements. One of the organization's stated aims was that the scheme should be under the control of the production teams from the outset.

DESIGN OF THE STUDY

A longitudinal research design backed by multiple data sources at two time periods constituted the basis for evaluating the extent to which the team concept was implemented as planned, and the impact of the overall strategy on quality of working life criteria. Data sources at these two time periods included questionnaires from all employees at the greenfield site, interviews with a random sample of operators and almost all first-line supervisors and managers, inspection of company records, participant observation, and unsystematic informal interactions with personnel in person or by telephone.

Researchers worked with an evaluation task-force comprising a representative cross-section of the workforce, including unions, during the period of the study. The task-force contributed to every phase of the study. Data reported in this study was collected eight months (Time I) and thirty months (Time III) from start-up from all personnel on site. An additional round of data collection, involving only outcome measures, was conducted nineteen months (Time II) after start-up. This was not considered for the present analysis because implementation issues were not addressed at that time.

Approximately ninety shift process workers, all male, completed questionnaires at both time periods (80 per cent response rate), and a random sample of 25 per cent were interviewed. Similar interviews were conducted with a random sample of maintenance workers, and with all first-line supervisors and managers.

FINDINGS

Degree of multi-skilling

It was expected that the degree of self-regulation experienced by shift process workers would depend on the success of the multi-skilling programme. Table 10.2 shows the increase in skills acquired as measured by the assessment points system. Time III data was collected almost two years after Time I, and it is clear that a steady increase in formal skill acquisition occurred during that time.

A team of fully multi-skilled shift process workers would have acquired 900 points. The results clearly show that only partial implementation of the multi-skilling programme had taken place within the shift process teams. From start-up, the job of control room operator was taken by experienced control room operators from other sites. These personnel were not multi-skilled, but were given an SP1 (shift process worker 1) classification on the basis of their pre-existing specialist skills, and were told that they would have to pick up the additional training and points over time in order to

Table 10.2 Acquisition of multi-skilling points by shift process workers

| | Points acquired | | |
Months after start-up	Shift process worker 3 (SP3)	Shift process worker 2 (SP2)	Shift process worker 1 (SP1)
18	29	241	243
21	76	310	281
24	75	389	321
27	105	220	445
30	145	526	467

maintain their wage standing. As a result, these personnel appear less multi-skilled than their SP2 counterparts.

Over the whole period of the study, shift process workers generally were strongly committed to the multi-skilling programme, many citing it as one of the reasons they had sought employment at the site in the first place. The guaranteed opportunity to learn and be paid for new skills was not available from any other employer in the mining sector at that time. One worker described the reasons for this:

> . . . because you change in different areas, you're learning something new all the time and it really broadens your outlook on the refinery, I think. There's a lot of opportunity there. A lot of opportunity.
>
> (Shift process worker, Time III)

However, over the three time periods, management choices appear to have played a role in limiting the extent of implementation of this design feature. This could most clearly be seen in terms of cuts to the number of training personnel and in training resources generally.

> There's not enough training available. . . . There's quite a lot of blokes been screaming about that, trying to get training and they just can't get it, to learn properly. A lot of blokes are going into some areas and then they can't do the job and they . . . get pushed out. They shouldn't be pushed out. They should have put someone in there to give them some intense training and give them a chance. . . . It is not the team pushing them. It is the other side [staff] not teaching them properly, not even trying to. Sometimes they have a [first-line supervisor] that doesn't know the job either, so he is no help. . . . Some of the boys are trained; they are OK within themselves, but when it comes to teaching somebody else, they can't do it. . . . There should be staff people available for training, intense training.
>
> (Shift process worker, Time III)

In other areas, management policy appeared to restrict worker acquisition of certain skills on the grounds that the usage would be very infrequent. Once two or three members of a team had acquired a skill, access by the remaining members to the relevant training programme seemed to be quite difficult. The relevant union felt that managers had reneged on the original agreement of unrestricted access to relevant training because they needed only two or three shift process workers with relevant skills in any team.

> In terms of other skills like crane tickets, bobcat tickets and things like that, that's zilch. We haven't even been trained yet because they reckon they haven't got time. Would be now two and a half years and I've been trying . . . . I think what they've done is got more or less one or two crane drivers on each shift . . . and I think they've just sort of been happy with that. There's been no really major attempt to try and get the shift workers through.
>
> (Shift process worker, Time III)

Although possessing a favourable attitude towards the programme, the survey results indicated that only 50 per cent of shift process workers felt that the multi-skilling programme had lived up to their early expectations.

Whilst the reining-in of opportunities for skill development may also be interpreted in terms of a management view that sufficient flexibility had been achieved by an existing combination of self-regulation, multi-skilling and job rotation, there was an additional reason for such cutbacks in this case. Initially, one of the main aims of the multi-skilling programme had been to achieve overlap between maintenance and semi-skilled occupations. A multi-skilling agreement was therefore also sought with craft personnel on site, but was not achieved, stalling over issues of the transferability of the approach to other sites. As the semi-skilled areas attempted to perform tasks such as tagging and isolating equipment for repair, they quickly came into conflict with maintenance tradesmen, who perceived that they were not receiving the same opportunities for skill development and reward enhancement.

> we have run into demarcation problems with the metal workers under that, so we are not as multi-skilled as we were originally.
>
> (Shift process worker, Time III)

This level of conflict led management to pull back from some of these issues (tagging was allocated to first-line supervisors). It also led to the development of a negative industrial relations climate, with employees in the process areas becoming increasingly sensitized to issues of demarcation, and less keen in some instances to pursue additional skill development under the existing employment contract.

Job rotation

At the outset, it was planned that within a fully multi-skilled team, employees would be free to choose their own patterns of rotation. In the early days of operation, rotation was constrained by the initial training requirements of unskilled operators, and by the need to staff particular control room positions with experienced operators. Thus employees were generally confined to the one area for between three and six months. In the first wave of interviews, shift process workers indicated a preference for minimal rotation, in order that they could develop their skills to a level that they felt comfortable with. First-line supervisors took on early responsibility for assessing competence and planning rotation through areas covered by a team. However, as time passed and the homogeneity of skills within teams increased, rotation increased only marginally, such that employees generally rotated between a subset of tasks within the one area or building.

Control over area rotation remained with first-level supervision. This is reflected in the finding that at Time III the number who felt they were able to rotate as they would wish had declined from 80 per cent to around 60 per cent of shift process workers. Particularly negative attitudes towards the lack of area rotation opportunities were expressed by SP1s who were stuck in control rooms, where attentional demands and consequences of error were perceived as higher (Martin and Wall, 1987).

Degree of self-regulation

A comparison between the plan for the development of self-regulation and the actual level of responsibility afforded teams led to the inescapable conclusion that only partial implementation of this component of the team concept had occurred. Whilst shift process workers experienced significantly greater work group autonomy than, say, maintenance work groups on site (Cordery *et al.* 1991) the degree of devolution fell well short of initial expectations. For example, while shift process workers were given collective responsibility for deciding on task rotation within a geographic region, responsibility for initiating rotation between areas remained the province of first-line supervision. Similarly, the maintenance of attendance and timekeeping records remained a supervisory responsibility. The reasons for this less than full implementation emerged clearly from interviews at Time III, and appears to have been the result of a conscious managerial choice to constrain the development of self-regulatory capacity within the teams. Views expressed in interviews by both managerial and non-managerial staff provide the following reasons for this.

First, it appears that, despite the existence of a guiding organization design plan detailing the areas in which delegated responsibility was to rest, there were differing views from the outset about how far and how quickly the self-regulation should develop. Many managers expressed the view that the shift process workers harboured unrealistic expectations about the ideal level of team decision-making responsibility to be developed, thereby questioning the plan which had been the basis of the organization design. In part, this may reflect the fact that a fair percentage of managers and first-line supervisors at the new site had not been part of the initial planning process.

> I think they were given a big dreamland idea of the concept when they started here and it causes a lot of friction when we are seen to be stopping them making decisions that they really shouldn't be entitled to make anyway . . . such as . . . manning numbers and who goes where, rotation through buildings, training requirements.
>
> (First-line supervisor, Time III)

The departure from the organization soon after start-up of senior organization development personnel, who had major involvement in the initial planning the approach, may have facilitated the development of such views. Shift process workers in turn recalled information provided to them during induction and early team development sessions, and felt that a shift in team concept definition had occurred, indicating that the goal of work humanization was no longer a significant one in the eyes of management. This in turn had lowered their initially high expectations for what the future might hold.

> People's expectations are not as high as they originally were, and I think that things are starting to settle down a bit. I think that it is working a lot better than the original concept, 'cause we were fairly well misled, in the beginning, as to the expectations on the team concept.
>
> (Shift process worker, Time III)

A second reason for a revised management view for the potential for self-regulation within the shift refinery groups relates to perceived performance control problems. Falling commodity prices, increasing maintenance difficulties with the new plant, and perceived labour cost over-runs in terms of absenteeism led to a view that the groups were not mature or skilled enough to take on many of the planned areas of responsibility. Soon after the first wave of data collection, senior managers began talking about full implementation of the self-regulation component in terms of being 'five years down the track', while instituting more direct supervisory controls over such matters as absence and the co-ordination of local maintenance. In the latter case, this involved the appointment of a range of additional floating first-line process and maintenance supervision.

> Well, it's just that they give us a loose lead when we come here and say, 'It's all yours', and then all of a sudden because some of the teams in certain sections were breaking down they put the collar back on and tightened it up and that is it and we are back to strictly a management/ worker situation. We used to see management. They used to stop and talk to you a lot. Now it is just refinery worker down this end; management – they stick to themselves.
>
> (Shift process worker, Time III)

Performance difficulties associated with the teams were related in part to the operation of the multi-skilling programme. Even in the more advanced teams, shift process workers were still only moderately multi-skilled at Time III. This meant that performance decrements occurred, because employees lacked the necessary skill and experience.

> these process workers that came in were expected to be, were going to become Superman overnight. They were going to be this, that and the other. They were just running riot, you know. And a lot of stuff that they were asking us to do was ridiculous. They did not know what they were talking about or going on about. So there was a bit of a problem at the beginning; but these, the fellows down there now know their job.
>
> (Shift mechanical fitter, Time III)

The limited development of the multi-skilling programme can be related to managerial decisions to dilute training resources, and to the restricted rotation of personnel through the various work areas, thereby creating something of a self-fulfilling prophecy in relation to the team's capacity to self-regulate.

Another reason for suboptimum performance within the teams appeared to be the geographical separation of the shift process team members. At start-up, managers attempted to counteract the effect of geographical separation by allowing teams to meet for half-an-hour before their shift. By Time I, this practice had already been abandoned by management, for economic reasons. Whilst monthly team meetings were held, the lack of any daily or weekly forum for operational decision-making on the part of the group tended to constrain severely the extent to which effective planning and organizing could occur at this level. This had the effect of pushing responsibility for many decisions back to the first-level supervisor or, in some instances, to an individual in a central position (e.g. computer control room operator).

As a changed view of the teams' capacity for self-regulation began to develop, it was reinforced by perceptions, particularly among middle-level management, that the plant was operating quite efficiently at that limited stage of implementation. Following the introduction of increased supervision, performance began to reach acceptable levels, absenteeism had been stabilized through the use of stricter supervisory controls, and maintenance co-ordination had been improved by the appointment of additional supervisory personnel with liaison responsibility.

After two years of operation, the plant was able to shed a number of technical and administrative support personnel as the first-line supervision became more technically competent. The organization also became flatter. The production manager left, and his duties were taken over by his immediate superior. This flattening, however, did not involve any further delegation of responsibility to the shop-floor. Any major effort to promote or develop the team concept further as a means of achieving flexibility and productivity was therefore seen as unnecessary.

Effects of partial implementation of team concept

The restrictions imposed on implementation of the original organization design appeared to have a negative effect on some employees' job perceptions and attitudes. Table 10.3 presents the results of repeated analysis of variance (ANOVA) measures of perceived intrinsic job characteristics (Warr *et al.* 1979), work role autonomy (Kemp *et al.* 1983), intrinsic and extrinsic job satisfaction (Warr *et al.* 1979), and organizational commitment (Cook and Wall 1980).

An earlier analysis (Cordery *et al.* 1991) compared the attitudes of shift process workers over the first eighteen months of operation with those of their counterparts in more traditionally run sister refineries, finding significant differences in favour of the multi-skilled teams, in terms of perceived job scope, job satisfaction, and organization commitment. Employees in self-regulating teams at both sites therefore saw their jobs as having more scope and autonomy than those in traditional, less autonomous work groups. Despite observable downwards trends in the greenfield site shift process worker scores in that study over the eighteen months, these failed to achieve significance, using both repeated measures and independent groups ANOVA.

Data collected some thirty months from start-up indicated that there had been a significant decrease in attitude scores over time, but only for those who had been present at all three time periods. Perceptions of the degree of job scope and work role autonomy, by contrast, had not changed

Table 10.3 Repeated measures one-way ANOVA results: perceived job content and attitudes at Times 1 and 3

	Repeated measures ANOVA				*Independent groups ANOVA*			
	T$_1$	T$_3$	N	Significance[a]	T1	T3	N	Significance[a]
Perceived intrinsic job characteristics	31.9[b]	29.3	38	n.s.	31.9	29.3	83/81	n.s.
Work role autonomy	36.5	36.6	38	n.s.	37.2	37.6	84/87	n.s.
Extrinsic satisfaction	38.7	34.8	40	sig.	37.6	36.6	86/87	n.s.
Intrinsic satisfaction	31.5	26.5	40	sig.	31.1	28.6	87/87	n.s.
Organizational commitment	47.2	41.6	41	sig.	45.8	43.4	86/88	n.s.

[a] set to .01
[b] higher scores represent higher levels of job scope, work role autonomy, satisfaction and commitment

significantly. Our interpretation of these findings, confirmed by views expressed within the interviews at Time III, is that those shift process workers who had been present at start-up felt that management had reneged on promises as to the level to which the 'team concept' would be allowed to develop, and that this has affected their work satisfaction and commitment to the organization. Supplementary analysis, in the form of a comparison between newcomers and stayers at Time III, added support to this view. Scores from those present at all three time periods were significantly lower (p<.01) at Time III for job satisfaction and commitment, though not for perceived intrinsic job characteristics and work group autonomy, than scores for those who were employed following the first data collection. It is worth noting that, when questioned during interview, such employees still drew a favourable distinction between work design and training opportunities at their own site, and those in force elsewhere.

CONCLUSIONS

Taken as a whole, the findings tend to indicate that the initial elements comprising the team concept had become fixed at a particular stage of implementation. Shift process workers who had been with the firm since start-up felt that management had deliberately impeded implementation. To the workers, this represented a lack of commitment to the human relations values which had been linked to the 'team concept' in early team development training and induction. The concept had been expressed in a 'philosophy statement' attached to the original organization design plan, and was a key objective of the socio-technical systems analysis. These unmet expectations appear to have influenced the ways in which those employees evaluated their job and commitment to the organization, as reflected in quantitative measures. In summary, it seems that the comparison made between what was promised and what was offered led to a process akin to resentful demoralization (Cook and Campbell 1979) for those workers.

It is our conclusion that management's decision to constrain the intervention stemmed from the realization that sufficient internal labour flexibility and control had already been achieved with partial implementation. Their attitude towards further development of the various elements outwardly had become one of 'we'll wait and see – when you are ready'. In terms of the notion of joint optimization referred to earlier, the pursuit of humanistic goals appears to have attained a lesser significance in management's eyes, in the face of an obviously workable alternative solution.

This chapter has underscored the role of managerial choice in determining work and organization design outcomes (Clegg 1984). It may be argued that most of the factors that appeared to be inhibiting both the multi-skilling programme and the development of self-regulating shift process teams were under the direct control of management. Certainly, this was the view of the initial intake of shift process workers:

> What happens is, middle management allows teams to go on, as long as they are doing the right thing, as they perceive it. It is advantageous to them. But if a practice or method is developed which, shall we say, tends to be liberal towards the team itself, then they start to assert themselves authoritatively in the traditional role. And to some extent the reason for that is because you have a few teams who do abuse privileges and liberties. So, what happens is the middle management, unable to cope with that in a progressive team method, asserts itself in a traditional role, you know what I mean?
>
> (Shift process worker, Time III)

The abandonment of pre-shift team meetings, the introduction of additional levels of supervision, the limitation of resources to the multi-skilling programme and restriction of the rotation of the most highly-skilled process workers to areas requiring considerable technical mastery and communication skills, all amount to a conscious reshaping of the original design concept based on what was seen by management as a manageable level of flexibility, providing a satisfactory level of organizational return. However, this conveyed the impression of a management whose actions were not

always compatible with their espoused commitment to the values attached
to the team concept at the outset.

In terms of lessons for academic researchers, these findings illustrate
well the difficulties of generalizing from organizational research. It is
common to call for more longitudinal research in organizational settings as
an aid to problems of generalizability and causality. Yet, had this research
project concluded after the second wave of data collection, or only included
quantitative data, the verdict as to the stability of attudinal outcomes over
time would have been somewhat misleading. If it is not possible to general-
ize within the one organization from one time period to another only two
years later, then this poses grave difficulties for the generalizability from
one organization to another within the publication time-lag of most book
and journal articles! As a goal of empirical research, we would therefore
favour extrapolation as a more useful goal than generalization for work and
organizational psychology, and one which is compatible with a constructivist perspective of social science. For organizational change agents
charged with the task of planning an organizational innovation, the act of
extrapolating from published studies means that previous research findings
can be placed on the agenda as part of the negotiation process in planning.
As an academic goal, extrapolation places greater publication pressure on
the contextual dependency of published findings. It is precisely this area
that is usually sacrificed for space in research papers.

REFERENCES

Cherns, A.B. (1976) 'The principles of sociotechnical design', *Human Relations*
   29: 783–92.
Clegg, C.W. (1984) 'The derivation of job designs', *Journal of Occupational
   Behaviour* 5: 131–46.
Cook, J.D. and Campbell, D.T. (1979) *Quasi-experimentation: Design and Analysis
   Issues for Field Settings*, Chicago: Rand-McNally.
Cook, J.D. and Wall, T.D. (1980) 'New work attitude measure of trust, organ-
   izational commitment and personal need non-fulfilment', *Journal of Occu-
   pational Psychology* 53: 39–52.
Cordery, J.L. (1985) 'Multi-skilling and its implications for work design', *Human
   Resource Management Australia* 23(3): 55–8.
Cordery, J.L. (1989) 'Multi-skilling: A discussion of proposed benefits of new
   approaches to labour flexibility within enterprises', *Personnel Review* 18:
   13–22.
Cordery, J.L., Mueller, W.S. and Smith, L.M. (1991) 'Attitudinal and behavioral
   outcomes of autonomous group working: A longitudinal field study. *Academy of
   Management Journal* (in press).
Cummings, T.G. (1978) 'Self-regulating work groups: A socio-technical synthesis',
   Academy of Management Review 3: 625–34.
Curtain, R. (1987) 'Skill formation and the enterprise', *Labour and Industry* 1:
   8–38.

Kelly, J.E. (1978) 'A reappraisal of sociotechnical systems theory', *Human Relations* 31: 1069–99.

Kemp, N.J., Wall, T.D., Clegg, C.W. and Cordery, J.L. (1983) 'Autonomous work groups in a greenfield site: A comparative study', *Journal of Occupational Psychology* 56: 271–88.

Martin, R. and Wall, T.D. (1987) 'Attentional demand and cost responsibility as stressors in shop-floor jobs', *Academy of Management Journal* 32: 69–86.

Mueller, W.S. (1991) 'New technology and flexible working', in J. Hartley and G. Stephenson (eds), *The Psychology of Employment Relations*, Oxford: Basil Blackwell (in press).

OECD (1986) *Flexibility in the Labour Market: The Current Debate*, Paris: OECD.

Pasmore, W.A. (1989) *Designing Effective Organizations: The Sociotechnical Systems Perspective*, New York: Wiley.

Wall, T.D., Kemp, N.J., Jackson, P.R. and Clegg, C.W. (1986) 'Outcomes of autonomous work groups: A long-term field experiment', *Academy of Management Journal* 29: 280–304.

Walton, R.E. and Susman, G.I. (1987) 'People policies for the new machines', *Harvard Business Review* (March–April): 98–106.

Warr, P., Cook, J. and Wall, T. (1979) 'Scales for the measurement of some work attitudes and aspects of psychological well-being', *Journal of Occupational Psychology* 52: 129–48.

11 Changing towards human-centred technology

Gillian Symon

INTRODUCTION

This chapter concerns alternative approaches to the design of technology for use in organizations. In particular, the focus is on the human-centred approach (Cooley 1987; Corbett 1988; Brodner 1990), which takes a specifically European perspective on work organization and technology. The opposing, underlying values of the traditional and human-centred approaches to the design of technology are outlined, and the application of the human-centred perspective in a European project is described. The chapter concludes with some discussion of the difficulties of changing from the traditional approach to the human-centred approach, particularly in terms of engineering practices and organizational contexts.

THE DESIGN OF TECHNOLOGY

Rosenbrock (1981) claims that current state-of-the-art computer-based technology is still designed according to the underlying principles of some of the earliest spinning machines of the Industrial Revolution. This is despite the infinitely greater flexibility and power of new forms of technology which present a range of new possibilities for utilization. In particular, there is still the tendency to pursue the complete automation of production processes, where human input is reduced to the performance of one or two simple (and often unrelated) actions which either cannot be automated, or would be too expensive to automate, the ultimate goal being unmanned production (Brodner 1986).

In a similar vein, it is argued that, in organizations, greater attention is generally paid to the technology than to the employees in the design of work systems. Clegg and Kemp (1986) maintain that in new technology implementations the majority of available resources (time, money, energy) are directed toward getting the technology 'right' – human and organizational factors being largely ignored. Cooley (1987) quotes an example of designers formally claiming parity with their CAD machines, where heating and ventilation were considered of paramount importance for the machines, but were barely considered for their human operators. Indeed, Cooley's book abounds with such examples, in which workers and their skills are considered insignificant in comparison with the needs of the technology.

Yet several sources have indicated that this approach is not necessarily the most appropriate or effective in many situations. In a survey of companies implementing information technology, Kearney (1984) discovered that most companies interviewed had only achieved around 50–60 per cent of the potential benefits of IT. The major factors they identified as determining successful IT implementation included quality of staff, and co-operation between users and technical staff (p. 33). Negative consequences for the use and development of skills have also been noted. It is now apparent that the distance between workers and the automated system means that workers have an inadequate model of the system, and are unable to intervene in the case of system failure (Bainbridge 1983). This lack of active intervention in the system by those closest to it also curtails severely the prospect of innovation or creativity at work (Brodner 1986).

It has been suggested by various observers that, for all the reasons for considering alternatives, there are particular beliefs or values underlying the design of technology which tend to foster a technology-centred approach. Rosenbrock (1981) has proposed that this comes from the nature of the engineering profession itself, although 'the engineering paradigm is not explicit, and it prevails not by a conscious choice, but by suppressing the ability to see an alternative' (p. 4).

From a more political perspective, Braverman (1974) and other proponents of the 'de-skilling' hypothesis, claim that the design of technology so as to exclude human intervention is another manifestation of management's desire to gain absolute control over the production process.

Symon and Clegg (1990) have hypothesized that the technology-led approach may simply be a 'satisficing' mechanism (March and Simon 1961) – a way for organizations to cope with the complex situations of organizational and technological change. By relying on the underlying belief that technology is neutral, the organization can claim that any changes resulting from its implementation (particularly those considered undesirable) are not the responsibility of any in-company group. Rather, such changes are unavoidable, a natural by-product of technological change.

It is probable that some combination of these motivations influences the design of technology; no single explanation would be sufficient. What is clear, however, is that for any alternative approach to be successful, it will have to outline not just different methods, but, at a more basic level, it will have to challenge the underlying values involved.

Such an alternative approach to the design of technology is outlined in this chapter. The human-centred approach takes an opposing perspective at a philosophical level, and puts forward a different set of guiding values for system design.

THE HUMAN-CENTRED APPROACH

The human-centred approach concentrates particularly on skill preservation and development, advocating the retention of human intervention in the work system, and using the new possibilities of advanced technology to aid the development of skill. As in the Scandinavian approach outlined below, in this view, the computer system should be regarded as a 'tool', which enables the recipients to carry out their work effectively, as an *extension* of their skill, rather than as a *replacement* for skill (Ehn 1988).

One of the justifications for this emphasis on human skill is that there are elements of knowledge and skill that cannot be quantified or represented as rules. That is to say, such aspects of knowledge and skill as the use of heuristics, and, in particular, the 'tacit' dimension (Polanyi 1962). For example, many situations are complex and may not necessarily be predicted or determined beforehand. Thus, we may need to draw on assumptions based on past experience (heuristics) in order to act in a given situation. In addition, we make judgements based on sensuous and subjective experience (tacit judgements) which we cannot fully articulate, unlike the rule-based knowledge we also possess. Judgements arising from these processes may be considered as legitimate as judgements arising from a purely logical and rational reasoning process.

Part of our inability to articulate some aspects of our experience may arise because they are only revealed in our actions, e.g. 'by watching the master and emulating his efforts in the presence of his example, the apprentice unconsciously picks up the rules of the art, including those which are not explicitly known to the master himself' (Polanyi 1973: 53). We only 'know' such knowledge as we act upon it; we cannot articulate it in the abstract. Thus tacit knowledge cannot be taught as sets of rules, because it is not accessible to that kind of description. Therefore, we must 'learn-by-doing' (Ehn 1988). In terms of system design, it follows that we could progress through 'design-by-doing'.

This experiential approach is clearly in conflict with the traditional approach to design, which takes the view that there is one 'best way' of designing systems. The human-centred approach rejects this concept, acknowledging the diversity of situations in which technology may be used.

What may be appropriate for a large industrial factory, may not be appropriate for an office, and yet the same technical considerations may drive both implementations (Clegg 1988). Furthermore, situations change, and systems should be designed to be flexible in order to adapt to new circumstances. It is only at the level of actual system operation that situational information becomes actively salient (see 'controlling variance at source', Cherns 1976), and it is at this point that the operator needs the necessary flexibility, both in the system and in his or her job to deal with unique situational constraints. Clearly, people vary too! Consequently, human-centred system design also takes into consideration, for example, varying levels of skill and varying levels of motivation.

At the organizational level of analysis lies the recognition that workers should have some autonomy and control over their everyday working lives, thereby rectifying the Taylorist drive toward the separation of physical labour and management, such that 'those conceptual and planning aspects of work should be integral to the labour process, thereby ensuring that those who do work also plan and manage it' (Cooley 1987: 133).

This viewpoint also implies that workers should have some influence over broader decisions that are taken in their organizations, particularly those that affect their jobs directly. In the case of system design, this may be in the form of user representation on the design team.

The traditional approach takes the view that the development of technology is a scientific and, therefore, socially neutral process. Yet, clearly technology is not neutral: the way it is designed can have profound effects on society – for example, the impact of the scientific management principles proposed by Ford (Wobbe 1990). Consequently, Rauner *et al.* (1988) argue that technology should be 'a union of the technologically possible and the socially desirable' (p. 48). An alternative approach such as human-centred technology should reflect in more detail what is socially desirable, particularly given that technological possibilities are now so much greater.

This social analysis clearly has a cultural component – particular technologies and approaches to the design of technology can arise from particular cultures. In Scandinavian cultures, participative approaches to system design are the norm, legitimized by government policy (e.g. Bjerknes *et al.* 1987). Cooley (1987) claims that the European work culture is based on craft skills (unlike North American or Asian approaches to work organization), and that Europeans should therefore build technology that reflects this fact.

In consequence of this broader perspective, technology should not be regarded as the preserve of technologists. Thus, for example, social scientists, who may have some understanding of the social issues involved in the design of technology, should also have some influence over the design process.

The human-centred approach to the design and implementation of computer-based technology claims to represent a fundamental change in perspective. Clearly, however, there are many other approaches which adopt an alternative view from the traditional model (see Clegg and Symon 1989 for a review). According to Gill (1990), the human-centred approach may be considered novel in its holistic perspective (cf. the user-centred approach, which is often confined to the interface) and the priority given to human abilities (cf. the socio-technical approach, where humans and technology are considered equal).

As it is presented so far, however, the human-centred approach to the design and implementation of technology is difficult to visualize as resulting in a concrete technical or organizational system. Consequently, Clegg and Symon (1989) have outlined a 'framework' for the design and evaluation of human-centred systems, which it is hoped can be used as a tool to make the conceptual analysis outlined above more accessible to the design process. In summarizing many of the issues outlined above, it can, itself, be thought of as an heuristic.

THE HUMAN-CENTRED FRAMEWORK

The formation of the framework was guided by relevant literature, but also arose from the experiences of the researchers in other organizations and in other projects. It is also written from the professional perspective of organizational psychologists, rather than (for example) sociologists, engineers or system designers (cf. Rauner *et al.* 1988; Craven 1986; Schael 1987).

In the tradition of 'design-by-doing', the framework evolved over the course of project number 1217 (outlined below) of the European strategic programme for research and development in information technology (ESPRIT). There is thus an interaction of ideas and experiences between the development of the project and the development of the framework. Therefore, this framework should not be considered as definitive; rather, it is open to further development in the light of future investigations. It is hoped that it may promote interdisciplinary discussion – particularly as an illustration of an alternative to technology-led system design. Because of this aim, it also represents a somewhat idealized view of the objectives the development of technology should be fulfilling.

The framework comprises five interrelated components:

Design philosophy

This drives the project and forms the basis of all the work carried out. The three main principles here are:

1 that people should not be subordinated to machines;
2 that technology should be considered as a tool to help people rather than replace labour;
3 that making better use of human skill, ingenuity, flexibility, creativity and knowledge will create a more effective organizational system, as well as a better quality of working environment.

Appropriation

More than user participation, the underlying principle here is that end-users should 'own' the technology they are eventually going to use. Thus users should be the prime decision-makers in its design and implementation.

Education and awareness

In most cases within industry, training on new technology tends to be 'technology-led' in that it is task-based, teaching people how to operate the machines. We advocate broader-based education strategies – where users are informed of potential benefits and costs of technology; how it can be made to work for them; and how it is implemented.

Design methods

There are four main areas here:

Parallel design process The aim here is that the human and technical aspects of a system are considered concurrently. This is in opposition to the traditional sequential approach, where the human aspects of an organizational system are generally under-resourced and considered after implementation (if at all). By this time, early design choices have often constrained possibilities for operation.

Interdisciplinary working An organizational system covers so many different areas of expertise that it is essential that there be diverse sources of knowledge available during the design process. Clearly, in these initial stages of human-centred technology design, the design team may need to include human factors specialists, for example.

User participation The idea of involving users in the design and implementation is not new (e.g. Mumford 1983; Briefs *et al.* 1983). As legitimate experts on the organizational model, and as legitimate 'concerned parties' who will ultimately be using the technology, potential users have a significant role to play in the design process. Indirect users, whose work may be affected by the use of new technology, should also have some influence over the outcomes. Consultation and negotiation are, therefore, necessary activities in the design process.

Human factors 'tools'   Much as the human-centred approach advocates, in general, the perception of the computer as tool, so the notion here is that we should also design specific techniques (tools) to enable designers to include human factors knowledge in design. Such tools include

- 'usability checklists', to evaluate the usability of the system software during design (e.g. Ravden and Johnson 1989);
- 'a design process model', which can be used as a decision aid for designers to assess when to incorporate certain human and organizational factors (e.g. Ravden *et al.* 1987);
- 'an allocation of functions decision aid', to help designers and engineers in the appropriate allocation of tasks between the human and the technology operating in the system (e.g. Clegg *et al.* 1989);
- 'scenarios', descriptions of different outcomes that can be expected from different methods of implementation, which can help inform organizational choices (e.g. Clegg and Corbett 1986).

Design goals

Although processes and goals may emerge during the design of human-centred technology, it is clearly beneficial (particularly for the designers and engineers involved) to have some objectives to aim towards. To fulfil this need, the framework includes sets of goals which are specific enough to guide design choices and aid evaluation, without being deterministic.

Five areas are identified here: hardware and software ergonomics; job and organization design; allocation of functions; information and control systems; and type and level of technology. Sets of criteria have been developed in the first four cases (see Table 11.1 for some examples).

In terms of the type and level of technology, the concern is that organizations and system designers consider the degree of automation that is necessary for their particular area. Thus, highly advanced technology may be inappropriate for simple work processes. Conversely, complex activity requiring a high level of flexibility in the system may require state-of-the-art technology which can support human intervention effectively.

Table 11.1 Sample criteria for design goals

Design goals	Sample criteria	
Hardware	Workspace design	Keyboard layout
	Environmental ergonomics	Lighting
Software	Visual clarity	Compatability
	Informative feedback	Explicitness
	Error prevention and correction	
	User guidance and support	Consistency
Job design	Control	Variety
	Feedback	Complete tasks
	Social contact	Cognitive demands
	Cost responsibility	Pay and recognition
	Opportunities for learning	
Information and control systems	Flexibility	Decentralization
	Local sub-system autonomy	
	Provision of diagnostic Information	
Allocation of system functions	Optimization	Systematic allocation
	Health and safety	Operational requirements
	Function characteristics	Sum total assessment
Organization design	Boundary management	Self containment
	Support	Minimum specialization

A EUROPEAN PERSPECTIVE

As outlined earlier, it has been claimed that the human-centred approach is particularly appropriate for the European tradition of craft-based production and the European tendency towards small batch manufacture. Indeed, similar programmes of work in this area in Europe have been attempted or are currently ongoing. Some of these bear a close relationship to the ESPRIT project, which forms the main focus of this chapter.

The UTOPIA Project in Sweden (Bodker *et al.* 1987), for example, which is based on the Scandinavian collective resources approach, has a primary objective of not just developing new technology, but also enhancing the professional skills of graphic workers through the use of that technology. Like the human-centred approach, the emphasis is on the computer as tool and the development of craft skills, including tacit knowledge. Furthermore, the project is interdisciplinary, involving graphic workers, computer scientists and social scientists.

Again like the ESPRIT programme of work, the German humanization of work programme, which has been running for the last ten years, is government-funded (Wilpert and Quintanilla 1984) and, as the title suggests, is concerned with improving workers' jobs as well as developing technology. Union involvement in this development work has been considerable. Trade unions are active at all levels of negotiation and consultation, including meetings with government officials. Dankbaar (1987) maintains that this has been made possible by a receptive attitude to technology on the part of German trade unions, an attitude not necessarily present in other cultures.

The ESPRIT project owes much to work carried out in the early 1980s at the University of Manchester Institute of Science and Technology (UMIST), which aimed to develop a programmable controller for a turning machine tool 'in which operators are not subordinate to machines' (Corbett 1986: 17). Broadly speaking, 'The hope was, that by a development effort parallel to the traditional one, and competitive with it, a divergent technological stream could be created, leading to an alternative 'human-centred' technology' (Rosenbrock 1987: 9). For the main part, the project concentrated on ways in which operator skill could be optimally utilized and further developed in interaction with the machine. Fundamental aspects of a programmable lathe were forthcoming and the work done at UMIST formed the basis for the British component of the ESPRIT project described below.

Another influential British initiative was the 'campaign to work for the right to work on socially useful products' (Cooley 1987: 117), which was pursued by the workers in Lucas Aerospace. Faced with a 'rationalization programme' which could have led to heavy redundancies, the workers at the various Lucas plants outlined a variety of socially useful products they could manufacture with the resources available to them. These included innovative energy-saving devices, appliances for the handicapped, and medical equipment. The design of these products involved the technologists working directly with the communities in need of their services, and demonstrated the creative ability of 'ordinary people'. However, the management of Lucas Aerospace would not allow the production of such products, on the basis that they were 'uneconomic' – an assertion disputed by Cooley (1987), who saw the decision as politically motivated. Cooley was one of the prime movers (along with Rosenbrock at UMIST) behind ESPRIT project number 1217.

ESPRIT PROJECT 1217: HUMAN-CENTRED CIM

The different European approaches, outlined above, were reflected in a project sponsored by the Commission of European Communities (CEC), involving participants from Germany, Britain, and Denmark.

This project is described here as an example of the application of the human-centred approach. However, the limited space available precludes a comprehensive evaluation of the project (see Clegg *et al.* 1989 for a fuller account).

The objective of the ESPRIT project was to design and implement (for real production work), a human-centred computer integrated manufacturing (CIM) system. In more detail, the aims were:

1 that the final system should enhance human skill, rather than replace it;
2 that both the technical and social aspects of the final organizational system should be optimized;
3 that the design process should follow a user orientation such that functionality, use, etc. is considered from the users' viewpoint, rather than according to the needs of the technical system.

Each element of the system was developed by a different country. In Denmark, the main focus was the design of a human-centred sketching module attached to a conventional computer aided design (CAD) system; in Germany, the design of a human-centred computer aided production planning (CAPP) system; and in the UK, the design of a computer aided manufacturing (CAM) system. In this description the British component (the CAM system) will be the focus.

The technical products included in the CAM system were control and scheduling systems for CNC machine tools, and shop-floor production scheduling and factory planning systems. These products were to be implemented in two main user sites respectively: a large engineering company manufacturing helicopters, and a smaller firm manufacturing telecommunications equipment.

In the first case, the two 'human-centred' machine tools were to be implemented in one small area of the organization, concerned with the manufacture of metal rings. Other workers in this area would still be operating traditional machine tools, and the rest of the organization (including the company-wide information and control systems) would not be changed. In contrast, the second user site (recipients of the production scheduling and factory planning systems) was already undergoing radical and company-wide changes to its working practices. As part of these changes, the shop-floor was being reorganized into product 'cells' – i.e. each cell to have all the necessary machines, raw materials etc. to manufacture a particular product. The human-centred computer-based systems would be supporting the new methods of working which these new arrangements entailed.

The role of the Social and Applied Psychology Unit in this project was to work with the engineers, systems designers and users, contributing knowledge and expertise concerning the human and organizational aspects of the design and implementation.

The design

As in a traditional design process, it was felt that a document outlining the goals (or requirements specification) was necessary. However, unlike the traditional approach, the initial specification for the system was given as a 'scenario' (Rosenbrock *et al.* 1987) – that is to say, a description of the new work system based on the work activities to be performed, rather than a technology-oriented description of system functions. This conception was founded on the notion of design and production islands, where the means and information to produce any product part is available within each island. The expectation was that more specific and detailed requirements would emerge 'in the doing', as the project team worked towards these broadly-defined goals.

In line with the philosophical commitment to 'design-by-doing', proto-typing of the emerging CAM systems was carried out, particularly as regards the CNC control system. Prototyping here included paper and computer simulations of the final system, for evaluation purposes. Un-fortunately, in the early stages, this prototyping tended to be confined to the design group which, although interdisciplinary, included few potential end-users.

One of the fundamental 'requirements' was that this project be inter-disciplinary, involving (in each country): systems designers; engineers and project managers from the user sites; potential end-users; and social scientists. To aid this collaboration, social scientific 'tools' were utilized to help incorporate psychological factors in the design (e.g. usability check-lists).

The implementation

In this description the focus will be on the CNC control system and the production scheduling system. Each system illustrates the human-centred approach at a different level: individual working and group working. These two systems were designed by different software houses working together along human-centred lines.

The CNC control system

The human-centred control system for the CNC lathe was designed along the principles of shop-floor programming. That is to say, the design of the computer program to cut the part is carried out on the shop-floor, rather than in the methods office. In this way, some of the 'craft' skills are given back to the operator. More specifically, the job design is expanded in various ways, including, for example: autonomy (having more control over how the work is carried out); variety (having more tasks to carry out); and decision-making (having to decide the best ways in which a part should be cut). In this latter case, the operator is able to use that judgement which comes from experience and knowledge of engineering (tacit and otherwise) to achieve an optimal solution, given current constraints.

The control system was designed with a graphic interface. In order to define the necessary cuts, the operator graphically 'draws' and 'cuts' the part on screen. This information is automatically translated into the G-codes which govern the automatic machining of the part. Thus, for the operator the interaction is in terms of the actual task to be accomplished, rather than a numerical representation of the same. The task is still an engineering task and has not become a computing task.

The operator is able to override any of the automatic processes (e.g. by editing the G-codes), but in order to encompass individual differences in the motivation to do so, the machine can be operated completely automatically. Tools, speeds, feeds etc, can be suggested by the computer program and simply accepted by the operator, or the operator can intervene at any of the stages to define particular parameters. The decision is the operator's.

Throughout the design process, the end-user organization was involved in the decision-making surrounding the CNC lathe control system. The company representative on the design group was also the line manager in charge of the production cell where the lathe would finally be installed. Thus he was able to have considerable influence over the way the project progressed, and some sense of ownership of the final product (appropriation). The company also set up an internal steering group, which included managers, supervisors and trade union representatives, who monitored the project. It was from this group that the suggestion came to modify some aspects of the operator's job at an organizational level, in line with the human-centred ideals. Thus, it was agreed that the 'operations sheet' (which normally gives very detailed instructions for manufacture) should be altered so that only minimum data was given, in order that the operator would have more control and autonomy over the production of the part. Furthermore, the eventual user of the system (the operator) made regular visits to the software house to comment on prototypes and working models of the system.

The production scheduling system

The design of the system was based on the objective of supporting autonomous working groups and group technology, which are concurrently
being implemented at the user site as product 'cells'. The technology
utilized in this case was not highly complex. As a relatively small company,
the scale of operations made a large automated solution unnecessary.
Instead, the solution was a series of networked software packages, some
generic, others bought in. The packages bought in included word-
processing, statistical process control, email, etc. This selection of packages were linked together by a common interface, designed as part of the
ESPRIT project. Thus, in this case, the computer as 'tool' became the
computer as 'tool-kit'. In the following description of the system, the focus
will be on the generic cell production scheduling system.

The scheduling system was designed to allow cells to have control over
their own work processes and to be, to a certain extent, self-determining.
Thus cell members can plan their production activities for the week, taking
into account specific situational constraints (e.g. a disabled machine in the
cell). Clearly, the cell members have, in this sense, more accurate information on which to draw.

In the company, the technology has not been the main focus of attention.
Most available resources have instead gone into the human and organizational aspects of the change programme, that is, the reorganization of the
shop-floor into product cells. In the product cells, staff now have new
grades, and promotion paths within the cell are clearly defined. Plans for
the reorganization were disseminated early; however, less information was
circulated concerning the technology. On the other hand, many potential
users did use the system at the software house to simulate production work,
before the system was installed at the user site.

Current stage of ESPRIT project 1217

The technology has been installed in the user sites for several months.
However, evaluation of its impact is still ongoing. A preliminary assessment is recorded in Clegg *et al.* (1989).

DISCUSSION

The discussion here will be confined to the process of design during the
ESPRIT project, and broader issues concerning technological and organizational change.

ESPRIT Project 1217

One of the fundamental issues in the ESPRIT project was achieving effective interdisciplinary working methods. Initially, the system designers and the social scientists could not understand each other's professional language and expressions, and neither could fully appreciate the practical problems faced by engineers in the user sites. The disciplines involved here have developed separately over decades; a common language is as yet not available. Neither are common techniques – while social scientists work with vague description, engineers traditionally work with formulae, programming languages and tight specifications. The most successful collaboration, in this sense, for the UK participants at least, was the usability check-lists (Ravden and Johnson 1989), which draw on social science knowledge, but expressed in precise and usable terms, which are 'to hand' (Ehn 1988). This is clearly a compromise, the check-lists do not deal with the fundamental issues of human-centredness, but they did help achieve effective collaboration.

Engineers claimed that at the end of the project, they felt their views and methods of designing had changed towards a more human-centred perspective. However, a three-year project was not long enough, and some maintained that it was a change in the British education system which was really required. Whatever happens in the future, the project was a first step towards achieving some kind of dialogue.

Similar problems were encountered in enabling user participation in the design process. In an iterative design model, where development progresses by experience ('design-by-doing'), the classic problem of 'who are the users?' is intensified. Furthermore, as with most studies of user participation (e.g. Mambrey and Schmidt-Belz 1983), those users who *were* involved in the process found it difficult to criticize. This arose because they felt themselves to be unknowledgeable and powerless in the face of expertise. Unfortunately, little time could be spent in educating and empowering users.

Clearly, as a consultative, empirical process, a human-centred approach to design will take longer. However, a protracted development cycle is notoriously unpopular with management in organizations. However, there is evidence (KPMG Peat Marwick 1990) that even traditional system design cycles can be prolonged due to 'management-related issues' e.g. inappropriate project management.

In a general sense there are always problems in implementing systems within systems. In both implementation sites (but particularly the helicopter plant), the new systems are only sub-systems within other much larger and well-established systems. Given that the human-centred methods of design and operation are so at odds with the usual 'technology-led' approach, it would not be surprising to find conflicts arising. If the old system emphasizes control and the new system autonomy, can the two be operated in parallel without cross-system interference? This remains to be seen in the ESPRIT project, but there is already some evidence that the process of change has been more effective in the site receiving the planning and scheduling systems than in the site receiving the CNC systems (Clegg *et al.* 1989). This may well be because, in the former case, the technological and organizational changes are proceeding concurrently and are fundamental to the company's structure. In the latter case, the change is confined to one area, and other organizational changes in support of the technological change are not deemed necessary.

Human-centred systems and organizational change

Most proponents of the human-centred approach pursue it at the level of the trade union or as a social issue. Clearly, all levels of analysis are legitimate; however, there appears to be little appreciation in the human-centred literature of organizational issues generally, even though 'it is of decisive importance which in-plant groups plan and implement technological innovations and what the former's interests and specific aims are' (Schultz-Wild 1990: 93).

Little account is taken of the (often conflicting) views of 'stakeholders' (Mitroff 1983) within an organization, and the manner in which opposing views of workers can be confronted. In fact the politics of the organizational situation are largely passed over, except in the very general sense of management interests versus workers' interests. Clearly, the organizational situation is more complex than this (e.g. Markus 1987; Symon and Clegg 1990).

Even though many researchers in this area do take a trade union perspective on initiating change, there seems little recognition of one of the fundamental problems in organizational change – what happens to displaced indirect workers when autonomy is moved downwards? In the case of shop-floor programming, for example, the resultant jobs for office programmers could be greatly reduced. This possible outcome might lead to a trade union backlash; thus in Scandinavia, for example, 'the lack of trade union co-operation, not the technology . . . may ironically become the decisive factor frustrating the dream of UTOPIA' (Booker *et al.* 1987: 260).

After decades of fragmented jobs, on which the current division of trade unions is based, demarcation lines are very clear, and trade unions are reluctant to change for fear of negative side-effects. Having had to cope with the Taylorism of jobs, workers are now in the position, ironically, of having to protect that fragmentation. Furthermore, an air of distrust, even for human-centred approaches, may pervade. Thus in the German programme, 'many workers considered the humanization programme nothing but a fig-leaf for rationalization policies' (Dankbaar 1987: 342).

These points serve to highlight the complex nature of change – both technological and organizational. The implication arising from this case is that the changes proposed here may be difficult, because they challenge a 'way of doing' and a set of beliefs that have been formulated over decades and even centuries.

CONCLUDING REMARKS

Clearly the human-centred approach represents a fundamental change in the design process. This new perspective is based on a different set of underlying values in the design process, in the belief that it is only at this level that the issues of fragmented jobs, large-scale automation, and the demise of skill-based working can be overcome. Given the years of engineering expertise that have gone into traditional system design, and the relative paucity of experience with human-centred design, problems are hardly surprising. However, the approach is clearly a workable one (as the ESPRIT project has demonstrated) and it is time (in the face of current developments in new technology) that such an alternative was seriously pursued.

This chapter has concentrated on the manufacturing and engineering industry; however, the same issues are pertinent to other technologies in other settings, and to other jobs which are now open to automation. The greater flexibility of that technology means that more possibilities for positive change are also open.

REFERENCES

Bainbridge, L. (1983) 'Ironies of automation', *Automatica* 19: 775–9.

Bjerknes, G., Ehn, P. and Kyng, M. (eds) (1987) *Computers and Democracy*, Aldershot: Avebury.

Bodker, S., Ehn, P., Kammersgard, J., Kyng, M. and Sundblad, Y. (1987) 'A UTOPIAN experience', in G. Bjerknes, P. Ehn and M. Kyng (eds) *Computers and Democracy*, Aldershot: Avebury.

Braverman, H. (1974) *Labour and Monopoly Capital*, New York: Monthly Review Press.

Briefs, U., Ciborra, C. and Schneider, L. (eds) (1983) *System Design For, With and By the Users*, New York: North-Holland.

Brodner, P. (1986) 'Skill-based manufacturing versus "unmanned factory" – Which is superior?', *International Journal of Industrial Ergonomics* 1: 145–53.

Brodner, P. (1990) 'Technocentric-anthropocentric approaches: Towards skill-based manufacturing', in M. Warner, W. Wobbe and P. Brodner (eds) *New Technology and Manufacturing Management*, Chichester: John Wiley.

Chems, A. (1976) 'The principles of socio-technical design', *Human Relations* 29: 783–92.

Clegg, C.W. (1988) 'Appropriate technology for manufacturing: Some management issues', *Applied Ergonomics* 19: 25–34.

Clegg, C.W. and Corbett, J.M. (1986) 'Psychological and organizational aspects of computer-aided manufacturing', *Current Psychological Research and Reviews* 5: 189–204.

Clegg, C.W. and Kemp, N. (1986) 'Information Technology: Personnel, where are you?', *Personnel Review* 15: 8–15.

Clegg, C.W., Ravden, S.J., Corbett, J.M. and Johnson, G.I. (1989) 'Allocating functions in computer integrated manufacturing: A review and a new method', *Behaviour and Information Technology* 8: 175–90.

Clegg, C.W. and Symon, G. (1989) 'A review of human-centred manufacturing technology and a framework for its design and evaluation', *International Reviews of Ergonomics* 3: 15–47.

Clegg, C.W., Symon, G. and Johnson, G.I. (in preparation) 'A formative evaluation of some 'human-centred' manufacturing technologies', SAPU Memo No 1093, University of Sheffield, MRC/ESRC Social and Applied Psychology Unit, UK.

Cooley, M. (1987) *Architect or Bee?* (2nd edn), London: The Hogarth Press.

Corbett, J.M. (1986) 'Human work design criteria and the design process: The devil in the detail', in P. Brodner (ed.) *Skill-Based Automated Manufacturing*, Oxford: Pergamon Press.

Corbett, J.M. (1988) 'Strategic options for CIM: Technology-centred versus human-centred systems design', *Computer Integrated Manufacturing Systems* 1: 76–81.

Craven, F. (1986) 'A human-centred turning cell', *Proceedings of the Third International Conference on Human Factors in Manufacturing*, November: 167–82.

Dankbaar, B. (1987) 'Social assessment of workplace technology – some experiences with the German programme "Humanization of work"', *Research Policy* 16: 337–52.

Ehn, P. (1988) *The Work-Oriented Design of Computer Artefacts*, Stockholm: Arbetslivscentrum.

Gill, K. (1990) *Summary of human-centred systems research in Europe*, The Centre for Social and Educational Applications of Knowledge Engineering (SEAKE), Brighton Polytechnic.

Kearney, A.T. (1984) *The barriers and the opportunities of Information Technology – A management perspective*, London: The Institute of Administrative Management and the Department of Trade and Industry.

KPMG Peat Marwick (1990) *Runaway computer systems*, London: KPMG Peat Marwick McLintock Management Consultants.

Mambrey, P. and Schmidt-Belz, B. (1983) 'System designers and users in a participative design process: Some fictions and facts', in U. Briefs, C. Ciborra and L. Schneider (eds) *System Design For, With and By the Users*, New York: North-Holland.

March, J. and Simon, H. (1961) *Organizations*, New York: John Wiley.

Markus, M.L. (1987) 'Power, politics and MIS implementation', in R. Baecker and W. Buxton (eds) *Readings in Human-Computer Interaction*, Los Altos, CA: Morgan Kaufmann.

Mitroff, I. (1983) *Stakeholders of the Organizational Mind*, San Francisco: Jossey-Bass.

Mumford, E. (1983) 'Participative systems design: Practice and theory', *Journal of Occupational Behaviour* 4: 47–57.

Polanyi, M. (1962) 'Tacit knowing: Its bearing on some problems of philosophy', *Review of Modern Physics* 34: 601–16.

Polanyi, M. (1973) *Personal Knowledge: Towards a Post-Critical Philosophy*, London: Routledge & Kegan Paul.

Rauner, F., Rasmussen, L. and Corbett, J.M. (1988) 'The social shaping of technology and work: Human-centred CIM systems', *AI & Society* 2: 47–61.

Ravden, S.J. and Johnson, G.I. (1989) *Evaluating the Usability of Human-Computer Interfaces*, Chichester: Ellis Horwood.

Ravden, S.J., Johnson, G.I., Clegg, C.W. and Corbett, J.M. (1987) 'Human factors in the design of a flexible assembly cell', in P. Brodner (ed.) *Skill-Based Automated Manufacturing*, Oxford: Pergamon Press.

Rosenbrock, H. (1981) 'Engineers and the work that people do', *IEEE Control Systems Magazine* 3 September.

Rosenbrock, H. (1987) 'Technology and Society', paper given as Cockcroft Lecture, 1986 Manchester Technology Association.

Rosenbrock, H., Corbett, M., Eriksen, E., Dreyer, K., Wellhausen, F. and Mackay, R. (1987) 'Overall System Specification', unpublished report ESPRIT 1217 (1199).

Schael, T. (1987) 'Design of a Production Cell', unpublished report ESPRIT 1217 (1199).

Schultz-Wild, R. (1990) 'Process-related skills: Future factory structures and training', in M. Warner, W. Wobbe and P. Brodner (eds) *New Technology and Manufacturing Management*, Chichester: John Wiley.

Symon, G. and Clegg, C.W. (1990) 'Managing technological and organizational change', SAPU Memo No 1143, University of Sheffield, MRC/ESRC Social and Applied Psychology Unit, UK.

Wilpert, B. and Quintanilla, S.A. (1984) 'The German humanization of work programme: Review of its first twenty publications', *Journal of Occupational Psychology* 57: 185–95.

Wobbe, W. (1990) Introduction, in M. Warner, W. Wobbe and P. Brodner (eds) *New Technology and Manufacturing Management*, Chichester: John Wiley.

12 Computer aided manufacturing and job design

Robin Martin and Keith Davids

INTRODUCTION

One of the major issues currently facing manufacturing organizations is how best to exploit recent developments in information technology. Advances in micro-electronics, particularly in computer technology, has led to a proliferation of information technology applications in industry. One example of this has been the development of computer aided manufacturing (CAM), a generic term for a variety of computer aided and computer controlled production machinery. Such technology is able to conduct a variety of different tasks under computer control with little, or no, human intervention.

Given the potential for such technology to profoundly affect the nature of shop-floor work, some commentators have likened the impact of CAM to a 'second industrial revolution' (Forester 1985). Barnes in Boddy and Buchanan (1982), comments 'It is no exaggeration to say that the impact of Information Technology, or IT, will be greater than that of any other technological developments that have come before – the invention of steam power, the telephone or electricity all included' (see Boddy and Buchanan 1986, p. 1). It is still too early to determine whether CAM can be considered to be 'revolution' or 'evolution'. Nonetheless, commentators do agree that CAM is having a dramatic impact upon manufacturing processes, and this trend is likely to continue for some time.

Clearly CAM influences a wide range of organizational issues, and space precludes a detailed consideration of all these factors (see Edwards 1989; Forrester 1985; Wall *et al.* 1987; Davids and Wall 1990; Wall and Davids 1991). While the developing literature is still in its infancy, a number of emerging themes can be identified. The aim of this chapter, however, is to describe briefly some of these main themes with reference to the job and organizational issues in general, and to the impact of CAM upon operator well-being and performance in particular.

The chapter is divided into five sections. The first section considers the nature of CAM and its current use in manufacturing industries. In the second section, we outline the impact CAM has had upon the jobs of shop-floor workers. The analysis is mainly at the level of operator skills and questions the widely held belief that CAM has the potential to radically reduce the skill levels of shop-floor operators. In the third section we examine the organizational implications of various approaches to the design of CAM jobs. Our aim is to evaluate the consequence of these job designs in terms of their effects upon the well-being of the operator and the performance of the system. The fourth section is concerned with the implications of CAM for industrial relations. Here we are specifically concerned with the potential of CAM to create conflict, and thus divisions, between sections of the workforce. In the final section, we offer some summary remarks and make some tentative suggestions for directions of future research.

THE NATURE OF CAM

CAM is a generic term for a wide range of computer controlled machines. Three levels of CAM can be identified. Firstly, there are 'stand alone' applications, such as computer numerically controlled (CNC) machines, used for such activities as drilling, grinding, cutting and insertion. Further examples include the use of robots for activities such as paint spraying and welding. As the name implies, these machines are operated in isolation from other applications, typically requiring human intervention only for such purposes as loading and unloading the machine. The operators' main responsibility is to monitor the machining process in case problems occur. In some situations, particularly with reliable technology, operators can have responsibility for several individual machines simultaneously (Martin and Wall 1990).

The second level of CAM occurs when several individual applications are linked together to form a flexible manufacturing system (FMS). The use of a common computer language coupled with compatible software allows several machines to work in co-ordination. In such systems, work can be transferred between a number of machines, by means of robots or conveyor belts, each machine being able to conduct a variety of different tasks. These types of systems still require human intervention, although less frequently than stand alone applications.

The third stage of CAM is arrived at when computer controlled manufacturing is linked into other organizational functions, such as production control, stores, and design. By achieving this it is possible to acquire total computer integrated manufacturing (CIM), where an entire production system is computer controlled. Such 'peopleless factories' are rare, and in reality are dependent upon indirect human support for their operation.

A number of general conclusions can be made concerning the nature of CAM. First, a wide variety of machines are being developed, which vary in their degree of computer and human control. In most cases the standard form of CAM is stand alone CNC machines which require human intervention. Second, the role of the operator in successful operation of CAM is critical. Thus, far from actually replacing humans, CAM is in many cases dependent upon them. Third, attempts are being made to integrate applications of CAM to achieve computer controlled manufacturing. However, few systems have been developed and, in reality, they are still dependent upon human support.

CAM AND OPERATOR SKILLS

One of the dominant themes in the literature on computer aided manufacturing concerns its potential to significantly reduce the skill levels of shop-floor operators. The origins of this argument can be traced through the work of Taylor (1911) and Gilbreth (1911), and is most recently represented with respect to CAM by Blauner (1964) and Braverman (1974). Put simply, the argument is that CAM, like any form of technological innovation, enhances the processes of the division of labour and job fragmentation. In this process the human skills associated with a task are broken down into their basic components, and jobs are designed such that the operator is required to perform as few of these components as possible. Among the organizational benefits of this approach is that training and learning times are shorter (as the operator has fewer skills to master) and operations are quicker (since only a limited number of movements are performed). A major consequence, however, is that the operator is left with a more specific, boring, and repetitive job.

Applying this perspective to computer aided manufacturing, Braverman argues that the introduction of such technology will further accelerate the process of job simplification (see also Cooley 1984; Noble 1977). He argues that the nature of the technology is such that it offers opportunities to transfer skill components from the operator's job and to allocate these to the machine. The important point of this perspective is that CAM does not inevitably lead to simplified jobs, rather it is the (mis)management of the technology in allocating the task functions between operator and the machine which result in this effect.

An example here highlights this process. Consider the operation of a lathe machine which cuts pieces of metal into a number of different shapes by moving a cutting tool into contact with a piece of rotating metal. The nature of the tool, speed of the object's rotation, and the angle and depth of cut determine the resulting shape of the metal. Traditionally, highly skilled operators were required to determine these parameters and execute these movements by manually moving the cutting tool into place. More recently, computerized (CNC) versions of lathe machines have been developed. In these machines the entire cutting process is controlled by the computer. The operator simply loads the machine, monitors the cutting cycle in case of error, and then unloads the finished product. All the knowledge required to control the cutting process (which hitherto the operator had been required to know) is contained in a computer program. Thus compared to traditional methods of working with a lathe machine, the CNC counterpart requires a less skilled operator, with the role of 'machine minder'.

The fact that CAM can lead to relative deskilling of jobs has been well documented in a number of studies across a variety of technologies and organizational settings (Butera and Thurman 1984; Shaiken 1979; Blumberg and Gerwin 1984). Additionally, such changes are typically associated with detrimental effects on operator well-being (Argote, Schkade and Goodman 1983). Two examples illustrate the effects typically associated with CAM. First, Patrickson (1986) reports on Australian newspaper printers' reactions to a change from traditional manual methods of work to an electronic production process. She found that two-thirds of the operators felt their jobs had become deskilled, and that they were 'subservient to the system'. Second, Wilson and Buchanan (1988) report a study involving three engineering companies which had introduced CNC machine tools for use in making components for power-generation equipment. The authors note that the resulting CAM jobs required much reduced decision-making skills and other associated job tasks. They conclude that as a result of the introduction of CAM, 'many turners feel that they have less control over their work process, feel less involved in their job and experience less job satisfaction and greater stress' (p. 378).

In the face of the evidence supporting a deskilling effect of CAM, a growing number of researchers have begun to question the generalizability of such a relationship (for example, Jones 1982). Indeed some applications of CAM have resulted in jobs which require greater operator skills, and consequently have a positive effect upon operator well-being (Kemp and Clegg 1987). Buchanan and Boddy (1983), for example, show that in a biscuit manufacturing company, the introduction of computer-controlled methods led to both positive and negative reactions.

Differential responses to CAM need not be linked to solely objective job changes, but are also linked to how operators perceive their computerized tasks. This was demonstrated in a study by Majchrzak and Cotton (1988) of a longitudinal survey of thirty-one machine operators changing from traditional mass assembly to computer-controlled assembly of telephone equipment. Initial inspection of the results showed a corresponding change to operators' perceptions of the new computer-controlled jobs, but no change in their well-being (psychological problems, job satisfaction and work commitment). Closer examination, however, showed that a differential pattern was evident, with the sample being split into two equal groups. Those operators who perceived their computer-based job as involving less automation and greater control over their work reported increased well-being. Thus it was the operators' perception of the CAM job which determined their well-being.

More damaging evidence for the deskilling hypothesis has come from a number of observations that both negative and positive operator reactions have been observed arising from the *same* application of CAM (Kemp, Clegg and Wall 1984) and from studies which have specifically aimed to enrich CAM jobs (the latter aspects are discussed in more detail later).

We conclude this section with a few summarizing statements. First, research into CAM has focused on the impact such applications have upon the skill level of shop-floor operator jobs. A number of researchers claim that the introduction of CAM will accelerate the process of job simplification which is prevalent in manufacturing industries. The main effect of this process will be an erosion of operator skill, which will consequently have a detrimental effect upon operator well-being. Whilst many examples of this process have been observed, such a relationship is neither universal nor deterministic. Organizations have choices over the design of shop-floor jobs, and the resulting impact this has upon the operator. In the next section we examine some of these organizational choices, and the effects these have upon the design of shop-floor work.

CAM AND SHOP-FLOOR JOB DESIGN

One of the conclusions drawn from research in the preceeding section is that CAM can lead to jobs which are either deskilled or enskilled. The key determinant of the direction of the effect is dependent upon at least two factors. The first factor concerns the nature of the technology. It is logical to assume that the range of tasks available to the operator is related directly to the capability of the machine. Some machines, by their design, are able to perform a complete task independent of the operator, while others rely to a greater extent on human input. Thus it is only possible to enhance operator skills where the technology allows. Given the fact that one of the primary aims of designers of CAM is to reduce operator involvement, it is thus not surprising that the operators of such systems have simplified jobs. To counter this trend, several researchers are active in the pursuit of designing CAM which facilitates rather than negates operator skills (see chapter 11).

Second, and more importantly to the present discussion, the nature of the job design depends upon choices made by management concerning the allocation of functions between the operator and the machine. To some extent this is dependent upon the first factor, namely the nature of the technology and the resultant range of tasks available. Whilst the range of tasks may be limited, there are alternatives and thus choices as to their allocation. These alternatives involve decisions concerning the allocation of tasks between the operator of the technology and specialists who support the production process (such as maintenance, engineering and programming personnel).

In many organizations, the allocation of tasks is such that as many as possible are assigned to specialists whilst leaving operators with the minimal number of tasks. The wisdom of this choice, which is often referred to as 'specialist control' (Clegg and Corbett 1986), is based upon a particular perception of the technology, and follows these lines. CAM consists of expensive and sensitive technology which requires expert guidance in its operation. Shop-floor operators do not have the skills or knowledge to handle the technology, and therefore it is necessary to place such responsibility in the hands of trained specialists. Such reasoning echoes the deskilling thesis discussed above. Elsewhere Majchrzak (1988) has aptly referred to a 'technical superstar' mentality, to describe this tendency.

The consequence of this choice, in terms of job design, is that the operator's job tends to become simplified and to consist mainly of a narrow range of simple and repetitive tasks. On the other hand, specialists' jobs become enriched, and they gain greater control over production. In this scenario, some have described the operator's role as that of a 'machine minder' (Martin and Jackson 1988), whose main responsibility is to visually monitor the machine and to alert the specialist whenever a problem occurs. It is thus not surprising that under these conditions operators often report low job satisfaction and motivation at work (Blumberg and Gerwin 1984; Scarborough and Moran 1985).

While many organizations have adopted the specialist choice option when introducing CAM, a minority of companies have taken a different route to the design of shop-floor jobs. Part of the reason for this has been the realization that the successful operation of CAM is more reliant upon human intervention than originally expected. As stated earlier, the anticipated 'peopleless factories' have not emerged, and it is clear that the majority of applications of CAM require human support (Adler 1988; Hirschorn 1986; Valery 1987). To this end the role of the operator has been critically examined, with the general conclusion that more, not less, control should be allocated to the users of the technology. This option, referred to as 'operator control' (Clegg and Corbett 1986), involves allocating as many tasks as possible to the operators of the technology. Moreover, these tasks should be of a nature which allows the operator to deal with operational problems, so that production is maintained with minimum recourse to specialist involvement.

Naturally, there is a limit to the nature of tasks which can be allocated to the operator, with major problems (requiring detailed knowledge) remaining under specialist control. Nonetheless, it is possible for the operator to deal with a wide range of problems which can occur with the machine, such as editing faulty computer programs, and basic maintenance. This choice of work design involves a greater active involvement of the operator in their work, correspondingly less reliance being placed upon specialist support. Wall (1986) has termed this role that of the 'operator midwife', drawing an analogy with that of the medical midwife, who is an expert but is nevertheless aware of certain problems which might occur for which outside help by a specialist (in this case a doctor) is required when they occur.

Given that organizations have choices concerning the design of jobs, this raises the important question of which design is more effective in terms of operator well-being and performance. To the best of our knowledge, only one study has been reported which has empirically compared the effects of specialist and operator control job designs. This study, by Wall *et al.* (1990) examined a group of nineteen operators in a company that manufactured printed circuit boards for use in computers. The operators worked on CNC machines, which automatically insert a wide range of electrical components into a computer board. When introducing these machines, the company's management had adopted the specialist control option when designing shop-floor jobs. The operator's job consisted of three main stages; loading the computer board into the machine, monitoring the insertion process for errors, and unloading completed boards. Thus the operators had little control over their work, and when errors occurred they were required to notify the relevant specialist (such as an engineer) who would make the necessary corrections. Not surprisingly, operators reported dissatisfaction with their jobs, and machine output was below expectations.

In order to remedy these problems, the company changed the operators' jobs in line with the operator control option described above. This involved identifying the key problems which cause machine breakdown, and then incorporating as many corrective tasks as possible into the operator's job. Thus instead of relying upon specialists, the operators played an active role, whereby they corrected many errors themselves. A comparison of breakdown data for fifty days before (specialist control) and fifty days after (operator control) the changes revealed a highly significant decrease (40 per cent) in machine downtime. Furthermore, questionnaire data revealed that the operators reported greater job satisfaction and lower job pressure under the operator control option compared to the specialist control option. Thus it is clear from this study that operator control led to enhanced well-being and performance. There are three main explanations for this, and these are described below.

The first explanation for the superiority of the operator control option draws upon traditional job design theory. It is widely accepted that jobs which offer greater variety, control and discretion over work are associated with improved job satisfaction and motivation (Herzberg 1966; Hackman and Oldham 1976). Thus the operator control option is one which leads to a 'good' job design and is one which should promote positive operator well-being and operator performance. Such an explanation is of limited utility however, due to the reliance upon a general conceptualization of motivation as an intervening variable between the effects of the job and performance (Wall and Martin 1987). While motivation may make people *want* to work harder, the extent to which such effort will result in increased performance depends upon a number of factors, particularly the opportunity to produce more work. When the work is highly constrained by external factors, as is the case with CAM, increased effort alone is unlikely to result in greater productivity, since the speed and capacity of the technology is fixed (Wall and Davids 1991). Thus while a favourable job design may motivate operators to increase their work effort, this is unlikely to result in improved performance, unless it is directed at reducing machine downtime.

The second explanation for the benefits of operator control draws upon the wider literature of organizational psychology. Research examining the relationship between technology and performance (for example, Woodward 1965; Perrow 1967) suggests that the most appropriate response to production uncertainty is to develop operators who have greater control over their work. This line of reasoning has been more explicitly stated by researchers advocating the socio-technical systems theory (for example, Cherns 1976; Trist *et al.* 1963). One of the main principles of this approach is the concept of 'controlling variances at source', where a variance is any unplanned deviation from expectation. Thus controlling these variances as close as possible to their point of occurrence should result in fewer production problems, which in turn leads to increased output. Within the context of CAM, a variance can be considered as any problem which results in machine stoppage (and consequently lost production). Therefore, controlling these variances at source will result in fewer production disruptions. Since the operator is the nearest person to the source of variances, they are in the ideal position to effectively correct them when they occur.

The third explanation for the superiority of operator control focuses on the role of tacit skills to operator performance (for example, Kusterer 1978;

Cavestro 1989; Wood 1990). Tacit skills are based on the subjective knowledge gained through direct work experience, rather than formal training programmes (Polanyi 1973; Koestler 1976) and has been identified as an important determinant of performance in CAM (Leplat 1990; Wall and Davids 1991). When faced with complex systems, individuals tend to enhance task efficacy at a tacit level by inducing rules and procedures which are often difficult to articulate. Thus one of the benefits of the operator control option is that it allows operators to gain detailed knowledge of the technology, facilitating the development of tacit skills, which had hitherto not been possible with specialist control.

However, the development of tacit skills alone is not sufficient unless there is a willingness to operate them (Blumberg and Pringle 1982). Thus although the operator may develop the capacity to enhance performance, the willingness to implement such skills may be a function of relevant factors such as incentive schemes. It has been shown that performance in an iron foundry was related to an incentive payment scheme, such that wage incentives stimulated employees to develop tacit skills which improved performance (Davids *et al.* 1991).

To summarize this section, a number of general points can be reiterated. First, there is variation, thus choice, as to the design of shop-floor CAM jobs. These choices are shaped by a number of factors, prominent among which is the perception of the technology held by key decision-makers in the organization. Second, the dominant organizational response to CAM has been to design jobs such that operators have a narrow and restricted role, while the major responsibility for the technology resides with specialists. Only a minority of organizations have attempted to counter this by enlarging the operators' job, to give them greater control over their work. Third, these two alternatives differ markedly with respect to their impact upon operator well-being and system performance. There is considerable theoretical, and limited research evidence, to suggest that the operator control option is one which will lead to enhanced operator well-being and performance. Three alternative explanations have been offered for the benefits of operator control, which focus on job design theory, organizational theory, and tacit skills.

CAM AND SHOP-FLOOR CONFLICT

The introduction of any new production system is often associated with resistance from the operators of such systems. The reasons for this are many and complex, but often arise from fears that the new system will have a negative effect upon their jobs. It is therefore not surprising that a technology with profound implications for jobs, such as CAM, should be associated with industrial conflict.

A full review of the causes of industrial conflict associated with CAM is beyond the scope of this chapter. However, two areas of concern are highlighted which are of particular relevance (see also Clark 1989; Carlopio 1988). First, there has been the belief that CAM would lead to industries which are technologically-driven, and that human input would be subordinate to that of machinery. In such a situation, people would have a supporting role, and consequently would be of secondary importance to technological considerations. Moreover, the types of jobs operators held would be boring and unskilled. It is this line of argument which underpins the deskilling thesis described earlier.

Second, and perhaps more damaging, there has been a widespread belief that CAM would replace operators, thus resulting in massive job losses. Ironically, some people have considered CAM to have a potentially positive effect for society by releasing humans from the mundane routine of work and providing ample leisure time. It soon became clear, however, that certain sections of the workforce are likely to be 'released' from work sooner than others, and that the anticipated 'extra leisure time' corresponded to long lengths of undesirable unemployment. For these groups of individuals CAM has come to represent a real threat to their livelihood.

The combination of these two fears, amongst others, has often led to considerable industrial conflict when CAM has been implemented (for example, Kemp and Clegg 1987). This conflict has resulted in a number of disputes between management and shop-floor personnel, particularly when the users of the technology have not been consulted prior to its implementation. Quite clearly, many operators were lacking in knowledge of the technology and the consequence it would have upon their jobs.

In some of our own research we have noted operator resistance to CAM which has resulted in industrial disputes (for example, Davids and Martin 1990). More recently, however, we have witnessed a new trend in industrial conflict associated with CAM, which has been related to a change in attitudes by shop-floor operators. While these attitudes were initially negative, for reasons outlined above, more recently they have tended to become increasingly favourable.

This change has occurred because of a greater awareness of the impact of CAM, together with the realization that many initial fears were unfounded. Hence, while jobs have been lost due to CAM, there have not been the widespread redundancies once forecast. In some cases CAM has in fact led to increased jobs, while in others it has made more secure those industries which were once threatened with closure. Furthermore, due to the complexity of CAM, human input has become more rather than less important, emphasizing the critical role the human operator has in such systems.

The improved attitude towards CAM by operators has greatly reduced conflict between management and shop-floor and has resulted in greater co-operation in implementation. Ironically, the improved image of CAM has resulted in a new type of conflict emerging. Given the importance of CAM for organizational competitiveness, coupled with a reduction of fear associated with the technology, many operators now perceive CAM-related jobs as being more important and having greater security than non-CAM-related jobs. Paradoxically, many operators are grasping at the opportunity to be trained in technological skills, in the belief that it will greatly enhance their job prospects. This has led to a growing competitiveness, and often conflict, between groups of operators on the shop-floor for control of the technology. More specifically, non-users of technology perceive themselves to be increasingly under threat from the users of CAM.

As suggested earlier, recent research by Davids and Martin (1990) illustrates the potential of CAM to result in significant levels of intra-workforce conflict. We examined a medium-sized engineering factory in the north of England which made industrial stamps and dies. The study was conducted in the machining shop, where seventeen operators worked on a number of cutting, milling, grinding and drilling machines. The operators manufactured a number of key metal components for use in other parts of the factory. The machining shop was typical, in terms of personnel and technology, of many found in light to medium engineering companies.

During a five-year period, seven stand alone CNC machines were introduced which were able to carry out a number of tasks, all under computer control. While CNC machines were operated alongside the conventional (manual) machines, both sets of machines had their own operators. While the CNC operators occasionally worked on the conventional machines, conventional machinists never worked on the CNC machines.

When the CNC machines were introduced, there was concern among the shop-floor operators. Some workers viewed the technology as a necessity for organizational development, while others believed that CAM implementation was the first step towards deskilling, lower work satisfaction, and job losses. Since there was little rationalization of the implementation of the technology to the shop-floor employees, opinions were varied, and were dominated by proactive individuals. This led to bad feelings between management and the shop-floor, and gradually relationships within the machine shop deteriorated.

As time progressed, the operators began to realize that many of their initial fears were unfounded. In particular, the introduction of CAM did not lead to the anticipated job losses. The improved operator attitudes towards CAM helped considerably towards reducing conflict between management and the operators. During this time shop-floor perception of the CNC machines changed. Initially, the new machines had been feared and resisted, but with reducing hostility they came to be viewed as an asset to the company. Many believed that the stability of the company depended upon their use, and that therefore those who worked on the CNC machines had a more prominent role within the company and thus had more secure jobs.

The changing perception of the CNC machines resulted in a new type of conflict emerging within the company, which centred on divisions between users of the CNC machine and the conventional machinists. Many of the conventional machinists resented the CNC operators, perceiving them as being more highly valued by management. This division between the conventional and CNC operators soon led to much conflict, and resulted in little co-operation between the two groups.

Four particular examples highlight the conflict between these two groups. First, conventional operators began to avoid the CNC operators, and withdrew from their social activities. Indeed, they formed their own informal social club which excluded CNC machinists. Second, in an attempt to increase their own identity, conventional technologists began to wear surplus-store East German army shirts as an unofficial 'uniform'. This served the purpose of highlighting the conventional group membership, making them appear different from the CNC operators. Third, derogatory graffiti concerning CNC operators and supervisors appeared on the walls of the facilities. Fourth, the two groups sat in separate, pre-designated sections in the canteen, which had hitherto not occurred prior to the introduction of CAM.

Our observations concerning the implications of CAM to shop-floor conflict can be simply summarized. Initially, operators fear the consequences of CAM in terms of its impact upon job content and job losses. These concerns often lead to a lack of co-operation during the implementation stage. More recently, however, a greater awareness of the technology, together with a reduction in the initial fears associated with CAM, has fostered more favourable attitudes among many shop-floor personnel. Consequently, users of CAM are perceived as having more stable and secure jobs compared to non-users, who often perceive their jobs as being threatened by the technology. This has resulted in a change in conflict, away from management and shop-floor, to between users and non-users of CAM.

SUMMARY

The aim of this chapter has been to consider some of the psychological and organizational implications of working with CAM. Much of the research in this area has focused on the potential for such technology to significantly reduce the skill level of operator jobs. In many cases CAM has resulted in simplified jobs which contain a narrow range of highly repetitive tasks. Not surprisingly, operators under these conditions report low job satisfaction and work motivation, and system performance is often below expectations. Whilst in many cases these (negative) effects do occur, a number of organizations have followed a different approach, with the aim of enriching rather than deskilling operator jobs.

Given that there are choices concerning the content of CAM jobs, an important question concerns the implication of these job designs for operator well-being and performance. We have argued for the operator control choice, whereby jobs are designed so that the operator has as much control as possible over the technology. Drawing from the wider literature in occupational psychology, there is ample support that giving operators greater control will lead to enhanced psychological well-being and improved system performance. To date there is little empirical research in this area, and clearly this issue warrants closer examination.

Another factor identified as important in this chapter of particular concern is the issue of industrial relations associated with CAM. We have raised this as a potential problem, since we have observed a change in focus in conflict on the shop-floor. Initially operators resisted CAM, which led to problems between management and shop-floor, in many cases leading to industrial action. More recently, however, CAM has come to be perceived as essential for manufacturing organizations, and those who work with it have a powerful role in the company. Thus CAM operators are often seen as having more important and secure jobs, compared to conventional (manual) operators. This in many instances is leading to intra-shopfloor conflict between users and non-users of CAM. We believe that the conflict between users and non-users is likely to increase, and could potentially lead to serious problems on the shop-floor.

We conclude this chapter with a comment on the research base (for more details see Wall and Davids 1991). To date, most research has analysed CAM on a macro level and has been of a case-study nature. While this research has been very important in its own right, there has been little complementary research on a micro level, particularly examining the implications of various job designs upon operator well-being and performance. Clearly, any area of investigation needs to take a multi-level approach, and we would argue that this is particularly true in the case of CAM. However, research in this area is clearly biased, with few empirical studies at the micro level. It is our belief that this bias should be redressed by systematic empirical research which closely examines the implications of CAM. It is only by conducting complementary research on all levels of enquiry that a complete understanding will be gained, and thus the full potential of CAM realized.

REFERENCES

Argote, L., Schkade, D. and Goodman, P.S. (1983) 'The human side of Robotics: How workers react to a robot', *Sloan Management Review* 24: 31–41.

Blauner, R. (1964) *Alienation and Freedom: The Factory Worker and his Industry*, Chicago: University of Chicago Press.

Blumberg, M. and Gerwin, D. (1984) 'Coping with advanced manufacturing technology', *Journal of Occupational Behaviour* 5: 113–30.

Blumberg, M. and Pringle, C. (1982) 'The missing opportunity in organizational research: Some implications for a theory of work performance', *Academy of Management Review* 7: 360–9.

Boddy, D. and Buchanan, D. (1986) *Managing New Technology*, Oxford: Blackwell.

Braverman, H. (1974) *Labor and Monopoly Capital*, New York: Monthly Review Press.

Buchanan, D.A. and Boddy, D. (1983) 'Advanced technology and the quality of working life: The effects of computerized controls on biscuit-making operators', *Journal of Occupational Psychology* 56: 109–19.

Butera, F. and Thurman, J.E. (eds) (1984) *Automation and Work Design*, New York: North-Holland.

Carlopio, J. (1988) 'A history of social psychological reactions to new technology', *Journal of Occupational Psychology* 61: 67–77.

Cavestro, W. (1989) 'Automation, new technology and work content', in S. Wood (ed.) *The Transformation of Work*, London: Unwin Hyman.

Cherns, A. (1976) 'The principles of sociotechnical systems design', *Human Relations* 29: 783–92.

Clark, J.A. (1989) 'New technology and industrial relations', *New Technology, Work and Employment* 4: 5–17.

Clegg, C.W. and Corbett, J.M. (1986) 'Psychological and organizational aspects of computer aided manufacturing', *Current Psychological Research and Reviews* 5: 189–204.

Cooley, M.J.E. (1984) 'Problems of automation', in T. Lupton (ed.) *Proceedings of the First Conference on Human Factors in Manufacturing*, New York: North-Holland.

Davids, K., Jackson, P. and Wall, T.D. (1991) 'Tacit knowledge and performance of complex manufacturing systems', manuscript in preparation: SAPU Memo No. 1216.

Davids, K. and Martin, R. (1990) 'Shop-floor rebellions', *Industrial Society* March: 26–7.

Davids, K. and Wall, T.D. (1990) 'Advanced manufacturing technology and shop-floor work organization', *Irish Journal of Psychology* 11: 109–29.

Edwards, J. (1989) 'Computer aided manufacturing and worker well being: A review of research', *Behaviour and Information Technology* 8: 157–74.

Forester, T. (1985) *The Information Technology Revolution*, Oxford: Blackwell.

Gilbreth, F. (1911) *Brick Laying System*, New York: Clark Publishing Co.

Hackman, J.R. and Oldham, G. (1976) 'Motivation through the design of work: Test of a theory', *Organizational Behaviour and Human Performance*, 16: 250–79.

Herzberg, F. (1966) *Work and the Nature of Man*, Cleveland, OH: World Publishing.

Jones, B. (1982) 'Destruction or redistribution of engineering skills? The case of numerical control', in S. Wood (ed.) *The Degradation of Work? Skill, Deskilling and the Labour Process*, London: Hutchinson.

Kemp, N.J. and Clegg, C.W. (1987) 'Information technology and job design. A case study in CNC machine tool working', *Behaviour and Information Technology* 6: 109–24.

Kemp, N.J., Clegg, C.W. and Wall, T.D. (1984) 'Human aspects of CAM', paper presented at IEE International Conference on Computer-Aided Engineering, University of Warwick, 10–12 December.

Koestler, A. (1976) *The Ghost in the Machine*, London: Picador.

Kusterer, K. (1978) *Know-How on the Job: The Important Working Knowledge of Unskilled Workers*, Boulder, CO: Westview Press.

Leplat, J. (1990) 'Skills and tacit skills: A psychological perspective', *Applied Psychology: An International Review* 39: 143–54.

Majchrzak, A. (1988) *The Human Side of Factory Automation*, San Francisco: Jossey Bass.

Majchrzak, A. and Cotton, J. (1988) 'A longitudinal study of adjustment to technological change: From mass to computer-automated batch production', *Journal of Occupational Psychology* 61: 43–66.

Martin, R. and Jackson, P.R. (1988) 'Matching AMT jobs to people', *Personnel Management*, December: 48–51.

Martin, R. and Wall, T.D. (1990) 'Double machine minding and psychological strain', *Work and Strain* 3: 323–6.

Noble, D.F. (1977) *American by Design: Science, Technology and the Rise of Corporate Capitalism*, New York: Alfred Knopf.

Patrickson, M. (1986) 'Adaptation by employees to new technology', *Journal of Occupational Psychology* 59: 1–11.

Perrow, C. (1967) 'A framework for the comparative analysis of organizations', *American Sociological Review* April: 194–208.

Polanyi, M. (1973) *Personal Knowledge* (2nd edn.), London: Routledge and Kegan Paul.

Scarborough, H. and Moran, P. (1985) 'How new technology won Longbridge', *New Society* 71: 207–9.

Shaiken, H. (1979) 'Impact of New Technology on Employees and their Organizations', Research Report, International Institute for Comparative Social Research, Berlin.

Taylor, F. (1911) *The Principles of Scientific Management*, New York: Harper.

Trist, E., Higgins, G., Murray, H. and Pollack, A. (1963) *Organizational Choice*, London: Tavistock.

Wall, T.D. (1986) 'Advanced manufacturing technology: The case for the operator midwife', in H. Noori (ed.) *Managing New Technology: Today's Competitive Weapon*, Waterloo, Ontario: Wilfred Laurier University and Government of Ontario Ministry of Trade and Technology.

Wall, T.D., Clegg, C.W. and Kemp, N.J. (eds) (1987) *The Human Side of Advanced Manufacturing Technology*, Chichester: Wiley.

Wall, T.D., Corbett, J.M., Martin, R., Clegg, C.W. and Jackson, P. (1990) 'Advanced manufacturing technology, work design and performance: A change study', *Journal of Applied Psychology* 75: 691–7.

Wall, T.D. and Davids, K. (1991) 'Shop-floor work organization and advanced manufacturing technology', in C.L. Cooper and I. Robertson (eds) *International Review of Industrial and Organizational Psychology 1991*, Chichester: Wiley.

Wall, T.D. and Martin, R. (1987) 'Job and Work Design', in C.L. Cooper and I. Robertson (eds) *International Review of Industrial and Organizational Psychology 1987*, Chichester: Wiley.

Wilson, F. and Buchanan, D. (1988) 'The effect of new technology in the engineering industry: cases of control and constraint', *Work, Employment and Society* 2: 366–80.

Wood, S. (1990) 'Tacit skills, the Japanese management model and new technology', *Applied Psychology: An International Review* 39: 169–90.

Woodward, J. (1965) *Industrial Organization: Theory and Practice*, Oxford: Oxford University Press.

Part IV

Change methods and methodologies

Introduction

Neil Anderson and Dian Marie Hosking

The three chapters in Part IV focus upon the methods and methodologies employed by work and organizational psychologists to understand, describe, and intervene in organizational change processes. Given the contributions already made by management scientists generally, and by organization development specialists and strategic management practitioners in particular, it is instructive to ask what organizational psychology might add. What methods are available to organizational psychologists? What are their merits and demerits? In which circumstances are certain methods more appropriate than others? With what criteria do we make judgements about our research methods and interventions? And ultimately, how are we to decide whether our methods generate accurate and comprehensive accounts of the multi-faceted phenomena of organizational change? Underlying this last question are the ubiquitous issues of the epistemological and ontological bases of our efforts to research into processes of organizational change. The three chapters in Part IV address these issues, but in quite differing ways.

In Chapter 13 Francescato and Tancredi explicitly offer an 'integrated approach' to change. In so doing, they set themselves apart from the many psychological and social-psychological approaches which focus narrowly on, for example, motivation, attitudes, skill or social relations. Of course there are other approaches to organizational change which claim to be 'integrative'. However, this has meant, for example, combining an emphasis on motivation, and social relations. When Francescato and Tancredi speak of 'integrative' they imply going beyond the disciplinary focus of many interventions. They intend to be multidisciplinary, to move away from the limited scope of, for example, approaches which focus primarily on process issues (as in OD), and to make use of a variety of perspectives to produce different pictures of organizational realities. Their underlying argument reflects what they refer to as an 'epistemology of complexity'. They take the view that different perspectives deal with different realities, and provide complementary descriptions and explanations. Each may provide a helpful way to analyse and understand organizations; each is valid in its own terms.

Their arguments about the need for, and the validity of, an integrative approach have a number of implications for the types of intervention they practice. Their change methods involve working with all participants in a particular organizational unit. To the extent that they have a theory of change, it seems to lie in an emphasis on increasing understanding (of the complexities of their organizations); reducing anxieties (through better understanding); and increasing problem-solving abilities. It is worth noting that this is another way in which they differ from other 'integrative approaches'. The emphasis on problem solving they share with traditional OD. However, unlike OD, they focus on the content of what is and should be, rather than the process. Their interventions are designed to get participants to work through four perspectives. Each of these is understood to emphasize different realities of organization. The perspectives are: strategic, functional, psychodynamic, and psycho-environmental. Participants are encouraged to attend to the many interconnections between 'variables', both within and between perspectives, and to consider what they imply for organizational change.

To conclude, Francescato and Tancredi outline their change methodology and link it to an argument in favour of an eclectic, multiple-perspective understanding of organizations. These arguments primarily concern epistemological and methodological issues; the former certainly justifies greater explicit attention than it typically has received in the organization change literatures.

Ernecq, in the following chapter, adopts a somewhat more case-specific focus of attention. He presents a detailed case study of a mail-order company in France in the throes of an intervention programme, from the perspective of a participant-observer in this process. The magnitude of the intervention itself, the introduction of educational programmes for less qualified staff, stands in stark contrast to the unplanned and wide-ranging effects upon organizational climate, working practices, and human resource management procedures which result. Ernecq presents results which attest to these unintended consequences. These results support assertions made by the editors in Chapter 1, that organizational change processes are actually far less manageable in practice than had previously been presumed. The major consequences in Ernecq's case were indeed unimagined, given that the focus of the intervention was solely upon the levels of education of organizational members. One is forced to question just how impotent senior management were to even influence these circumstances even if they had been foreseen in advance? Appropriately, to conclude this

chapter, Ernecq considers the role of the W/O psychologist in such intervention programmes and attempts to place his own actions in context by
reviewing his role as participant-observer to this organizational
intervention.

The final chapter, by Catherine Cassell and Mike Fitter, reports on a
project intended to provide the unwaged with access to information technology resources in two local community centres in Sheffield, UK. An
action research methodology is employed to evaluate the project and to
provide feedback to the participants. In reviewing this methodology, the
authors elaborate and redesign Lewin's original model of action research,
arguing that their extended model should facilitate future research by
organizational psychologists interested in this approach. Specifically, they
superimpose a number of feedback loops to illustrate the different types of
feedback (operational, strategic, and policy-making) provided by the action
researcher to the organization at different stages in their research relationship. Developing this process to consider the vested interests of different
groups involved, a stakeholder perspective is explored to describe matches
and mismatches in perceptions of user interests. The authors conclude their
chapter by examining their experiences as W/O psychologists utilizing
their modified version of the action research approach.

13 Methodologies of organizational change

The need for an integrated approach

Donata Francescato and Mario Tancredi

In this chapter we will review briefly some of the main approaches to the study of organizations to show how each gives a distinctive but partial contribution to the understanding of organizational phenomena. We shall argue for a multidimensional perspective to promote organizational change. We finish by presenting a multi-dimensional training and intervention technique we have developed to promote organizational change.

WHY WE NEED A MULTIDIMENSIONAL APPROACH

Society has undergone rapid and dramatic social, political, technological and cultural changes over the last fifty years. These have deeply affected the way organizations and individuals live and think about themselves (De Masi 1985, 1987; Naisbitt and Aburdene 1990).

While society itself has changed rapidly, this has not been true of approaches to the study of organizations. In a major review of organizational theories, Bruscaglioni (1982) states that they can be grouped into four main approaches: sociological-structural; systems-functional; socio-analytical; and psychosocial. These are summarized in figure 13.1. Bruscaglioni stresses that in organizational studies, it is not so much a question of having competing theories, using different concepts and arguments to explain the same aspect or problems, but rather that theories use different concepts to explain *different* aspects or problems of organizations. For example, we might find that a theory which clarifies the conflictual aspects of organizations, neglects to explain the cooperative components; while another approach explains clearly why organizations are co-operative, at the same time failing to explain why they are conflictual.

The fact that a theory or paradigm reveals only a portion of the truth is in part a consequence of the historical period in which it arose, and the kinds of questions it tries to answer. To some degree, theories depend upon

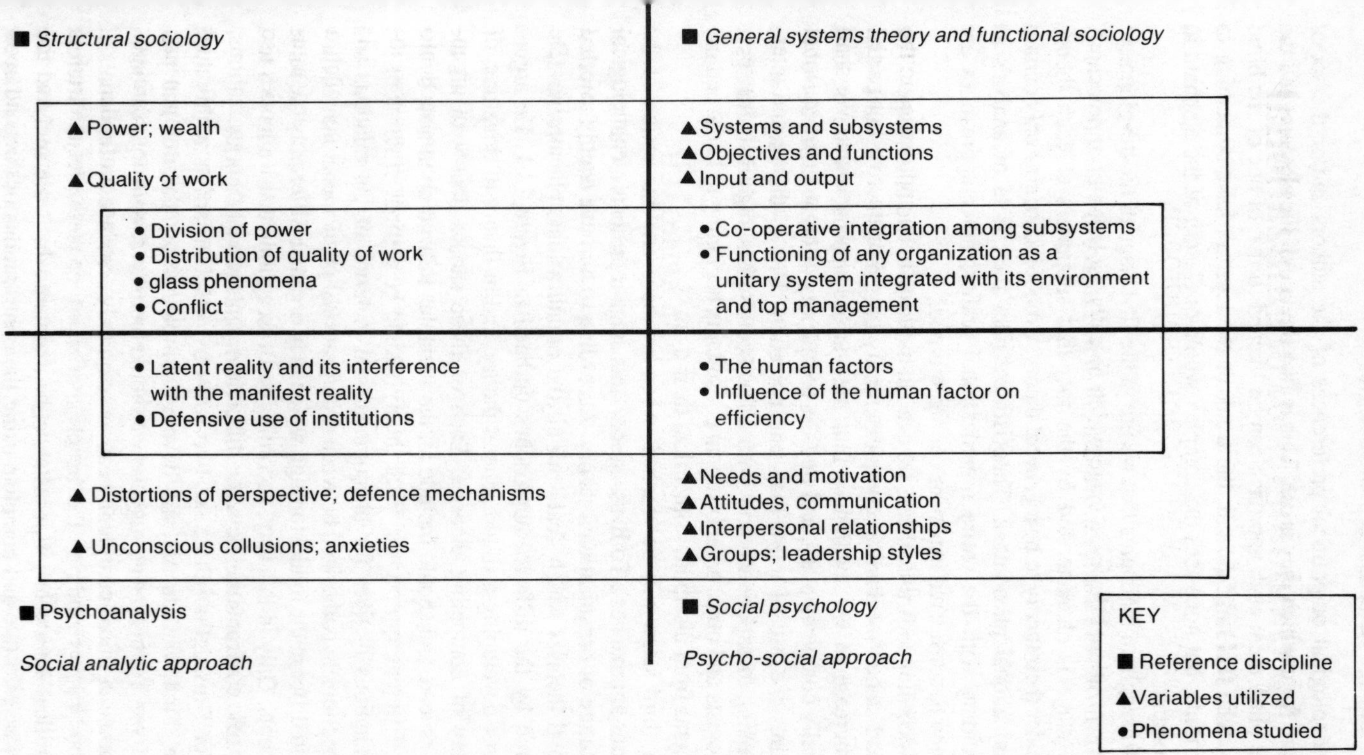

Figure 13.1 Variables, phenomena and reference disciplines of the main approaches to the study of organizations (Bruscaglioni 1982)

the ideological or political preferences of the authors and/or the social culture from which they arose. This is like the tale of the elephant and the three blind men: each approach can be likened to that of one of the blind men, who feel only the tail, the trunk or the legs; all have something to contribute, but none sees the complex whole or *Gestalt* of the elephant in its context.

Bruscaglioni maintains that we are in the first stage of the development of organizational theory, a stage which he calls 'isolation of approaches'. This stage is characterized by the fact that supporters of each theory consider their theory to be a *general* theory, even if it concerns only certain organizational phenomena. Theorists consider their field of analysis as coinciding with the entire organizational reality; other approaches are unknown, considered irrelevant, or are spurned.

According to Bruscaglioni, we need to move on to two other stages. The second stage, 'mechanical complementarity of approaches', is marked by an increase in the awareness that the various approaches are at least partially complementary, and that the complexity of organizational reality requires the use of more than one approach. This is the stage we are beginning to experience now with a few sociologists, organizational psychologists and other organizational consultants beginning to know and use concepts from disciplines other than their own.

A third stage will be reached, when we have an 'integration of the various approaches'. To Bruscaglioni, this stage represents a challenge for the future of organizational theory. According to him, we could formulate general theories which deal with all the organizational phenomena considered by the different approaches outlined in Figure 13.1. He argues against developing a single general theory, and in favour of developing a variety of competing theories. Each of these should deal with all the phenomena, and should include all the variables utilized up to now by the four different approaches. Each theory should be distinct in terms of the explanations it gives for phenomena, and in terms of the relations and connections hypothesized between organizational phenomena: that is, they would differ in the model through which they organize differently the same elements. Only in this way, according to Bruscaglioni, can we have a real scientific confrontation between different organizational theories.

For Bruscaglioni there are two ways by which to arrive at this third stage. First, we can use and develop complementary theories and perspectives. To this end he suggests we should focus on certain organizational phenomena whose complexity can more quickly convince professionals of various backgrounds of the benefits of using concepts from different theoretical approaches. For instance, he maintains that 'role analysis' can be more effective and complete using the contributions of three different theories: the systemic functional approach, to understand the dynamics of organizational functions; the sociostructural approach, to deal with themes of class identity and class conflict; and the psychological approach, which has more to offer on the topic of interpersonal relations within the organization.

A second path to the third stage passes through the development of what Bruscaglioni calls 'the technique of crossing variables and phenomena of the various approaches': by this, he means we should study phenomena traditionally investigated by one approach, using variables traditionally associated with another approach. The numerous approaches he cites include the study of the influence of structural variables, such as power and income, on unconscious perceptions of individuals and groups in organizations (such as anxiety, intraphysic conflict, perceptual distortions); relations between psychosocial variables (such as work motivation) and functional variables (such as different ways to organize a task, or allocate functional responsibilities); and relations between psychosocial variables and sociostructural variables (working for a private or public institution, with decentralized or centralized decision-making structures, etc).

By following these two paths, Bruscaglioni feels that we can accommodate the epistemological and ontological differences which characterize the four main approaches (Figure 13.1). Bruscaglioni seems to adhere to the theory of complexity proposed by Morin (1988), believing that as we accumulate knowledge through the different approaches, we also raise our awareness of phenomena not previously examined. In giving up the dream of one 'all-encompassing' theory, Bruscaglioni maintains there is no single perspective from which all reality can be made to converge, but that there is a multiplicity of aspects, each coexisting and each valid in its own terms.

We also believe that we are witnessing the passage from linear epistemology to the epistemology of complexity. Applying this to our present discussion we argue that there is no single 'best way' to look at organizations, but many satisfactory ways. Further, by using more than one way, we will increase both our knowledge and our capability to find more valid solutions to the complex problems facing organizations.

One example of the above may be found in the potential value of integrating the socio-analytical approach with the system-functional schools, which will become more important as we move increasingly towards a service economy. To illustrate: Barassi (1988) argues that the organization of services must be seen partly as a problem in interpersonal communication – because there is no material product, as in industry, to act as a buffer between producer and consumer. In farming and manufacturing, the mental emotive worlds of the farmer or skilled worker, and the consumers of food or artefacts, can be independent of one another. A farmer can produce good or bad grapes, whether or not he/she likes the person who will buy them in the supermarket. The quality of the product does not depend on the interaction of producer and consumer. With services, however, the quality of performance may depend not only on economic and functional dimensions, but also on the motives of people, who have to interact and give each other feedback by which to reach a common goal (such as in teaching, consulting, psychotherapy, etc.).

Moreover the quality control in face-to-face services comes *after* the service is performed, while in back-office service, or in manufacturing, quality control can be done before the product/service is rendered to the client. Motivating a professional to perform a crucial face-to-face part of a job will become more important, and the need for participative decision making may increase, giving more relevance to the contributions of the psychosocial approach.

We need to move in the direction indicated by Thompson (1967), when he pointed to the desirability of identifying typical variables common to all kinds of organizational realities, because they are ways of coping with uncertainty. Thompson made one of the first attempts to integrate different approaches to understanding complexity. He underlined the interplay between the task environment, the level of technological innovation, the business domain, and organizational structure. He stressed that by moving to a service economy, and from homogeneous and stable environments to heterogeneous and unstable environments, we were maximizing uncertainty. He recognized the irrational component of organizational behaviour, underlying the subjectivity involved in all strategic decision making when preferred outcomes are unclear and the technology of how to produce the desired effect is also uncertain.

In addition to these challenges from theory a vital stimulus, again favouring multiple perspectives and integration, came from our work as trainers and consultants. Again and again we found that our clients lacked a clear picture of the complexity of organizational functioning. This was true whether or not they belonged to top or middle management in a manufacturing firm; whether they were nurses, doctors, or administrators in a health setting; or principals, teachers or parents in a school. It was as if the isolation of approaches denounced by Bruscaglioni in relation to theories, could be seen in the daily working lives of people in organizations. Often we observed that individuals or subgroups tended to overvalue their own functions, minimizing or not recognizing the contributions of other professions or work-units. Even more interesting was the failure to understand interactions between the legal, economic, functional and psychological dimensions of organizational life. It was as if a person's discipline and training, and their role in an organization, promotes a tendency to look at one particular dimension only of organizational functioning. Perhaps this behaviour may also be a response to the anxiety felt in the face of uncertainty and complexity. This attitude, in turn, can lead to intergroup conflicts, feelings of powerlessness, and a decrease in operational efficiency.

MULTIDIMENSIONAL ORGANIZATIONAL READING: A TRAINING AND INTERVENTION METHODOLOGY

For these theoretical and empirical reasons we felt the need to elaborate a methodology which could be used both as a diagnostic tool and as a training technique to increase participants' understanding of the complexities of their organizations. By this methodology each participant is helped to understand that different theories share a common interest in the same organizational phenomena, and each tries to measure certain variables of organizational functioning. Each has its own methodology: an ensemble of tools and techniques producing certain kinds of data which allow a certain 'reading' of organizational functioning. But just as we see different images through a kaleidoscope as we adjust it, so different theoretical approaches lead us to gather different kind of data. None of these data are more or less 'true'; they are simply different views of reality.[1]

Why use more than one 'reading'? First, it increases people's capacity to identify both problem areas and strong points of organizational functioning. In other words, to use the data as a basis for a multifaceted diagnosis of organizational functioning. Second, more than one reading enlarges participants' awareness of the interconnections between the variables they have to take into account when they want to promote organizational change. Third, multiple perspectives empower participants to face uncertainty with less anxiety, and to find new ways of handling problems.

In our multidimensional organizational analysis we train participants to consider four major approaches, which focus on what we called strategic, functional, psychodynamic and psycho-environmental dimensions.[2] The dimensions are summarized below.

The strategic dimension

This deals with the juridical, political and economic aspects of the task environment. We include in this dimension the analysis of the strategic history that brought the organization into existence. This includes its primary aim in relation to certain environmental variables (what kind of business it should be, what goals it should pursue, and by what technologies they could be achieved) and how this evolved.

We have developed a set of guidelines which direct participants to look at a variety of materials[3] from which they can ascertain the opportunities and the limitations within which the organization has been functioning. For instance, working in a co-operative which provides health services we found, through examining EC laws that the co-op could obtain free training for their workers (an unused opportunity). In another case we found that EC regulations limited the steel output a particular factory could produce, forcing it to operate below capacity.

The functional dimension

This includes organizational components related more directly to operational achievement of the organizational objectives. As a tool for analysis at this level, we chose a schema designed by Tancredi (1981, 1985, 1989). He examined the interaction between three subsystems of functioning, all of which are necessary to reach organizational aims.

The management control system includes the main functions of planning, organizing and efficiency control. It is the system in charge of decision making, taking into account strategic aims and environmental constraints.

The operating system's main function is to produce actions. It involves the functions of resource acquisition, transformation, and distribution. It also deals with acquisition and training of personnel, and with acquisition of knowledge and finance.

Finally, the information system deals with gathering, coding and transmission of data, which in turn are used by management to control and to plan.

Examining how each function is performed in the organization, one can detect a problem area in which some function is not done well, or lacks connections with other functions or with the task environment. Consequently one can find possible functional improvements and consider their repercussions on other organizational functions.

The psychodynamic dimension

This tries to explore the unconscious aspects of organizational life at the individual, group and cultural levels. We make use of the works of Carli and Paniccia 1981, Cotinaud 1975, Enriquez 1980, Lapassade 1975, and Muti 1986. We have developed a variety of subjective techniques to explore this dimension. These include individual and group drawings and free associations, 'work short stories', jokes, sayings, and analysis of materials hanging on office walls etc. For instance, we may divide the group into professional subgroups. The longest-working member of each subgroup tells the others the history of the organization through what they perceive to have been its main events. Each worker is then interviewed by the others on their work history, both before and after they entered the target organization. While one talks, others are instructed to look for constant themes of both content (what the person is telling) and process (how, with what emotion, voice, expression etc.) as they appear in the work story. They are also asked to note beliefs and attitudes toward work, expectations, relations with peers and authority figures. Listeners are also helped to consider their feelings while hearing the different work stories, and to find out what the various professional stories have in common, or how they differ, and so on. Then each professional subgroup relates the results of their discussion, and all groups, together, try to distinguish common elements and differences that may illustrate the cultural and psychodynamic climate of the work group and its subgroups.

The psycho-environmental dimension

This includes many of the phenomena studied by industrial and organizational psychologists. These include leadership styles, communication patterns, and motivation. We have also introduced concepts borrowed from environmental psychology such as 'behaviour settings' and 'environmental pressure' (Francescato and Ghirelli 1988, Moos and Mitchell 1982). We look for the amount of psychosocial fit between environmental pressure and individual expectations.

The tools used for the analysis of this dimension vary. They include individual and group interviews, scales, questionnaires, action research, and group discussions. We have also used scales that measure various cultural characteristics (Spaltro 1981, Moos and Mitchell 1982).

After all four dimensions have been explored by all participants, and after they have produced a list of problems and areas of strength for each separate dimension, the participants then look for connections among various dimensions, which problems seem to come up with different aspects in most dimensions, etc. Then the participants elaborate a final diagnosis of strengths, problems areas, and contributing factors, and the results of this organizational diagnosis are compared with those of the preliminary analysis, done informally by the group at the beginning of the seminar. Then the group works on establishing priorities for change, and decides which dimension is best to start implementing them.

We do our multidimensional organizational reading with people working together in a service or in the same organizational sub-unit of a big company. When professionals or managers approach us with some organizational problem, we offer to try our multidimensional analysis as a means of understanding the problems and suggesting possible solutions. We explain its aims and methods as outlined earlier. Regardless of who is paying (a private firm, local or regional government) we consider our client to be all the people belonging to the organizational unit under study (see Francescato and Ghirelli 1988). We do not run this kind of seminar unless this condition is agreed: the methodology relies on the confrontation among different kinds of knowledge, competences and subjectivities, so we require the active participation of people in all functions and hierarchical levels. Final position papers or change plans formulated during the seminar are shared in written form with all participants, and not just with top management. Sometimes this participatory style is too foreign to the culture of the organization, however, and therefore the intervention is not attempted.

A CASE STUDY

The target of our case study was a public drug addiction unit, located in central Rome. The unit is one of many belonging to the public health agency (USL) in Rome. We held a training seminar with the entire professional staff: four nurses, eight doctors, four psychologists, four social workers, one head medical co-ordinator, and four administrative workers. We also included three members of the board of directors of USL, who had direct responsibilities for the drug addiction service, and two members of the political board of control who legally, financially and politically were responsible for the entire health agency.

We had a total of nine meetings, each three hours long, which were held every other week for about five months. We began by asking the entire group to list strong and weak points of their service, and to indicate factors that either contributed to the creation of problem areas or were points of strength. It turned out that the main problems were lack of motivation on the part of the professional staff, and disorganization. They attributed these problems to worker burn-out, lack of interest in drug addiction, indifference on the part of the political board members, and poor management skills. A tendency for each group to blame other organizational components for inadequacies of organizational functioning was especially obvious (professionals blamed politicians, who blamed administrative staff, who felt misunderstood by professionals, etc.).

We used two meetings to examine the strategic dimension. The entire group was divided into professional subgroups to examine relevant national, regional and local legislation as well as economic data. Each received guidelines which contained a series of questions they had to try to answer together. At the end of their analysis they found out, for instance, that local political and professional management had interpreted the national law in an unduly restrictive sense – giving methadone to drug addicts, and neglecting those points of the law which emphasized prevention or sanctioned intervention in cases of other addictions, such as alcohol, smoking and food abuse. Also, politicians had not allowed doctors to take blood samples to test for AIDS, because of an alleged lack of insurance coverage. Examining documents from other drug centres in Italy, however, revealed a legal loophole by which they could get insurance cover. It was also concluded that the drug centre had been set up with poor strategic goals, because no real study had been made of the catchment area, to ascertain prevalent needs and to help formulate specific goals.

During the functional analysis (two meetings), each professional subgroup examined how it fulfilled its own operational functions. Subgroups then discussed together how the information system and the management control system functions were handled in the service as a whole, using the schema previously described as a guideline for their discussions.

After the functional analysis, participants were able to identify a series of functions that had not been performed, but which could be done under existing structural conditions (economic, legal, staff and space limits). These included: the recruiting of ex-addicts for tasks of prevention, through school discussions and assistance to in-treatment addicts; the creation of a network of important professionals and other interested parties (relatives, police agents, pharmacists) who could be helpful in organizing educational activities; and outreach programmes on local radio and TV shows.

Subgroups also produced numerous recommendations for better internal functioning. These included the improvement of information gathering and data transmission, to produce better plan and outcome evaluations, and the promotion of better integration among different professionals, through better run staff meetings (to meet this goal they decided they needed further training, which they later received).

Analysis of the psychodynamic dimension required two meetings. The methodology included using word association with drawings of the drug-addiction centre drawn by each participant; and the associations made to all drawings together; and connecting these associations with the key words emerging from the tales of their work short stories. Analysis showed that the group perceived there was a climate of conflict and depression, connected at least in part with disagreement between different professions, and associated with difficulties with their co-ordinator, who had been promoted from within the ranks. His former colleagues wanted him to behave like a real 'boss' when confronting politicians, administrators or prominent members of the community, and yet to be 'one of the boys' inside the service. The group of professionals both longed to have a professional leader and refused to have one. This ambivalence lay behind many of the functional problems which had arisen, when the co-ordinator had proposed new procedures.

The psycho-environmental dimension was examined in two meetings. Specially constructed interviews were used, which tried to probe the fit between individuals' work-related desires and organizational goals, as well as scales which measure organizational stress, motivation, feelings of power, leadership styles, and optimism to solve problems (Spaltro 1977). The group found there was a huge discrepancy between the kind of tasks different professionals wanted to do, and what they felt the organization required of them. There was a lot of conscious dissatisfaction, and low professional self-esteem. There was a strong need, expressed especially by social workers and psychologists, to further their professional development.

The last meeting was dedicated to examining the interconnections between the various dimensions, and establishing priorities for desired changes. An important point that emerged was the interplay between the strategic and psychodynamic dimensions. The restricted interpretation of the law had focused the entire drug service primarily on the use of methadone for rehabilitation. This had severely limited the professional role of doctors, giving them an impossible task: to stop drug addiction by creating another drug addiction. Furthermore, by focusing on rehabilitation of hard core addicts instead of prevention, the service had attracted a concentration of criminal, violent and often deranged clients. These clients behaved very differently from ordinary medical clients, upsetting and even threatening their doctors. This produced on a psychodynamic level feelings of panic, rage, and impotence. These personal feelings interfered with the therapeutic work, patients being seen as 'enemies', and created a tendency to blame others (other staff members, politicians, etc.). This fostered interpersonal and professional friction, which in turn contributed to lowering of the capacity for group cohesion in goal setting and implementation.

There was an interplay between functional and psychodynamic dimensions as well. The political and higher level directors did not plan regularly, and did not therefore give operational objectives to the professionals, who were left to decide more or less on their own what to do with their time, besides giving methadone. This lack of planning and control was experienced on a psychodynamic level as a feeling of 'being abandoned', 'cast off as the drug addicts themselves'.

After outlining the kinds of problems that were most common, we had participants work on the two or three they considered more urgent and had some power to do something about. We concentrated on opportunities within the limits the organization presented. For instance, the lack of firm guidance from top management could be seen as an opportunity for a high degree of professional autonomy. So professionals were asked how they could spend their time more rewardingly, and plans were made taking into account both unmet needs of clients and professional preferences. These plans were later presented to top management, and permission was obtained to experiment with them. For instance, two psychologists began working with parents of schoolchildren with educational problems; another worked with the families of drug addicts. Some social workers and nurses started a programme for alcohol dependency. The medical staff, while still bound by law to give methadone, found a way to distribute it only on some days of the week, on a fixed schedule, in order to have time to carry out more meaningful professional work (research on drug-related diseases, check-ups, etc.).

We did a follow up after two years and we found that meetings were scheduled regularly, and the entire staff had received further training in group skills. Both through individual interviews and through observation of staff meetings, we found that these functional changes had had an impact both on the psychosocial dimension (workers' satisfaction improving) and also on the strategic dimension. This was one of the few drug centres in Rome which obtained extra funding from the regional government for new pilot projects.

Since we developed this method in 1982 we have applied it in work settings as diverse as steelmills, chemical plants, health agencies, and educational and recreational facilities (Francescato and Ghirelli 1988, Tancredi and Francescato 1989). Seminars are generally conducted by two trainers: a work or community psychologist, and an organizational consultant (systems engineer or economist). The systems engineer plays a major role in the analysis of the first two dimensions, while the psychologist is more active in the analysis of the latter two, but they work together as a team. Both stimulate the entire group to look for connections among the four dimensions, to come up with the final diagnosis. Observations of group processes made by the psychologists during the first sessions on strategic and functional analysis are offered and discussed as data during the psychodynamic and psycho-environmental analyses.

In conclusion, we would say that examining an organization from a perspective that takes in both broad environmental variables and deep unconscious feelings allows one to develop professional modesty and confirms the need for interdisciplinary teams. The participatory process we use during our seminar has persuaded us of the need to share knowledge and know-how with participants, who want to learn how to monitor their own organizational development. We think organizational analysis in the future could become more and more part of a continuous educational process, and therefore intervention, consultancy and training may become more integrated.

NOTES

1 The various approaches can be seen to lie on a continuum on the level of data validation. Some of the approaches deal with hard, objective variables, on which consensual validation is easily obtained or which are long established (such as geographical boundaries, number and types of shares, machines, buildings, laws, statutes, credits and debts, market share, level of schooling of work force, etc.). Some deal with soft subjective variables which are not easily measured, or whose existence and measurement are subject to much controversy. These include unconscious images of work settings, deep-seated attitudes toward work and power, and intergroup conflicts. We were convinced that in spite of these differences on the level of data validation, we had to include approaches which dealt with variables on both 'objective' and 'subjective' levels of organizational functioning. We also accepted that we had to use methodologies which were different, but were valid within each approach for our dimensional readings. We then had to look for the connections between the phenomena on which the different approaches focused in order to diagnose weak and strong points of organizational functioning for our final organizational check-up.

2 An organization has at least four dimensions. We include in the word 'dimension' all the phenomena and variables taken into account, and the methods used to measure the phenomena and variables. Each theoretical approach is an ensemble of theories which focus on the same dimension of organizational reality.

3 Obviously the materials gathered differ according to the target organization. However, we have a list of general variables we look at in all organizations. For instance, we can look at organigrams, statutes, laws, level of technology employed, share of market, age and schooling of workforce, etc.

REFERENCES

Barassi, D. (1988) *The Service Idea*, Edizioni Il Sole 24 ore.

Bruscaglioni, M. (1982) 'Il comportamento organizzativo' ('Organizational behaviour'), in M. Bruscaglioni and C. Spaltro (eds) *La psicologia organizzativa (Organizational psychology)*, Milan: Angeli.

Carli, R. and Paniccia R. (1981) *Psicosociologia delle organizzazioni e delle istituzioni (Psychosocial analysis of organizations and institutions)*, Bologna: Il Mulino.

Cotinaud, O. (1975) *Groupe et analyse institutionelle*, Paris: Editions du Centurion.

De Masi, D. and Bonzanini, A. (eds) (1984, 1987, 1988) *Trattato di sociologia del lavoro e dell'organizzazione (Textbook of work and organizational sociology)* (three volumes), Milan: Angeli.

Enriquez, E. (1980) 'Interrogation ou paranoia, enjeu de l'intervention', *Sociologie et société* 9(2): 79–104.

Francescato, D. (1975) *Psicologia ambientale (Environmental psychology)*, Rome: Bulzoni.

Francescato, D., Cudini, S. and Putton, A. (1986) *Star bene insieme a scuola. Strategie per un'educazione socioaffettiva dalla scuola materna alla scuola media inferiore (Getting along well in school. Strategies for a socio-affective education from nursery school to secondary school)*, Rome: Nuova Italia Scientifica.

Francescato, D. and Ghirelli, G. (1988) *Fondamenti di psicologia di comunità (Foundation of community psychology)*, Rome: Nuova Italia Scientifica.

Lapassade, G. (1975) *Socioanalyse et potentiel humain*, Paris: Gauthier Villars. Paris 1975.

Lorau, R. (1975) *L'analyse institutionelle*, Paris: Les Editions de Minuit.

Morin, E. (1988) *La methode III, La connaissance de la connaissance*, Paris: Editions du Seuil.

Moos, E.H. and Mitchell, R.E. (1982) *Multiphasic environmental assessment procedure manual, data collection forms and handbook*, Palo Alto: Stanford University.

Muti, P. (1986) *Il lavoro di gruppo (Working in groups)*, Milan: Angeli.

Naisbitt, J. and Aburdene, P. (1990) *Megatrends 2000*, New York: William Morrow.

Spaltro, E. (1977) *Il check-up organizzativo (The Organizational check-up)*, Milan: Isedi.

Tancredi, M. (1981) 'Un modello dinamico del processo aziendale' ('A dynamic model of the business process'), *Direzione aziendale* 2: 73–8.

Tancredi, M., Francescato, D., Giammarco, I., Prezza, M. (1985) 'Politica del personale, controllo di gestione, sistema informativo e prestazioni di prevenzione primaria e secondaria nei consultori, familiari delle Unità Sanitarie locali di quattro regioni italiane ('Personnel policy, management control, information system and primary and secondary prevention activities in family counselling centres of public health agencies in four Italian regions'), *Psicologia Clinica* 3: 364–91.

Tancredi, M. and Francescato, D. (1989) 'L'analisi organizzativa come strumento di formazione-intervento' ('The organizational analysis as a tool for training and intervention'), *Rivista AIF* 6: 37–42.

Thompson, J. (1967) *Organizations in Action*, New York: McGraw Hill.

14 Planned and unplanned organizational change

Consequences and implications

Jocelyne M. Ernecq

INTRODUCTION

Recent literature and massive interest in organizational change may lead one to believe either that social science has discovered a new concept, or that change has become the fashionable thing to study. But what do we mean when we speak of 'change'? Is it an event, a phenomenon, a sociological mutation, a variable or a variance, a stimulus or a response? Does one study change *and* organizations, changes *in* organizations, or organizational change?

Raimbault and Saussois (1983) wrote that the term 'change' is 'overused; behind it one finds a spectre of multiple meanings and contradicting interpretations'. Some authors use the word to refer to developments external to organizations. For example, Landier (1984) and Wilpert (1987) write that in order to survive, firms must adapt to economic, technological, and sociological changes in their environment. Pémartin (1987) distinguished 'intrinsic' changes, in aspects of the firm itself, from 'extrinsic' changes, environmental evolutions over which firms have no control, such as monetary fluctuations, consumer protection laws, or improved technology of competitors. According to him, extrinsic change plays the role of independent variables; organizations, however, may introduce intrinsic change not only as a reaction to environmental changes, but also as a means by which to modify relations with the environment.

Gilbert (1988) pursues this idea, and prescribes that organizations should not submit passively to external changes, but should manage, and even provoke, the necessary internal transformations in the organization. One notes here not only the shift in the use of the term 'change' but also in the focus of interest, from external environmental change to internal organizational change; from the study of change *and* organizations, to that of changes *in* organizations.

Interest further shifts to how internal changes can be brought about in the organization. The term 'OD' refers to a specific approach of creating desired changes in the functioning of an organization (Schein and Bennis 1965; French and Bell 1973). The term 'planned change', used by Huse (1980), Tessier and Tellier (1973), and Gilbert (1988) seems to have wider applications, and may be used to refer to different methods of carrying out desired changes, including those interventions with purposes and phases different from those of OD. Raimbault and Saussois (1983) propose to study the 'process of organizational change'. For them, organizational change exists whenever there are transformations in the rules, tools, and norms of the organization. In OD, 'planned change', and 'process of organizational change', the main focus is on the actual carrying out of desired changes in the organization.

When the word 'change' refers to environmental mutations external to the organization, it is a stimulus-change, provoking internal adaptations on the part of the organization. When the term refers to these internal adaptations in the organization, it is a response-change. In OD and planned change, these internal adaptations may function either as stimuli or responses, or both. French and Bell (1973) describe the OD process as consisting of interventions in the client system, and responses to the interventions. 'Planned change' and 'process of organizational change' may be viewed as an ensemble of stimulus-changes voluntarily carried out to bring about desired response-changes in the organization; a sequence of stimulus-response chains carried out in specific parts of an organization. However, the systems approach emphasizes that, because organizational phenomena and dynamics are interrelated, interdependent, and are in constant interaction, one cannot change one part of a system-organization without changing other parts in some ways, and without changing the total organization itself (French and Bell 1973). It is in this way that OD interventions and planned change may be viewed as multiple-stimulus-change and multiple-responses changes, bringing about organizational change.

OD or planned change processes involve carrying out changes in the organization with the purpose, and inevitable result, of changing the organization itself. The objective of OD is to improve the organization's problem-solving and renewal process (French and Bell 1973). The focus is on the organization's capacity to adapt to its environment, to respond to external stimuli-changes, to become or remain more viable. This link to external stimuli-changes provides OD and planned change purpose and direction, and a context for evaluating and interpreting results (Pémartin 1987).

While the purpose and end result of OD and planned change is the development of the whole organization and not just its component parts, the process consists of carrying out changes in component parts. Evaluation of the impact of planned change may take the form of measuring resulting changes in the organization's capacity to adapt to its environment, or simply demonstrating that 'organizational change' has been achieved, by identifying and measuring changes in the organizational components, both anticipated and unanticipated in the intervention. Pémartin (1987) acknowledges that in the evaluation of planned change, the common temptation is to look only at obtained anticipated changes. The systems approach analysis in terms of multiple causes and multiple effects is a safeguard against this temptation; the model does predict 'organizational change', meaning changes in the organization's members, rules, structures, and tools other than those directly specified or involved in the planned change; these should, therefore, not come as a surprise. One just has to track them down and include them in reporting the results of the intervention.

In this case study, the author presents as an illustration of 'planned change', an experience with a firm's project designed to improve the organization's adaptive capacities by developing the skills of certain members. Brought in by the organization to monitor and facilitate the implementation of the project, the author was in an appropriate position to observe and participate in a planned change, and to evaluate its impact in terms of the 'organizational change' obtained. Difficulties were encountered in the selection of changes to include in the evaluation. Which resulting unintended change can be reasonably linked to the planned change? Undoubtedly, the training in organizational psychology and the active involvement of the author influenced his perceptions and selection. The inevitable influence of 'subjective' factors in research has been studied by other authors, who conclude that it is highly important that researchers identify the theories and models they utilize (Curie and Cellier 1987; Fouchard 1989; Touati 1985).

In this case study, the author uses OD and systems concepts and models in order to demonstrate that 'planned change' results in 'organizational change', that changes carried out in one part of the organization system bring about changes in the total system. The objective is not to describe the process itself, but more modestly to draw out concrete illustrations of organizational change in terms of observed and measured transformations and modifications apparent in the organization's members, rules, structures and tools.

BACKGROUND OF THE CASE

The organization which provided the setting for this case study was a private mail-order firm in the north of France. About two-thirds of the company's 3,500 employees had barely completed primary school, and had clerical and manual jobs such as packing parcels or unloading trucks. Of 649 employees tested by a university educational institute, 52 per cent were found to have language abilities equivalent to that of eight-year-olds in the third year of primary school. They had few qualifications and were at risk of unemployment in the near future, due to the company's plan to increase robotization and automation, and due to the growing demand for greater technical and intellectual abilities. It was against traditional company policy and practice to make workers redundant, yet to remain competitive the company had to undertake programmes of modernization and rationalization. Future jobs, such as machine repairmen, credit analysts, and robot technicians, required levels of technical and commercial skill equivalent to at least those of secondary school leavers, much higher than that possessed by the majority of the company's clerical employees and workers.

The planned change

Convinced of the potential aptitudes and willingness of its employees and workers, the company decided to introduce general education courses in its training programmes. The objective was to upgrade the low academic levels of volunteer employees and workers, making them eligible for technical or commercial courses which would develop the skills and capacities required to hold jobs in the future.

Traditionally, the company's training programmes were concerned only with job-related matters, and most seminars were reserved for executives and supervisors. In September 1985, however, general education subjects such as spelling and grammar were introduced in the training programmes, and were made available to volunteer clerical employees and workers. Courses were held during working hours in company premises, at no cost to trainees. Eleven courses of four types were offered to volunteer employees:

1 Courses of general interest, intended to attract employees to enroll by providing positive non-threatening experiences of the training situation. Examples of this type of courses were 'Basic Notions of Economics', 'Introduction to Computers', 'Law in Daily Life' and a 'Self Assessment' course, designed to help trainees take charge of their own professional career development, to identify strengths and weaknesses, and to elaborate an appropriate project of self-development. Courses averaged thirty-five hours each, held once or twice a week in half-day or whole-day sessions.

2 General education courses, intended to upgrade low academic levels in language (reading, writing, spelling, and grammar) and in mathematics (arithmetic operations, percentages, and algebra). Courses were for sixty hours per term, held twice weekly in two-hour sessions.

3 Courses intended to develop problem-solving and reasoning skills. A course entitled 'Logical Action' was created by a university institute for adult continuing education. It was run by a multi-disciplinary team for a total of ninety hours, one day a week. It was created after an analysis revealed that most future jobs required improved or enhanced capacities of logical reasoning.

4 Semi-professional courses, intended to develop skills required in administrative types of office work. There were thirty-hour courses in typing, in writing business letters, in presentation of graphs and tables, and in basic statistics.

Methods of evaluation

The project was monitored continuously by the author, an organizational psychologist working in the company's training office. In June 1988, after three years of operation, a comprehensive evaluation of the project was made. Methods typically used in OD diagnosis were used to identify and, whenever possible, measure the changes in individual and group behaviour. Performance in pencil and paper achievement tests were used by teachers to monitor trainee performance before and after courses. A local university educational institute administered standardized language and mathematics achievement tests, using French national norms to transform levels of achievement into a six-point scale with equivalents in terms of primary and secondary school levels. Satisfaction and attitude changes were measured by questionnaires, group and individual interviews conducted by the university's educational counsellors, and by the company's training and recruitment staff. In regular contacts with supervisors, with trainees and their co-workers, and with the personnel department, the author collected verbal reports of their observations and opinions, and added these to his personal observations and diagnoses.

SUMMARY RESULTS

The first measure of the project's impact was the number of persons it affected directly. A total of 1,046 persons underwent training in one or more of the eleven courses. That 46 per cent of the target population manifested the expected behaviours in terms of their agreed personal development objectives may be interpreted as the first change in the organization.

The second measure of impact was the actual improvement in the qualifications and skills of the trainees. The upgrading of language and mathematical abilities of the trainees were clearly demonstrated by performance in tests before and after training. Teachers used tests to determine whether a trainee could be promoted to the next-level course. At the end of a term, an average of 46 per cent of language trainees and 72 per cent of mathematics trainees would be promoted. The graphs of the distribution of the total 392 language trainees before and after training on the university's normalized six-level scale of language achievement showed that the mean, median and mode increased by one level: from that equivalent to the third year of primary school, to that of the second year of secondary school. Two-hundred-and-eight or 53 per cent of language trainees attained the next superior level to their pre-training level; twenty persons changed two levels. Of the 190 mathematics students, 80 per cent changed levels, and ten attained the second highest level, equivalent to that of a secondary school leaver.

In order to evaluate the project in relation to its objectives, data on the professional development of the employees were also collected. Various measures of job mobility were used, including a random sample of a hundred trainees compared with a matched group of non-trainees. The rate of vertical job mobility, defined as an actual change of jobs with an increase in qualification, was 24 per cent in the trainee group compared to 17 per cent among the non-trainees. Of the 228 trainees who attended the 'Self Assessment' course, 47 per cent displayed subsequent professional development, such as applying for better jobs, enrolling in professional training courses, obtaining promotion, requesting aptitude testing and counselling. The recruitment office of the company reported that in the year following the start of the project, trainees represented 78 per cent of first-time job applicants, and in general were perceived by the recruiters as being more confident, and as displaying less anxiety in test and interview situations than non-trainees. Twelve supervisors reported observations that their workers taking language courses demonstrated increased willingness to speak out in group meetings and to volunteer written information to the meeting.

Finally, to really measure the impact of the project on the company's development strategy and to provide figures useful to company executives, data were interpreted in economic and employment terms. The number of persons at the level of language mastery required for secretarial types of jobs increased by 15 per cent, from 94 to 108 persons. Half of the eighty-eight persons who started training at levels equivalent only to primary school attained higher levels, enabling them to be eligible for pre-professional training. A total of 104 persons were accepted in training programmes designed for jobs with better employment prospects; 27 per cent had taken general education courses. Had it not been for the general education courses, these twenty-eight employees would not have been eligible for the professional training programmes; and had it not been for the project, these 104 persons would surely have joined the ranks of the unemployed in a couple of years' time.

Economic figures and pay-back estimates showed that the costs of the project were far overweighed by what would have been the financial and social costs of making redundant employees who were low-qualified, but high-tenured, experienced, and loyal workers. This was in addition to the potential costs of hiring persons who might have been more qualified, but who would have needed time and investment to learn the company ways and methods.

The non-anticipated changes

The changes observed in persons, groups, procedures and norms *not* directly involved with the project illustrate the interrelated dynamics in a human organization. The company is indeed a system wherein a change in one domain necessarily has repercussions throughout the whole system. A comprehensive evaluation of the impact of a planned change on the whole organization requires going beyond the sub-systems targeted by the planned change, and identifying and, if possible, quantifying the modifications which took place in other components of the organization. The lack of appropriate instruments available to measure these unanticipated changes limited the author to the use of observations and verbal reports of the presence or absence of changes.

Other changes in the trainees

Changes in the trainees were not limited to acquisition of the skills and knowledge taught in the eleven courses. There were changes in individual attitudes and receptiveness to learning in general, for example familiarity with test situations and working with groups. Trainees learned about the company structure and practices through their co-trainees; in some cases friendship bonds were created. In 87 per cent of group interviews held at the end of courses, an increase in knowledge about the company's diverse activities and functions was ranked by the trainees as being among the three most important gains from the training. Behaviour modifications which could be categorized as 'personality' changes were also reported; such attitudes were transferred to work and non-work situations. In individual interviews of random samples of trainees of the self-assessment courses, 84 per cent cited an increase in assertiveness and self-confidence. Supervisors reported that trainees demonstrated better understanding of instructions, more fluent expression of opinions, an increased ability to propose solutions, not only in work but also in quality circle meetings. Observers also noted fewer errors in spelling and grammar, in speeches and pamphlets written by trainees.

Activities which fell outside the sphere of work were likewise affected. In individual interviews with counsellors, more than one-third of trainees reported an increase in their abilities and self-confidence in helping their own children in school work. In some instances there was a re-distribution of tasks and responsibilities in housework and childcare among family members, especially between spouses, in order to enable the trainees, the majority of whom were working mothers, to adapt to the course schedules and to study at home.

Changes in individuals and groups other than the trainees

Twenty professional trainers and educators were brought in from public and private institutions to run the courses. Those directly concerned were not only the volunteer trainees actually enrolled in the courses, but also the target population of 2,200 low-ranking employees and workers who received information concerning the project and its results. The supervisors of these persons were also directly concerned, because they had to integrate the project in their daily schedules and accountability systems. Other staff and line members of the company became indirectly involved by the adaptations that had to be made to the company's policies and procedures. Government agencies became involved when the company obtained state funding for its efforts in improving the qualifications of the labour supply in the north of France.

Managers of the company were confronted with the conflict between strict norms of productivity and time 'lost in unproductive training'. They had to adjust their notions of production to a new notion of training as part of working hours. What was until then a vague notion of 'human resources development' became more concrete, and had to be integrated in the existing management practices and rewards system. Supervisors had to learn the meaning and uses of aptitude tests, skills acquisition tests, language and mathematics mastery levels, professional development, career planning – things which had always been regarded as the exclusive domain of professionals in education or personnel. First-line supervisors so clearly understood the importance of general education courses in assuring professional development, that in 1987 fifteen of them enrolled in language and grammar courses. A term later, eleven supervisors started arithmetic courses.

Co-workers of trainees had to cope with changes in the behaviour and work schedules of trainees. Work teams experimented with innovative methods, such as job-sharing and flexible hours. The information campaign conducted in order to reduce resistance to the project was directed at all employees; for many, it was an occasion to learn certain concepts, such as 'aptitude'. Employees who discovered they did *not* need remedial training gained enough self-confidence to apply for better jobs. Slowly but surely, some employees started to feel personally responsible for their own professional evolution, instead of continuing to expect to be 'taken care of' by the personnel office of the company. Counsellors reported that about 85 per cent of trainees interviewed in their first term of training expected the recruitment office to indicate which future jobs to prepare for, and which training courses to take. Over time, this attitude changed; 58 per cent of trainees interviewed in their fourth or fifth semester had personally selected the type of future job they desired, and had drawn up personalized training programmes based upon an introspective assessment of their needs and strengths.

Changes in the organization's climate, rules, methods, policies

A net improvement in employees' attitudes towards the company was shown by the climate audits made by an outside consultant in 1985 and again in 1988. The project was cited by more than 25 per cent of respondents in the survey as one of the positive actions of the company. There was strong approval of the company's efforts to minimize the risks of future unemployment among its personnel, by investing in training.

The organization's procedures and norms were also affected by the project. The systems for accounting for hours worked and production time had to be changed to integrate training hours during working time. Changes in the organization of work and team structures were implemented, such as job-sharing, rotation, shifts, task redistribution, and extensions of beginning and leaving times. Performance-appraisal criteria were modified to avoid penalizing individuals and teams whose measures of production were affected by the absence of trainees who were attending courses. Factors included to calculate productivity were changed; efforts for human resources development were introduced as a criterion for evaluating the managerial performance of supervisors.

THE ROLE OF THE ORGANIZATIONAL PSYCHOLOGIST

Officially commissioned by the training department to supervise the project, the author functioned as co-ordinator and centralizing figure for all parties involved in the project. There was direct access to information and decisions concerning the introduction and actual running of the eleven courses. Quite often the author assured the flow of communication between different decision makers, and gave feedback of information and data concerning the ongoing changes for them to decide on further actions. For example, the author helped first-line supervisors draw up a proposal to upper management executives based on an analysis of their difficulties in integrating training hours in their calculations of working hours. It resulted in changes in the methods used throughout the company to calculate production time.

Although a member of the organization, the author was a 'third party': not a teacher, nor a trainee, nor a manager, therefore external to the subsystems initiating and directly affected by the planned change. Actively involved in the implementation of the project, especially in the collection and feedback of relevant information and data, the author acted partly as a 'change agent'. Brought in to facilitate the implementation of the project, the author did not participate in the first phase of diagnosis and problem identification which resulted in the decision and choice of the project; his mission was clearly to help carry out a 'planned change', rather than conduct an OD intervention. To overcome resistance, much time was spent informing all parties concerned; there were new concepts and procedures to be explained, suspicions and fears to be allayed. The author was in direct contact with the different persons concerned, in their offices, their work sites, and in the training rooms. In these day-to-day relations, the author solicited remarks, opinions, suggestions and gathered information and data on how the organization and its members were changing as it assimilated the project in its daily functions. It was indeed an ideal position for a participant-observer from which to accompany and study 'organizational change'.

Perhaps due to his personal involvement in the project, and to his training in organizational psychology, the author attempted to optimize the experience and extend the simple project evaluation required of him by the company, to draw a first-hand demonstration of 'organizational change' by identifying and, when possible, measuring those modifications which illustrated how an organization's system and sub-systems react to a 'planned change'.

CONCLUSIONS ABOUT THE STUDY OF CHANGE

This case study reports changes that were observed and measured at individual and group levels in terms of modifications in behaviours and attitudes, and at organizational levels in terms of transformations in rules, tools, and methods. This study goes beyond a simple narration of these observed changes, by using the model which fixes the project as a planned-stimulus-change, and the organization as an open system.

The term 'planned change' has been used to refer to a project, an ensemble of events and activities carried out to bring about desired changes; it also brings about other unintended unanticipated changes. It is clear that these changes are part of the ongoing dynamics in a system; the organization is constantly changing. When can we say that a 'change' has begun or has ended? To what extent can one say that the observed changes were consequences of the stimulus-change? Why these changes and not others? The OD approach based on system analysis assumes structures and stability within some arbitrarily separated and frozen time period (French and Bell 1973). Our measures and models attempt to take a photograph of a constantly changing phenomenon, fixing it in time, giving it artificial beginnings and ends, and attributing causal linkages to the stimulus-change fixed by the model as the starting point of the analysis.

It is in the actual use of social science concepts and models in the study of real-life phenomena that the researcher realizes that they are mere intellectual tools, created in order to make sense of ongoing reality. They are useful for labelling and fixing phenomena, making explanations possible. The notion of 'change' as a subject of study is doubly elusive; it must be artificially fixed in time and space if it is to be understood. It helps to remember that, despite their limitations, these models and concepts are what organizational psychologists have to offer to make sense of constantly changing reality, and eventually contribute to the prediction, control, and implementation of desired changes, thus reducing haphazard changes. The final goal is to improve the anticipation of consequences of behaviour, in order to increase responsibility for our behaviour.

Conscious of the responsibilities of consultant-psychologists working with organizations, and of his partial role as a change agent, the author seized the opportunity offered by the requested project evaluation as a feedback to help increase awareness of organization members of the management of change. Data and information, findings and conclusions had to be translated into economic and business terms corresponding to the culture and objectives of the client organization. The case study was rewritten for use in training seminars on decision-making, for company managers to illustrate not only the predicted consequences but especially the unanticipated repercussions on different components of the organization of a 'planned change'. The objective was an increase in the organization's managerial skills in anticipating organizational changes resulting from, or accompanying, types of change that managers are often called upon to decide or to implement.

In this way, the psychologist employed in a business organization assumes the role prescribed by Michael Beer and Anna Walton in their chapter 'Organization Change and Development' in the 1987 *Annual Review of Psychology*. Psychologists leave the front stage to managers, whose main responsibility is to see to the continued survival and development of the organization in its daily operations. The psychologist may translate his or her social science concepts and tools into terms understandable and useful to the manager, and use economic models and measuring instruments highly valued by the business actors. It is surely one way in which the psychologist can earn the respect of the manager and become a partner, working together with change. After all, both manager and psychologist are concerned with studying, controlling, and implementing desired changes and reducing the existence of haphazard changes, to make sense of the continually changing realities of the business organization.

REFERENCES

Curie, J. and Cellier, J.M. (1987) 'Stratégie de la recherche en psychologie du travail' ('Research strategy in work psychology'), in C. Levy-Leboyer and J.C. Sperandio, (eds) *Traité de Psychologie du Travail*, Paris: Presses Universitaires de France.

Fouchard, P. (1989) *La Psychologie dans L'Entreprise (Psychology in the Business Firm)*, Paris: Collection Devenir et Exercices, Le Journal des Psychologues, numéro hors série.

French, W.L. and Bell, Jr., C.H. (1973) *Organization Development*, New Jersey: Prentice-Hall.

Gilbert, P. (1988) *Gérer Le Changement Dans L'Entreprise (Managing Change in the Business Firm)*, Paris: Les Editions ESF.

Huse, E.F. (1980) *Organization Development and Change* (2nd edn), New York: West Publishing Company.

Landier, H. (1984) *L'Entreprise Face au Changement (The Business Firm Confronted with Change)*, Paris: Les Editions ESF.

Pémartin, D. (1987) *Réussir le Changement, Mutations des Entreprises et Problèmes Humains (Successful Change, Mutations of Business Firms and Human Problems)*, Paris: Les Editions ESF.

Raimbault, M. and Saussois, J.M. (1983) *Organiser le Changement (Organizing Change)*, Paris: Les Editions D'Organisation.

Schein, E.H. and Bennis, W.G. (1965) *Personal and Organizational Change Through Group Methods*, New York: John Wiley and Sons.

Tessier, R. and Tellier, Y. (eds) (1973) *Changement Planifié et Développement des Organisations (Planned Change and Organization Development)*, Paris: Les Editions de l'Institut Francais de la Gastion.

Touati, A. (1985) 'Conclusion du troisième forum professionnel des psychologues', Cannes, in *Intervention Psychologigues et Changements, (Psychological Interventions and Change)*, Paris: Le Journal des Psychologues, numéro hors série.

Wilpert, G. (1987) 'Aspects psychologiques du changement technique' ('Psychological aspects of technical change'), in C. Levy-Leboyer and J.C. Sperandio (eds) *Traité de Psychologie du Travail*, Paris: Presses Universitaires de France.

15 Responding to a changing environment

An action research case study

Catherine Cassell and Mike Fitter

INTRODUCTION

This chapter presents a case study of a three-year project called SPRITE (Sheffield People's Resource for Information Technology). The SPRITE project was set up as a response to the changing economic environment within Sheffield, the fourth largest city in England. The emphasis of this chapter is the methodology used in the evaluation of the project. The results of the evaluation can be found elsewhere (Cassell *et al.* 1988; Cassell and Fitter 1988, 1989). An action research methodology was used to evaluate the impact of the project and identify its strengths and weaknesses, providing regular feedback on the processes by which the project was developing. This chapter outlines the project and its evaluation, and reviews the appropriateness of the evaluation methodology. A model for understanding the processes of feedback within action research is described and evaluated. Finally, some general comments are made about action research that address some of the common criticisms of the methodology.

Responding to a changing environment: action research

The evaluation of SPRITE is set in the methodological tradition of action research. Action research originated in the work of a practitioner, John Collier, and a social psychologist, Kurt Lewin (French and Bell 1984). Both were interested in how knowledge from the social sciences could be applied to contemporary social problems. They believed that application of this knowledge would arise from the combined efforts of researchers and practitioners. Lewin (1951) recommended how this could be achieved with his now famous comment:

> Close co-operation between theoretical and applied psychology can be accomplished if the theorist does not look towards applied problems

with highbrow aversion or with a fear of social problems, and if the applied psychologist realises that there is nothing so practical as a good theory.

(Lewin 1951: 169)

The major generic characteristics of action research are this emphasis on collaboration between practitioner and researcher, and an emphasis on feedback. Feedback is crucial for action to be prescribed, or goals to be modified. Therefore the action research process is essentially about change. Action research also stresses the utilization and dissemination of research products. Findings from evaluation need to be accessible to practitioners, so that they can be acted upon.

Action research is used in many of the areas in which industrial and organizational psychologists work, in particular in the field of organizational development (Froham *et al.* 1976). The methodology is not without its critics, however. The two most common criticisms are based on issues of generalizability and objectivity. These criticisms will be addressed later within the paper.

Responding to a changing environment: unemployment

The beginning of the 1980s saw a rapid increase in the number of unemployed people in Britain. Figures from the 1981 census, and subsequent figures, suggested that in Sheffield over 50 per cent of the adult population came into the category of 'unwaged'. By 'unwaged' we mean those groups such as women with childcare responsibilities, people with disabilities, and senior citizens, as well as those on the unemployment register. As a response to the increase in unemployment in the 1980s, many psychologists studied the effects of unemployment on individuals, showing that the psychological effects can be harmful (Warr 1982; Swinbourne 1981). Additionally, practitioners and service providers have attempted to set up projects designed to compensate for these harmful effects (Cassell *et al.* 1988). This evaluation fits into the latter category of action. The aim of SPRITE is to enable unwaged people to develop skills that are useful to themselves and to their local community.

Responding to a changing environment: IT

Developments in micro-electronics over the last ten years have meant that the 'information society' is now clearly upon us. Skills in using IT, and access to IT, are important resources. This has led some authors to question the wider implications of this revolution. Bevan (1988), for example, offers the following interpretation:

The new conventional wisdom on Information Technology is that an IT-led revolution is in progress with a new kind of society emerging. This society will facilitate the empowerment and liberation of previously excluded groups of people by bringing them the power of information, a technological cure for information disability. I suggest that we need to examine this idea more critically. There is a strong argument for the opposite case; that the new technologies will all too easily serve to reinforce existing power relationships. There could be increased inequalities of access. The rich and powerful will have the up-to-date equipment and software, leaving the rest of us struggling to adapt yesterday's technologies.

(Bevan 1988: 330)

In acknowledging the importance of access to IT resources, Nowotny (1982) suggests the appearances of various disadvantaged groups on the margins of an information society. Inequalities have developed to the extent that 'information rich' and 'information poor' groups are clearly emerging. She argues that:

Whilst it is a truism that every society has its marginals, we owe it to those who are likely to be the most affected by the incumbent changes to look towards their plight in order to intervene when and wherever possible.

(Nowotny 1982: 106)

In the distinction between the information rich and the information poor there is, in particular, a growing gap between the waged and the unwaged in terms of access to computer resources and skills (Darwin *et al.* 1985). The unwaged have no contact with computers at the workplace, and rarely have the disposable income to purchase them for home use.

The SPRITE project was set up to evaluate the extent to which this division between the waged and unwaged in terms of access to IT resources could be addressed. As an intervention, the project aimed to provide access to IT resources for unwaged people within their local communities.

CASE STUDY: THE SPRITE PROJECT

SPRITE was a three-year project that began in November 1985 with two full-time project officers and a part-time administrative worker. The project was funded jointly by the European Social Fund and Sheffield City Council, and was administered by the Workers' Educational Association.

The philosophy behind the project recognized that within the category of unwaged people, particular groups have been traditionally denied access to resources. These groups – women, ethnic minorities, older people, and people with disabilities – are therefore target groups for the project. It is also recognized that these groups are best aware of their own interests and for a project to serve the interests of these groups, it must be responsive to their needs. Consequently, one of the aims of the project was to ensure that community centre users determined the way in which SPRITE worked within their local centre, having as much say as possible in the implementation process.

SPRITE was implemented in three community centres in May 1986. Each centre was provided with five machines, together with introductory training sessions in computing. Over the next two years the project developed considerably, and by September 1987 it was located within nine community centres in Sheffield. Each of the centres was different in terms of their user groups and their aims in using IT. In order to describe how SPRITE worked in practice, the rest of this section focuses on the implementation of SPRITE in two particular centres.

The Frontier Centre

The Frontier is a new community centre on the first floor of a municipal library that serves several major housing estates in Sheffield. The centre is used by a number of groups from the local community, including Adult Education, who run a variety of classes in the centre, an Asian women's sewing group, a local history workshop, and a local theatre group. Most of the users come from the local area and use the centre for a variety of activities. When SPRITE made contact with the Frontier there was already a computer club that met on the premises. They had considerable experience of using computers for playing games. However, they expressed an interest in becoming involved with SPRITE because they wished to learn about the more serious side of computing. In particular, they were keen to learn aspects of desk-top publishing which would enable them to produce a newsletter to distribute around the local community. This newsletter would publicize activities at the Frontier and would, it was hoped, bring more people into the centre.

The group that SPRITE worked with in the centre were all male, aged between 20 and 45, the majority of whom had previously been involved with the computer club. Through the training provided by SPRITE they developed their skills considerably, and results from the evaluation suggested that their confidence as a group was enhanced. After the initial training sessions the group began to work on community projects. The first project began when the Frontier was approached by a representative from the 'Consortium', a co-ordinating group for people with disabilities in Sheffield. The Consortium expressed an interest in learning how to use a computer to improve their administration procedures, and turned to the Frontier users for advice on computer applications. Over the next few months, Frontier users designed a database for the Consortium users to implement and use for their administration. As well as providing the organization with a mailing list system, it was hoped that the database would be useful to the Consortium in other ways.

As well as developing computer skills, this exercise required the Frontier users to think about issues such as the meaning of disability and the difficulties involved with labelling people as 'disabled'. Users also learnt some of the skills of relating to clients and working to the specifications of those clients.

Other community groups began to request databases from the Frontier users and they worked with two tenants' groups on databases designed to monitor the repairs that were necessary to the houses on their respective estates, as well as the design of effective membership systems.

The experience of SPRITE at the Frontier centre was clearly successful. By providing training to a group of unwaged users, they could develop their skills to work on products that were useful to the local community. These users then went on to train other users through the process of skill-sharing, and a few of them found work as part-time computer tutors.

Woodvale

The Woodvale group are based within a school in the middle of a large council estate in Sheffield. As a community centre the school has few resources, apart from a number of rooms that are well-used by adult education workers. The group consisted of eleven women, who had originally attempted to enrol for an adult education course in office skills. On finding that the course was full they decided to form themselves into a group and to try to find some other resources through which they could learn office and computer skills. The group was directed towards SPRITE by a local adult education worker.

The women in the group were aged between 20 and 35, and all had young children, mostly of school age. They were particularly interested in developing computer skills so that they could re-enter the labour market.

SPRITE provided the Woodvale centre with three BBC machines and began regular training sessions in the centre in March 1987. After these first training sessions it became apparent that the women wished to have some formal training in computing. SPRITE negotiated a ten week course for the group at the Women's Technology Training Workshop in Sheffield. This course was organized around the aspects of computing that they were particularly interested in. Meanwhile the SPRITE workers were running introductory sessions for a new group of women at the centre.

The commitment of this group to the development of computer skills was impressive. During 1987 they made an application for urban programme funding of £18,000, to finance the development of computing within their centre. This application was successful, and the money was used to buy some of their own equipment and to improve the security within the computer room at the school. They also employed a trainer who could devise the formal training courses they required.

The involvement of SPRITE at Woodvale is an example of the impetus that SPRITE has given and can give to community groups. In this case an informal introduction to computers, and the development of computer literacy, meant that the group could make an informed decision about the kind of project and the kind of skills they wanted to acquire.

These two cases highlight the successes of SPRITE, and provide examples of the different groups with which the project worked.

THE EVALUATION OF SPRITE

The evaluation of SPRITE is set in the methodological tradition of action research. Action research arose as a response to the division between theory and practice which is generally evident in research where, rather than the two having a symbiotic relationship, they are often seen as being independent. Kurt Lewin (1951) was the most influential exponent of action research.

Ketterer *et al.* (1980) suggest that the most important aspect of Lewin's model of action research is that it involves the cyclical process of fact-finding, action and evaluation. The fact-finding stage leads to the establishment of structured goals, which are then converted to action strategies to pursue. Finally, the process is evaluated and the information gained can lead to the formation of further goals. This model is shown in figure 15.1.

Within the model we have included an additional element: ideological perspective. This arises from the recognition that the process of, and the results of research have to be seen in the appropriate ideological framework within which the research takes place. With SPRITE this framework is that of making IT resources accessible to unwaged people, and also encouraging centre users to determine the nature of the project within their own particular centre. The framework has clearly influenced our research, in that we have identified centre users as the major 'stakeholder' group within the project that we especially want the evaluation to serve (Fitter 1987). Therefore our framework is consistent with the philosophy of the project.

Action research, based on Lewin's model, is regularly used in the areas where organizational psychologists work. Marrow (1969) suggests that Lewin's greatest contribution was the idea of studying things through, changing them, and then seeing the effects of those changes. He points out

Figure 15.1 The action research process

that to some people this may seem like common sense, but to Lewin, involvement with practical problems was a continual source of theoretical ideas and knowledge about fundamental social-psychological relationships. Lewin's model was designed initially for the evaluation of social programmes. Action research is now widely applied in the area of organizational development (OD) (French and Bell 1984) and a number of other models of action research have emerged from that literature. These models focus on action research as a problem-solving activity, designed to help in the process of planned organizational change. French (1969), for example, presents a model of the process of action research as it relates to OD. The important aspects of his model are diagnosis, data-gathering, feedback to the client group, action planning, and action. He suggests that the sequence is cyclical, with a focus on new or advanced problems as the client group learns to work together.

French and Bell suggest that there are two different ways in which action research can be seen as a process. These aspects are common to all models of action research:

> Action research is a process in two different ways: it is a sequence of events and activities within each iteration (data collection, feedback and working the data, and taking action based on the data); and it is a cycle of iterations of these activities sometimes treating the same problem through several cycles and sometimes moving to different problems in each cycle. Both aspects point up the ongoing nature of action research.
>
> (French and Bell 1984: 109)

The characteristics of action research make it different from other perspectives. One way it differs from traditional research is that it is concerned to a greater or lesser extent with bringing about change, as well as attempting to evaluate it. Ketterer *et al.* (1980) also suggest that within a community setting, action research seeks out social problems and issues that can serve as the context for continuing research and evaluation activities. Therefore, maintaining a problem focus is seen to be a strategy for testing and developing theory, as well as for solving practical problems. As French and Bell suggest:

> The payoff from a good action research project is high: practical problems get solved, a contribution is made to theory and to practice in behavioural science, and greater understanding grows amongst scientist, practitioner, and layperson.
>
> (French and Bell 1984: 118)

The major generic characteristic of action research is its emphasis on feedback. This is crucial in order that action can be prescribed, or goals modified. Feedback ensures that evaluation is a continuous process, as in Lewin's cyclical model. Feedback channels can use formal organizational channels, such as management committee meetings, or be informal, for instance through word of mouth. The SPRITE evaluation was set in the context of Lewin's model, and provided the project with feedback, to enable it to change in line with the needs of centre users and the aims and objectives of the project.

The focus of SPRITE's evaluation was on the processes by which the project developed, and a number of methods of data collection were used. These included regular interviews with SPRITE users, participant observation, and analysis of documents and discussion groups. One of the authors (Catherine Cassell) was a full-time action researcher for the first two years of the project. This involved visiting the centres on a regular basis, keeping a research diary of each visit, and working closely with the SPRITE workers and users. Most of the feedback into the project was provided by the action researcher.

Within the feedback process itself we identified three loops through which the results of the evaluation were fed back into the project.

The feedback loops

The operational loop

The first feedback loop was at the operational level. The purpose of this loop was to feed back information on a day-to-day basis within the centres.

In practice this was a continual process, with feedback being directed to the SPRITE workers. This generally occurred through talking with them during and after centre visits, or at the regular meetings the action researcher had with them to discuss the progress of the project. Much of the information fed back was descriptive and informal. Within these discussions we would negotiate our understandings of situations from the basis of our interpretation of events. We would then consider ways of dealing with any problems that emerged, where necessary.

The information in this feedback loop was used to make decisions about the daily implementation of the project. One example concerns the planning and provision of training. Users would often make comments to the action researcher about the nature of SPRITE training, such as the pace at which it was progressing. She would then pass these comments on to the project workers. This example also indicates one of the perceptions that SPRITE users had about the role of the action researcher, that of a go-between between themselves and the project workers. It was at this level that she had most contact with the SPRITE users. During the first set of interviews with users, one of the questions in the interview schedule referred to what they thought the impact of the evaluation had been within their centre. It is interesting that the majority of responses to this question referred to the role of the action researcher. This role was perceived by users in a number of ways. For example, 'Well you're a spokesperson aren't you, anything that needs to be known about SPRITE, you'll let them know, so in a way it's a good thing isn't it?' In this case the function of the researcher is seen as a go-between. There were a number of other functions that users thought the evaluation had. As one commented, 'Well it's important to evaluate, it's no good going along at the same level, you've got to get better and if you're an independent person saying "Oh what did you do?" then we're not slacking all the time. I mean we could sit here to our heart's content, but as long as you know that somebody is going to evaluate it then you may as well do the best job you can . . .'. Here the evaluation role is almost one of social control. To the majority of regular users, however, feedback was viewed as the most important aspect of the evaluator's role.

The other image of the role that emerged from the interviews was the idea of the evaluator as 'fixer', noticing when things were going wrong: 'If something is going wrong then hopefully you can say, "Well if you steer it this way a bit it'll be all right." I think you're pretty good at doing things like that, maybe it's your university background, I don't know . . .'. Therefore it was at the operational level that the researcher had most contact with the users, and where the majority of informal feedback took place. Feedback at this level was usually acted upon quite quickly.

The strategic loop

The second level of feedback was at the strategic level of the project. Feedback here was used to make medium-term reports on the project, enabling strategic decisions to be made. This feedback would often take the form of written documents that were provided to the management committee of the project to aid strategic planning, for example deciding which would be the next SPRITE centres. The project management committee was constituted of a group of project users and interested professionals who met every six weeks to discuss the implementation of the project and to make executive decisions about developments within SPRITE. An evaluation report was given verbally to each meeting of the management committee, and therefore although the audience included some of the people who had received feedback about the project at the operational level, such as project users and workers, it also included the managers of the project. This feedback emerged from a careful analysis of all the data collected within the project over a given period, for example from interviews and the notes made from participant observation. Therefore this feedback loop provided the link between the day-to-day implementation of the project and the management of the project.

The policy-making loop

The third feedback loop was at the policy-making level. The aim of this loop was to provide general lessons and information about the results of SPRITE. Feedback at this level was directed primarily towards the project's funding bodies. Some of this feedback has already been given. For example in April 1988, some of the SPRITE users and ourselves provided a presentation to officers from the Sheffield City Council about issues that had emerged within the project as a whole. We presented the information in the form of a play, which gave us the opportunity to put forward users' opinions about how they wanted to see SPRITE continue, in a way that was accessible and amusing to the audience. Therefore the presentation focused on our collective recommendations as a result of the research, combined with their experience.

However, most of the feedback from this loop has still to be given. At the time of writing, the final report on SPRITE for Sheffield City Council and the European Social Fund is still being written. The aim of that report is to provide guidelines to funding bodies for the establishment of future projects similar to SPRITE, as well as to describe how the funding for the project was spent. Therefore, feedback at this level can be characterized as being in a formal style and directed towards funding bodies.

Links between the loops

These feedback loops did not exist in isolation, but rather information from one loop fed into the next loop. An example of this process can be found in an intervention, made by the evaluation, at the Frontier centre. At the Frontier problems emerged in trying to get women involved with the project. At the operational level it was identified that women may have difficulties breaking into an all-male computer user group, and that the lack of crèche facilities meant that women who wanted to attend SPRITE sessions had nowhere to leave their children. Feedback from meetings that the researcher had with users and local community workers led to a decision at the strategic level about setting up a series of women-only computer classes, with a crèche provided by the local adult education workers. This intervention took place and the results were evaluated. Information from the evaluation of the intervention was fed into the policy-making level. For example, the recommendations in the final report for future projects proposed that all centres in which a computer project works should have crèche facilities. Additionally, that a project such as SPRITE should have a full-time female worker. This is an example of how the results of interventions are fed into the policy-making process.

In describing how feedback is used at each of these three levels, it is possible to provide a general analysis of the nature of feedback in action research. The ways in which feedback can be characterized at each of these levels are shown in Table 15.1.

Within the table, the differences in feedback at the three levels are characterized in terms of the stakeholder groups to which the feedback is addressed, the medium of communication that is used to convey the feedback, the interval between the occasions on which feedback is provided, and the time-span of a single iteration of the feedback loop. Additionally, the different roles of the action researcher as interventionist are highlighted. This framework assumes that the findings of action research will be utilized in practice, and provides suggestions about appropriate ways in which to conceptualize the feedback process. Therefore the framework should be useful to other action research programmes in organizations both inside and outside the voluntary sector.

AN ACTION RESEARCH MODEL

Lewin's model of action research has been put forward as the model on which the SPRITE evaluation was based. The framework of feedback loops can extend Lewin's model, in a number of ways. If the various types of feedback are mapped on to this model, it shows what kind of feedback is appropriate at each stage. It also suggests a stage where the circular process will

Table 15.1 Characteristics of feedback loops

	Stakeholders (Nature of client group)	Medium (Type of feedback)	Time-span (Between feedback and action)	Role of interventionist
Operational	users/project workers (clients)	verbal informal	short-term continual	data-collector/ fixer
Strategic	management committee (service providers)	verbal/ written formal	medium-term regular	reporter and adviser
Policy-making	funding organizations (service organization)	formal	occasional/ final	advocator

eventually stop, when the policy-making loop has been completed. There is also a recognition that after the first stage of evaluation, feedback will be taking place at more than one level. Figure 15.2 illustrates this process.

The combined model presupposes that information from action research is cumulative, that information at the operational level will always be fed into the strategic level. This stage of the model is an iteration process that can happen countless times. The accumulation of all this information forms the basis for the policy recommendations that occur, at the end of the research. The model also suggests that particular forms of feedback are relevant to particular stages of the evaluation process. Information from the policy-making loop, for example, will enable a review of the original ideological perspective within which the project was set.

By describing and analysing three feedback loops it is also possible to identify the different aspects of the change agent's role at each of the levels. Although active at all levels of the change process, at the operational level the researcher is more concerned with collecting data and reacting to any everyday problems that arise. At the strategic level the role becomes one of reporting findings and advising on possible directions for a change programme or project. Finally, at the policy-making level the interventionist becomes primarily an advocator providing policy recommendations for new projects and comments on appropriate ideological perspectives.

Additionally, while Lewin's model suggests that action research is circular, a consideration of the different types of feedback allows an under-

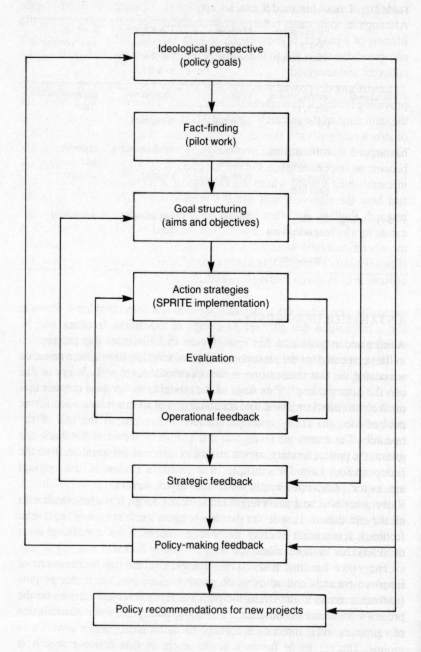

Figure 15.2 The action research model

standing of how his model can be applied to a project of fixed length. Although in some cases policy recommendations may be made during the lifetime of a project, in most cases, as with SPRITE, the making of policy recommendations is left to the end of a project, when all the data has been collected and analysed.

Lewin's model proved very useful as a starting point for a framework for providing feedback throughout the evaluation. It also provided a model for the utilization of the research findings which were fed back into the process of structuring goals and the development of action strategies. Legge (1985) has argued that the utilization of findings within evaluation research has become an important issue. One of the barriers to utilization is uncertainty in establishing toward whom the findings of action research are directed, and how the receivers will use the results. As Patton (1978) suggests, research findings are often ignored in programme decision-making. The extent to which action with SPRITE has occurred as a result of feedback at the operational and strategic levels is clear, and is reported elsewhere (Cassell 1989). However it is likely to be at the policy-making level that the utilization of research findings will be questioned.

A STAKEHOLDER PERSPECTIVE

A fuller understanding of this argument comes from locating the discussion in the perspective of the stakeholder (Fitter 1987). The SPRITE evaluation advocated the interests of one of the stakeholder groups as primary (the users). Other stakeholder groups (such as project workers and the management committee) perceived the users' interests as an important priority and goal of the project. It is therefore understandable that feedback at the operational and strategic levels was acted upon. However, one stakeholder group, the project funders, appear to have a different perspective. With the European Social Fund it is difficult to see what their interests in the project are, as they were not directly involved with the first two feedback loops. Rather, they will be given a report at the end of the project about the results of the evaluation. It will then be up to them how they deal with that feedback. It is unclear whether they will use the results for the development of SPRITE or for other related projects.

The other funding body, Sheffield City Council's Department of Employment and Economic Development (DEED), were involved with the feedback process at the strategic level, as they had representatives on the project management committee. As their current priority is rationalization of resources, their interests are likely to conflict with other stakeholder groups. The results of the evaluation which suggest that the project is beneficial and should be continued will need to be reconciled with their strategic plans. However, because DEED is part of the feedback loop, there is substantial pressure to reconcile potentially conflicting perspectives. We see the difference between inclusion (DEED) and exclusion (ESF) in the strategic loop as being a vital factor in the influence of the project at the policy level. Therefore when suggesting that evaluation research findings are often ignored, it is important to point out which stakeholder groups ignore findings, as this will be different in different cases. Is it the funders of the project? Those who implement the project? Or those on the receiving end? To comprehend the crisis in the utilization of evaluation research findings, an understanding of the particular stakeholder groups and their interests is necessary.

SOME CRITICISMS OF ACTION RESEARCH

Before drawing some conclusions about the action research process within SPRITE, it is worth addressing some of the criticisms that have been levelled at action research as a methodology used by organizational psychologists. The first common criticism emerges from the role of the action researcher, and suggests that action research findings are not objective, because the researcher is involved in the planning and implementation of the project as well as the evaluation. In response to this criticism it is worth questioning whether evaluation of programmes can ever be objective, in that it takes place in a political environment where knowledge is socially constructed. It would appear that the evaluators will of necessity have a stake in the project as a whole. This stake may not necessarily be identified as the success of the project in question, but at a more basic level, the researchers will be concerned about the collection of high-quality data from the project and the subsequent use of that data. This interest may materialize in a variety of ways, which are largely unpredictable. However this complexity of influence does not remove the material nature of that influence. Thus, rather than addressing the question of objectivity, one can fairly address the question of the researchers' involvement within a project. Rather than saying that the interpretations of a participant researcher are biased, it is more fruitful to show the extent and manner in which the researcher influences the project. The major interventions that were made with SPRITE have been fully described (Cassell 1989), together with the results from the evaluation of those interventions. It is important then that the action research role becomes analysed as part of the research findings. The role in itself is interesting 'data'. Additionally we would suggest that having an action researcher participating within SPRITE ensured that the methods used were sensitive to the people who were essentially the 'subjects' within the study: the SPRITE users. Without their trust, the results of this evaluation would have been qualitatively poor. Therefore as long as an action researcher can describe their input into a programme and analyse the implications of that input, there is no more, and possibly less threat of bias than in other, less overtly interventionist research methods.

The other major criticism of action research refers to the applicability of findings and generalization. To counteract the criticism that the results of action research are not generalizable, we would argue that the results of this study are not aimed to be generalizable to the population at large. Rather they give insights into the processes that enable the development of community projects and allow the generalizability of these findings to other community projects, and more specifically to those projects that seek to enable and provide resources to people at a collective level. The results of this study, like most action research, have produced knowledge that is not achieved by some statistical analysis, but rather by the understanding of processes and their effects. It is through this understanding of context, process and effect that the applicability of findings to other contexts can be judged.

SUMMARY AND CONCLUSIONS

The aim of this chapter has been to describe some of the issues that have arisen from the use of the action research framework as a basis for the SPRITE evaluation. The paper has described the SPRITE project and its implementation, and has produced a framework for examining the nature of feedback within action research. This framework analyses feedback to different stakeholder groups at different levels. In conclusion, it is argued that this framework will be useful for the analysis of feedback within other action research projects.

Acknowledgements

We would like to thank the SPRITE users and the two workers, Ted Baldwin and Steve Jackson, for their contributions to, and support for, the work described in this chapter.

REFERENCES

Bevan, E.D. (1988) 'The task for a new professionalism', in B. Glastonbury, W. La Mendola, and S. Toole (eds) *Information Technology and the Human Services*, Chichester: John Wiley and Sons.

Cassell, C.M. (1989) 'The development and use of information technology in the community', unpublished PhD. thesis, University of Sheffield.

Cassell, C.M. and Fitter, M.J. (1988) 'The impact of organizational characteristics on computer education in community centres: an evaluation', *Computers in Adult Education and Training* 1(1): 55–70.

Cassell, C.M. and Fitter, M.J. (1989) 'The evaluation of the SPRITE project: the final report', available from MRC/ESRC Social and Applied Psychology Unit, University of Sheffield.

Cassell, C.M., Fitter, M.J., Fryer, D.M. and Smith, L. (1988) 'The development of computer applications by non-employed people in community settings', *Journal of Occupational Psychology* 61: 89–102.

Darwin, J., Fitter, M.J., Fryer, D.M. and Smith, L. (1985) 'Developing IT in the community with unwaged groups', paper presented to the working conference on the development and use of computer-based systems and tools, Aarhus, Denmark, 19–23 August.

Fitter, M.J. (1987) 'The development and use of IT in healthcare', in F. Blackler and D. Osborne (eds) *Information technology and people: designing for the future*, Leicester: British Psychological Society.

French, W. (1969) 'Organizational development: objectives, assumptions and strategies', *California Management Review* 12: 23–34.

French, W.L. and Bell, C.H. (1984) *Organizational development: behavioural science interventions for organization improvement* (3rd edn), Englewood Cliffs, NJ: Prentice Hall.

Froham, M.A., Sashkin, M. and Kavanagh, M.J. (1976) 'Action research as applied to organization development', *Organization and Administrative Sciences* 7: 129–61.

Fryer, D. (1986) 'Employment deprivation and personal agency during un-employment: a critical discussion of Jahoda's explanation of the psychological effects of unemployment', *Social Behaviour* 1: 3–23.

Ketterer, R.F., Price, R.H. and Politser, P.E. (1980) 'The action research paradigm', in R.H. Price and P.E. Politser (eds) *Evaluation and Action in the Social Environment*, London: Academic Press.

Legge, K. (1984) *Evaluating planned organizational change*, London: Academic Press.

Lewin, K. (1951) *Field theory in social science*, New York: Harper & Row.

Marrow, A.J. (1969) *The practical theorist: the life and work of Kurt Lewin*, New York: Basic Books.

Nowotny, H. (1982) 'The information society: its impact on the home, local community and marginal groups', in N. Bjorn-Anderson, M. Earl, O. Holst, O. and E. Mumford (eds) *Information Society: For Richer, For Poorer*, New York: North-Holland.

Patton, M.Q. (1978) *Utilization-focused Evaluation*, London: Sage Publications.

Swinbourne, P. (1981) 'The psychological impact of unemployment on managerial and professional staff', *Journal of Occupational Psychology* 54: 47–64.

Warr, P.B. (1982) 'Psychological aspects of employment and unemployment', *Psychological Medicine* 12: 7–11.

CHESTER COLLEGE LIBRARY

Author index

Subject index